D1528095

Hospitals and charity

Manchester University Press

Hospitals and charity

Religious culture and civic life in
medieval northern Italy

SALLY MAYALL BRASHER

Manchester University Press

Published by Manchester University Press
Altrincham Street, Manchester M1 7JA

www.manchesteruniversitypress.co.uk

British Library Cataloguing-in-Publication Data
A catalogue record for this book is available from the British Library

ISBN 978 1 5261 1928 5 hardback

First published 2017

The publisher has no responsibility for the persistence or accuracy of URLs for any external or third-party internet websites referred to in this book, and does not guarantee that any content on such websites is, or will remain, accurate or appropriate.

Typeset
by Toppan Best-set Premedia Limited
Printed in Great Britain
by TJ International Ltd, Padstow

For Kelsey, Charlie, and Meghan

Contents

Figures

Figures 4.1–4.6 have been reproduced from the *Liber Regulae S. Spiritus* (Archivio di Stato di Roma, Ms.3193) with the permission of the Ministry of Cultural Heritage, Activities and Tourism, Rome, ASRM 52/2016. No reproduction without permission.

Acknowledgements

For a historian of the Middle Ages researching in Italy is a labour of love. There can be no greater pleasure than seeking out the *Archivio di Stato* in Pavia or Milan and spending pleasant days in the company of archivists whose work ethic includes a frequent cappuccino break and a long lunch. I owe much to the many archivists in the state archives of Bergamo, Como, Cremona, Lodi, Milan, Parma, and Pavia.

This project evolved out of my earlier work on the *Humiliati* and I must thank Katherine Jansen for starting me down this path so many years ago. For the current work I have been supported by a number of colleagues, friends, and family to whom I am eternally grateful. First, I am indebted to Marianne Davis for her meticulous reading of draft after draft, her constructive suggestions, her cheerleading me through many a frustration, and generally making me a better writer. To the extraordinary cartographer and world's greatest son, Charles Brasher, thank you for giving visual life to my findings. Melba Mayall, at ninety-five years young, once again proved to be an able research assistant, helping to catalogue information for the appendix.

To my colleagues at Shepherd University, I am grateful for your support and encouragement. In particular, Anders Henriksson, thank you for allowing me the time and space to carry out my research while fulfilling my teaching and departmental responsibilities. Over the years Josh DiSalvo, of the Shepherd University library, has been instrumental in accessing hundreds of sources for me, sometimes from very obscure locations, which has also greatly enabled me to carry out my research in addition to my university duties. I must thank Steven Rigby for the very thorough and constructive comments he provided as well as those of Cynthia

Botteron, Mark Sachleben, and several anonymous readers. Additional thanks for editorial assistance to Carlo Bella and Lucia del Moro. Finally, and most importantly, none of this work would have been completed, much less begun, without the unwavering support and unfailing encouragement of my travel agent, reader, research assistant, and world's greatest husband, Niel Brasher.

Abbreviations

ASBg	*Archivio di Stato di Bergamo*
ASCO	*Archivio di Stato di Como*
ASCOs.a.	*Archivio Ospedale di S. Anna*
ASCr	*Archivio di Stato di Cremona*
ASCr OSM	*Ospedale S. Maria della Pietà*
ASF	*Archivio di Stato Firenze*
ASMi	*Archivio di Stato di Milano*
ASMi, AOM	*Archivio Ospedale Maggiore Milano*
ASMi, OM	*Consiglio degli Orfanotrofi del pio Albergo Trivulzio, Orfanotrofio Maschile*
ASP	*Archivio Comunale Pavia*
ASPr	*Archivio di Stato di Parma*
AST	*Archivio di Stato di Treviso*
ASVat	*Archivio Segreto Vaticano*
BCBg	*Biblioteca Civico Bergamo*
CDC	*Codice Diplomatica Cremonese*
CDF	*Constitutiones dedicatorum familiarium servitialium et omnium in Hospitali Sancti Spiritus de la caritate civitatis Laude commoriantum*
CDL	*Codice diplomatico laudense*
LR	*Liber Regulae S. Spiritus Regola*
OPC	*Office of the Poor of Christ*

Introduction

The current political maelstrom that revolves around social welfare, health care coverage, and emerging pandemic scares may seem to be a specifically modern concern. However, these issues also loomed large in earlier historical eras. Today, while perhaps debating the politics of health care economics, most people would agree that the hospital functions as one of the 'first duties of an organized society'[1] as a public service for those members of the community who are in need. This ideal is not a recent conception. It emerged as early as the twelfth century in Western Europe in communities that were experiencing economic, social, and political upheaval. Throughout the high Middle Ages, the debate over whose responsibility it was to take care of the ill and indigent as well as the public's concern over poverty and crime led to a grand experiment in creating a social welfare system for the poor and sick. One that has served as a model for social service institutions that still exist today. In Italy, the emergence of institutions to care for the needy coincided with the rise of the city and the birth of European capitalism. The leaders of independent city-states vied for political control with local bishops and distant emperors and popes, and created innovative civic institutions to replace traditional rural-based, class- and religion-centred, facilities. The case of Ospedale Santa Caterina serves as an example of the path taken by citizens as well as the civic and ecclesiastical authorities to organize a response to the needs of the community.

In his will, recorded on 31 March 1335, Moderno Caccialepre entrusted his wife and three children into the care of his brother and requested that within one year of his death, money from his estate be used to purchase existing buildings in his family's neighbourhood to establish a small hospital of twelve beds. He specifically

requested that this facility be located near the heavily trafficked
gate, Porta Ticines, in his home city of Pavia and that it was to serve
the ill and needy of his community. Caccialepre also stipulated that
members of his family should serve as *advocati* and *dominari*[2] of
the facility, allowing them to choose a director and to oversee the
hospital's administration. However, such a proposed institution
required ecclesiastical approval. Within two years of the writing of
this final testament the archbishop of Milan granted the bequest
and the hospital, called Santa Caterina, opened its doors. It was
staffed by a community of lay men and women who were appointed
by members of the Caccialepre family. The facility fulfilled an unmet
need and by 1345 had grown and merged with two similar facilities
in the same community. It was at this point in time the archbishop
of Milan issued a decree reminding the now numerous lay brothers
and sisters running this facility of the ecclesiastical jurisdiction over
its administration and encouraging them to follow faithfully the
rule of S. Augustine.[3]

Although for a century Ospedale Santa Caterina served thousands of pilgrims, the sick, and indigent men, women, and children
very successfully, the city of Pavia closed it down in 1444 when the
municipal government consolidated its assets and staff with many
similar institutions to create one major, municipal, professionalized
hospital. This central hospital was administered by the city-state
with a much circumscribed, mostly symbolic role left to the bishop
of Milan and little that reflected Signor Caccialepre's original
purpose. The familial, community-focused facility, whose intent was
to respond to social and spiritual ills, was lost to a new organization
that treated physical illness and served a much larger constituency.
Throughout Italy, from the twelfth through the fifteenth centuries,
city after city would witness a similar institutional and philosophical evolution in the approach to providing social services for the ill
and needy. The evolution of the medieval hospital illuminates the
transition of influence, status, wealth, and power from early ecclesiastical governance of the regional bishop and papal court, to
grassroots activism of the lay citizenry and from them, finally, to
the control by civic authorities of the budding early modern state.
The medieval hospital provides an excellent vehicle for examining
the alteration of the civic jurisdictional landscape of the medieval
city as well as constituting a model for the nature of religious life
and charitable activity among the lay citizens.

Between the twelfth and the fifteenth centuries medieval hospitals evolved from primarily religious institutions, reflecting communal and personal piety intended to house pilgrims and succour the dying, to civic facilities. These new institutions still welcomed pilgrims and the gravely ill, but expanded to include the poor, the homeless, the indigent, lepers, and orphans. In response to the ravages of disease that plagued growing urban areas, they eventually even attempted to understand and cure illness.[4] The mission and administration of these institutions evolved, along with the evolution of the concept of charity from one of obligatory help for those with whom one has a close relationship, either as family or as constituents and congregants, to that of social assistance for the needy in general, that is, charity as a civic responsibility.[5] In addition to providing much needed care for a growing urban community, this charitable activity offered unprecedented access to spiritual life and encouraged civic participation by an increasing number of lay citizens from an ever-wider spectrum of society. Over the course of three centuries, these institutions lost much of their spiritual purpose and reflected more and more the social, political, and economic interests of their communities.

Specifically, in Italy both the ecclesiastical and civic institutions, all the while jockeying for political power, were pressed to meet the growing needs of an urban population and somewhat ambivalently allowed for lay religious groups and individuals to step in and to temporarily dominate the foundation and administration of hospitals. Increasingly over this period, emanating from the papal reform efforts of the eleventh century,[6] ecclesiastical authorities attempted to rein in much of the autonomous activity of the laity, but by the middle of the fifteenth century the civic fathers had all but usurped much of the authority originally held by local bishops and ultimately the papacy. Political leaders were thus able to consolidate the small independent hospitals and replace the laity with municipal workers, creating a nascent, bureaucratically ruled, social security system. In addition, while not completely abandoning their religious identity, hospitals developed a more secular, specialized approach to the care and treatment of the sick. The 'care of the body' began to take precedence over the 'care of the soul'. The institutional outcome of this change was the medicalization of the hospital.[7] The growth of the medieval hospital reflected an overall change in civic life in which the compelling needs of an increasingly

urbanized society marginalized both ecclesiastical authority and
the influence of the *popolo* and necessitated a more bureaucra-
tized, secular public service industry that served the aims of the
growing state.[8]

The commercial centres of northern and central Italy witnessed
this evolution to the greatest extent. Independent communal governments emerged in the late eleventh and twelfth centuries in more
than two hundred distinct city-states. Men of an emerging class of
cittadini, or bourgeois merchants and lesser noblemen, ran these
newly formed republican governments. The incessant struggle for
supremacy between the Hohenstaufen imperial house in Germany
and the medieval papacy lasted over two centuries and was played
out to a large degree in northern and central Italy. The *boni homines*,
or good men, of hundreds of small to large cities throughout the
peninsula played politics with these international powers and forced
them to cede greater and greater freedom from external rule.
However, the resulting commune governments soon found that
once they rid themselves from the authoritative oversight of bishops
and aristocratic overlords, they had to take over many of the functions of government that these individuals and institutions had
provided. Urban Italian society was more complex than earlier
medieval rural society and the demands on government to meet
social welfare needs were much greater.[9] The Italian city-states were
unique in Western Europe in the degree to which they created independent governments and in the novel institutions of welfare that
they were forced to conceive.

It was at this point in the development of the Italian commune
that hospitals took on their most expansive role. They provided
a social security net for the urban community by protecting the
marginalized from destitution and desperation; they helped alleviate crime, indigence, and the spread of disease. They offered a
measure of control by the city over those who passed through
its gates by serving as hostels for individuals who could not
afford private accommodation.[10] Pilgrims and wayfarers were
common in the medieval city and the hospital provided them a
safe, but supervised place of respite.[11] The need for such assistance
increased dramatically over the course of the high Middle Ages.
The crowded city and increased contact of wandering merchants
and pilgrims facilitated the spread of plague, leprosy, and other
deadly diseases.[12] The Commercial Revolution, which expanded

international and regional trade and led to massive urbanization and unequally distributed prosperity, peaked by the late thirteenth century.[13] By the end of the thirteenth century, wages in cities were stagnant or in decline while the cost of living was steadily rising.[14]

Hospitals were more than just an institutional answer to a communal need, they also provided an opportunity for pious urban dwellers to contribute to their community and to fulfil the commandment for Christian charity. Hospitals represented a nexus of exchange between church officials, the community, the needy, and the pious or ambitious individual. These symbiotic relationships were unique for the period. In a highly religious society in which care for the soul and the body were inseparable and where health and prosperity were inexorably linked to the beneficence of God, the hospital was both a substantive benefactor as well as a symbolic presence in the community.

Organization

This study synthesizes information from primary and secondary sources written in both Italian and English to provide a comprehensive examination of the foundation, administration, and evolution of the medieval hospital in northern Italy between the twelfth and fifteenth centuries.[15] This research is focused primarily on hospitals in the Lombardy region of northern Italy. However, in the twelfth and thirteenth centuries this regional designation is somewhat meaningless due to the independence of the individual city-states and the overlapping episcopal jurisdictional designations and therefore includes some areas outside Lombardy. Cities considered here are primarily representative of the urban trade and pilgrimage routes in the region, which had an important impact on the hospital movement.[16]

Any examination of the role of the medieval hospital must take into consideration the relationship between the various constituents, especially when the institution itself is undergoing change. This survey offers a much-needed overview of the role of the hospital in affairs of the urban community as well as suggests how changes within that community were reflected in the activities of the hospital. It provides documentary evidence to encourage and enable further investigation into individual cities and hospitals in this region of northern Italy. While there have been a number of studies in English dealing with charity and the medieval hospital movement in Western Europe there are few that focus on the phenomenon in Italy, which is regretful given that it is a region of dynamic and varied experimentation in civic response to the needs of the community.[17]

Chapter 1 locates the rise of the hospital movement in northern Italy within the context of the changing religious, social, and political environment of the city-states. It traces the evolution of the ideas of charity and poverty from the early to high Middle Ages suggesting that a fundamental shift occurred in both the mechanisms of collecting and distributing charity, and in the perception of poverty and need. The chapter introduces the hospital's central function in this distribution and administration of charity and illustrates how the hospital and other charitable organizations played a role in the appropriation of power and influence by urban citizens. Chapters 2 to 6 delve into the dynamics, internal workings, and social and political contexts of specific hospitals in northern Italy.

Chapter 2 examines the phenomenon of the rapid growth of the foundation of hospitals in the twelfth and thirteenth centuries. A comprehensive investigation of these hospitals' foundational charters provides insight into the location, purpose, need, and political context of the origins of the hospital movement. Chapter 3 provides an analysis of the groups and individuals who administered the hospitals and their affiliations with other larger religious and community entities. Chapter 4 delves into a detailed description of the physical plant of the hospital, the daily life of individuals, and rules and statutes followed by its members. Chapter 4 also considers the social composition of donors, workers, and recipients of hospital services. Chapter 5 tracks the jurisdictional disputes among the city leaders, the community, individual religious orders, ecclesiastical authorities, and larger political forces. Lastly, Chapter 6 explores the process of consolidation and bureaucratization of hospitals in the fifteenth century and the emergence of state control over social services. The fifteenth century saw nearly universal consolidation of the many small neighbourhood hospitals into larger, centralized, state-run facilities. The result was the creation of singular civic institutions that included a conscious plan for not only caring for the poor and ill but also reflected an emerging understanding of health care as one of curing illness and preventing contagion of the body.

Notes

1 A. Caretta, 'Gli ospedali altomedievali di Lodi', in *Archivio Storico Lodigiano Ser. II Anno XV* (Lodi, 1967), 3.

2 Representatives in legal and administrative capacities.

3 *Antichi diplomi degli arcivescovi di Milano e note di diplomatica episcopale,* ed. G. C. Bascape, Firenze, 1937, cit. doc. n. 41, 112–13. See discussion in G. Albini, *Città e ospedali nella Lombardi a medievale* (Bologna, 1993), 74–5.

4 J. Henderson, *The Renaissance Hospital: Healing the Body and Healing the Soul* (New Haven, CT, 2006), xxx. Henderson introduces this idea of the civic role of the hospital in the Renaissance and suggests the medieval foundations of this model. Italy led the way in the hospital movement throughout Europe but he concentrates mostly on the Tuscan region. In fact, it can be argued that Northern Italy was as instrumental, if not more so, in this process. Also, Henderson places the origins of the Renaissance hospital in the mid-thirteenth century. As this research will show, however, the hospital movement was already established by that time and had even experienced the first of many alterations in its nature by then. D. M. D'Andrea, *Civic Christianity in Renaissance Italy: The Hospital of Treviso, 1400–1530* (Rochester, NY, 2007), provides an excellent case study for the emergence of the Renaissance hospital within the civic religious context with particular attention to the role of the confraternity in the administration of the emergent unified hospitals. See also F. Bianchi, 'Italian Renaissance Hospitals: An Overview of the Recent Historiography', *Mitteilungen des Instituts für Österreichische Geschichtsforschung,* 115 (2007), 394–403.

5 J. W. Brodman, *Charity and Religion in Medieval Europe* (Washington, DC, 2009), 3–5.

6 Emanating from, but not confined to the papacy, reform efforts beginning in the middle of the eleventh century sought to strengthen and codify doctrinal law and eradicate localized ecclesiastical abuse and corruption. Pious lay groups in cities such as Milan joined with the papacy to challenge corrupt local clergy and as well as imperial and localized episcopate authority. The papacy welcomed this assistance but by the time of the Lateran Councils of the thirteenth century found the need to control over-zealous lay activity. For information on the papal reform movement of the era see C. Morris, *The Papal Monarchy, the Western Church from 1050–1250* (Oxford, 1989), 79–108; K. Pennington, *Pope and Bishops; the Papal Monarchy in the Twelfth and Thirteenth Centuries* (Philadelphia, PA, 1984).

7 Henderson, *The Renaissance Hospital,* 27–8.

8 L. Little, *Religious, Poverty, and the Profit Economy in Medieval Europe* (Ithaca, NY, 1978), remains the seminal work on the economic

revival of the high Middle Ages and its effect on the religious culture of the time remains the standard for the study of religion, economics, and society of the period.

9 For overall analysis of the history of the city-states in the period see D. P. Waley and T. Dean, *The Italian City Republics* (New York, 4th edn, 2009). For information on the external power struggle see D. Abulafia, *Frederick II, A Medieval Emperor* (London, 1988); P. Brezzi, 'Le relazioni tra i comuni italiani e l'impero', in *Questione di storia medioevali* (Milan, 1964); D. P. Waley, *The Papal State in the 13th Century* (London, 1961); C. Wickham, *Sleepwalking into a New World: The Emergence of Italian City Communes in the Twelfth Century*. The Lawrence Stone Lectures (Princeton, NJ, 2015). For overall analysis of the history of the city-states in the period see Waley and Dean, *The Italian City Republics*.

10 Caretta, 'Gli ospedali altomedievali'.

11 Studies that consider the medieval hospital movement in other areas of Europe and give a different regional perspective include, J. W. Brodman, *Charity and Welfare: Hospitals and the Poor in Medieval Catalonia,*. Middle Ages series (Philadelphia, PA, 1998); and T. Huguet-Termes, *Ciudad y hospital en el occidente Europeo, 1300–1700* (Lleida, 2014). For England see B. Bowers, *The Medieval Hospital and Medical Practice* (Aldershot, 2007); N. Orme and M. Webster, *The English Hospital 1070–1570* (New Haven, CN, 1995); C. Rawcliffe, *The Hospitals of Medieval Norwich* (Norwich, 1995); also by Rawcliffe see *Leprosy in Medieval England* (Woodbridge, 2006); *Medicine for the Soul: The Life, Death, and Resurrection of an English Medieval Hospital: St Giles's, Norwich, C. 1249–1550* (Stroud, 1999); and *Sources for the History of Medicine in Late Medieval England* (Kalamazoo, MI, 1995).

12 Plague epidemics and leprosy were familiar, recurrent scourges of the medieval city. Their increased incidence in the high Middle Ages was coupled with the appearance of other novel maladies such as a disease known as St Anthony's Fire, caused by infected rye grain. For further information on medieval plague and disease epidemics see D. Herlihy and S. K. Cohen, *The Black Death and the Transformation of the West* (Cambridge, MA, 1997).

13 The impact of the commercial revolution and urbanization on the city-state of Italy is discussed in depth in S. Epstein, *Genoa & the Genoese, 958–1528* (Chapel Hill, NC, 1996); *Wage Labor & Guilds in Medieval Europe* (Chapel Hill, NC, 1991); and R.L. Reynolds, D. Herlihy, R. S. Lopez and V. Slessarev, *Economy, Society, and Government in Medieval Italy: Essays in Memory of Robert L. Reynolds.* (Kent, OH, 1969).

14 P. Racine, 'Il sistema ospedaliero lombardo (secoli XII–XV)', in *Città e servizi sociali nell' Italia dei secoli 12–15, Dodicesimo Convegno di Studi: Pistoia, 9–12 Ottobre 1987* (Pistoia, 1987), 367.

15 The state archival system of Italy, decentralized to such an extent that virtually every city of over ten thousand people or so has its own archive office, ensures the accumulation and preservation of thousands of localized documents. This is a boon (and bane) for researchers but also leads to the decentralized nature of the historiography for the period. The challenge is to accumulate and synthesize these sources without losing the distinctness of each community. For instance, while Milan was a relatively large metropolis even in the twelfth century, Cremona was much smaller and had to contend with very different political realities than its giant neighbour. The economy of Bergamo was quite different from that of Padua as was its physical location. Many of the smaller northern Italian cities became subject states of Milan or Venice; their political fortunes and misfortunes were tied to those larger entities, which were often in competition and confrontation with one another. In addition, the incessant conflict between the Holy Roman emperor and the papacy that played out in the region rearranged the alliances and fortunes of various cities on a frequent basis. One must consider these factors when attempting to generalize across all of northern Italy.

16 See maps in Chapter 2, Figures 2.1 and 2.2.

17 There are a number of very good studies of elements of the hospital system in Italian, most outstanding in this are the works by Giuliana Albini. See Albini, *Carità e governo delle povertà: Secoli XII–XV* (Milan, 2002); *Città e ospedali*; 'El rostro asistencial de las ciudades: la Italia septentrional entre los singlos XIII y XV', in T. Huguet-Termes (ed.), *Ciudad y hospital en el Occidente Europeo (1300–1700)* (Lleida, 2014), 115–35; 'Fondazioni di ospedali in area Padana (secoli XI–XIII.)', in *La conversione alla povertà nell' Italia dei secoli XII–XIV: Atti del XVII. convegno storico internazionale Todi, 14–17 Ottobre, 1990* (Spoletto, 1990); 'La gestione dell'ospedale Maggiore di Milano nel quattrocento: Un esempio di concentrazione ospedaliera', in *Ospedali e città / a Cura Di Allen J. Grieco E Lucia Sandri*, 157–178; 'Ospedali e società urbana: Italia centro-settentrionale secoli XIII–XVI', in F. Datini and F. Ammannati (eds), *Assistenza e solidarieta in Europa, secc. XIII-*: Atti della quarantaquattresima settimana di studi, 22–26 Aprile 2012 (Florence, 2013). See also Pierre Racine, 'Il sistema ospedaliero', 355–80. Marina Gazzini has compiled a comprehensive guide to the individual archival collections for medieval hospitals throughout Italy. See M. Gazzini, *Reti medievali Rivista,* 13,1 (2012): http://rm.univr.it/repertorio/

rm_gazzini_ospedali_medioevo.html; see also *Codice diplomatico della Lombardia medieval 9secoli VIII–XII.* http://cdlm.unipv.it/progetto/piano, a collection and directory for accessing more general archival information for the region of Lombardy in the eighth through the twelfth centuries. Also by Gazzini, see 'Rodolfo Tanzi, l'ospedale e le società cittàdina nei secoli XII e XIII', and 'Una communita di 'fratres' e 'sorores', both in R. Greci, *L'ospedale Rodolfo Tanzi di Parma in età Medieval* (Bologna, 2004), 3–28. Also, *L'ospedale a Parma nei secoli XII–XIII* (Parma, 2002).

1

Hospitals and charity: history and context

The hospital movement in Europe arose out of a tradition of charity and religious life that originated in the earliest days of Christianity. The perception of who deserved charity and whose responsibility it was to provide such relief changed considerably by the twelfth century as the populations of cities grew and the ability of ecclesiastical institutions to serve them diminished. The perception of personal charity shifted from the idea of *caritas* to *misericordia*. *Caritas*, the term employed in the earlier Middle Ages, refers to the idea of a personal obligation to assist those with whom one is in close relation.[1] *Misericordia* reflects the twelfth-century perception of the necessity for assisting the poor and needy for the common good of the community and the social security of all.[2] The establishment of hundreds of small, independent hospitals throughout northern Italy in this period reflects the reaction by nearly all segments of society at multiple levels of authority to a new urban context and a shift toward communal responsibility. An examination of the medieval hospital movement in Italy must consider the rise of these essential charitable institutions within the context of the major evolution in medieval society, religious culture, and the political orientation of the newly independent city-states of northern Italy.

Taking care of the ill and needy, and administering and distributing pious bequests was originally an ecclesiastical responsibility. Church fathers of the fourth and fifth centuries, faced with the need to build a unified Christian society and to establish a fiscally sound Christian institution, wrote and preached on the necessity and centrality of taking care of the poor in society through charity.[3] The nature of ecclesiastical charity in the early Middle Ages was that of 'ritualistic charity', that is, charity was an affirmation of one's piety,

an expression of one's love of God, and the church was the intermediary between the donor and God.[4] Charitable institutions often
served a fixed number (usually twelve, representing the apostles) of
poor individuals and administered charity in a fashion that spoke
more to symbol and mission rather than actual requirements of the
needy. There was not the sense of a specific 'poor' as recipients of
charity; charity was a gift to God, through the church, to help the
faceless 'poor' spoken of so frequently in the Bible. Charity overall
came to be viewed as a reflection of the piety of the individual. The
success of chartable collections reflected the piety of the institution.
As ecclesiastical authorities saw caring for God's poor as part of
their mission, going directly to the rich with an appeal for alms,
the actual poor became an abstraction.[5]

The lack of an effective centralized state in the early Middle Ages
allowed the papacy to step in and create institutions that would
provide the security needed to maintain all levels of society.[6] The
medieval monastery was a central part of this system, and the public
supported it through charitable donations. While these donations,
mainly in the form of land and bequests upon admittance or at
death, sustained and even allowed the monastic institutions to
prosper, religious officials were the only ones allowed to administer
them. In the reciprocal relations of the rural medieval community,
this was the monastery's role and responsibility. The paternalistic
power of ecclesiastical authority over the care of the community
cemented the larger institutional church's moral supremacy and
authority, and ensured its own continual protection in the form of
economic sustenance and political influence.[7]

The ecclesiastical response to need in the early Middle Ages took
the form of small, rural monastic facilities that functioned as nascent
hospitals scattered throughout Europe. There is evidence, although
scarce, of shelters for pilgrims and the poor as early as the patristic
era. The earliest references to the establishment of houses for the
sick or poor come from France in the sixth century.[8] Centuries later,
Merovingian and Carolingian bishops established small houses for
pilgrims near public roads. The foundation and administration of
these hospices moved from the purview of bishops to monasteries
in the late Carolingian era. The priority of these institutions appears
to have been primarily hospitality rather than poor relief or care
for the ill. These were generally small shelters frequently established
by the local bishop and often attached to a monastery. Members of

the hospital community were commonly required to follow monastic rules and priests were on hand to hear obligatory confessions of patients before their treatment.[9]

There is also evidence for some urban hospitals in Italy prior to the communal age. In the seventh century, the hospital of Santa Maria in Aquiro in Rome had beds for one hundred individuals.[10] As Rome was the major pilgrimage centre of Europe, this large institution was probably unique. Between the ninth and the twelfth centuries there were several episcopal houses established in the larger cities such as Milan. Documents refer to the foundation in 876 of a *xenodochio*[11] in Milan for the poor and pilgrims that was dependent upon the monastery of San Ambrogio.[12] Various Milanese archbishops founded hospices for the needy in 881, 903, and 996.[13] Carolingian law required monastic and canonical institutions to be jurisdictionally linked and provide care for the poor.[14] There appears to be a decline in the foundation of new hospitals after that, with the re-emergence, in an altered form, of the hospitals as part of the reform movements of the twelfth century.

Challenges to traditional responses to poverty and need

Beginning in the twelfth century, a convergence of changing economic, religious, political, and social currents demanded a comprehensive re-evaluation of poverty, need, illness, and the appropriate institutional response to such challenges. The extensive, fast paced, urbanization of the high Middle Ages, nowhere more pronounced than in Italy, challenged the earlier ecclesiastical model of charity. The establishment of new forms of community created novel social, economic, and political relationships that tested the traditional authority of both the secular and ecclesiastical hierarchies. The emergence of corporate and artisanal guilds, and patronage systems based on material wealth and labour status instead of bloodline or land ownership, altered the political balance within the cities. The ensuing economic and social stressors created by these far-reaching socio-political changes challenged existing institutional structures.[15]

Urbanization and a revitalized commercial economy brought opportunity and prosperity to some, but it also attracted an increasing flow of individuals who were displaced and often desperate. Throughout the twelfth and thirteenth centuries many merchants, pilgrims, and crusaders passed through the urban areas of northern

Italy on their way to the ports of Venice and Genoa, and on the road to Rome. The roads and waterways also brought an increasing number of vagrants, beggars, and thieves to the cities along the routes.[16] Increased mobility, urbanization, and economic diversification created a growing disparity between the rich and the poor within the confines of the community and that resulted in more and more individuals being pushed into the margins of society.[17]

The monastery, a predominately rural institution, was not organized to respond to the demand of urban inhabitants. Increasingly, urban bishops were called upon to collect and administer poor relief in the cities.[18] Bishops did rise to the occasion and there are copious examples of this ecclesiastical response. For instance in Lombardy, Bishop Lanfranco of Pavia, appointed in 1070, was known feed twelve poor inhabitants of the city at his table every day.[19] Earlier in the eleventh century, in response to a famine in Milan, Bishop Lanfranco, stressing his role as 'father of the poor', encouraged bakers to bake bread for the poor and organized them for its distribution. These bakers in turn formed a permanent organization of bakers for charity.[20] In 1140 the jurist Gratian articulated the official ecclesiastical call to duty of bishops saying, 'The bishop ought to be solicitous and vigilant concerning defence of the poor and the relief of the oppressed and protection of the monasteries.'[21]

However, larger jurisdictional struggles of the eleventh and twelfth centuries challenged the bishoprics' ability to respond adequately to ever increasing communal need. As the papacy worked to codify its temporal authority and create a papal monarchy, it found itself locked in an epic struggle with secular imperial powers and its own bishops. Often, the local bishops suffered a decline in personal authority as a result. In Italy in particular, bishops were frequently caught in the middle of the fight, as there were overlapping layers of secular and religious authority, which meant they often served two masters.[22] Although, in some instances the transition to the communal era was smooth and the bishop and cathedral church (*duomo*) remained central symbols of authority within the city, even if they did retain power their practical ability to respond to communal need was tested. Support, in the form of income and property, was often lost in the larger power struggle between secular and religious powers.[23] Over the course of the late

thirteenth and fourteenth centuries, bishops ceded more and more
control over social assistance to corporate bodies and civic government as a result.

Redefining poverty and charity

As the challenges of providing for an increasingly needy constituency escalated, church and civic authorities found it necessary to
redefine poverty and need, and to create legal and cultural designations that could guide them to a determination of the level of
assistance required. As Miri Rubin has suggested, poverty is a relative term best defined as, 'the want of something which can reason-
ably be expected based on social status'.[24] Officials attempted to
codify such need, but medieval statutes were not always unambigu-
ous as to what these expectations or requirements were. Major
changes to social status required the regular redefinition of such
designations. In twelfth- and thirteenth-century England, legal statutes defined those who did not have enough goods to 'live rightly'[25]
as poor, but much examination was required to determine what
constituted 'living rightly'.

From the highest intellectual circles to the common workers'
associations discourse revolved around these issues. The eleventh
and twelfth centuries witnessed a pan-European flourishing of pious
activity among all individuals in society and created a revival of
Christian theological discourse and an institutional reordering.
Monastic reform, combined with the introduction of vibrant theological debate within the nascent university system and the rise of
grassroots mendicant movements, fostered an era of the active
pursuit of religiosity between both the educated elites within the
ecclesiastical system as well as common citizens.[26] Much of this
renewed religious activity focused on service to the community and
aiding the disadvantaged.

By the eleventh century, theological discourse regarding charity
evolved to reflect changes to society. Individuals such as Peter
Abelard, Albertus Magnus, and ultimately Thomas Aquinas, birthed
a novel Christian philosophy, Scholasticism, which challenged and
revived doctrinal discourse. At the same time, men like St Francis
and St Dominic, the women of the beguines, as well as countless
other nameless lay persons pursued a new passion for the apostolic
life within their communities.[27] Urban ecclesiastical reformers like

Arnold of Brescia articulated the idea of a civic-centred lay apostolic activism.[28] The papacy, under the leadership of such intellectual popes as Innocent III, utilized scholarly justification to assert
papal authority over all ecclesiastical as well as many temporal
affairs.[29]

Lay activism

Some scholars have viewed the rise of lay religious and semi-
religious movements throughout medieval Europe as a result of
theological reform and ecclesiastical leadership. J. Brodman, viewing
religious charitable movements throughout Western Europe, argues
for the primacy of ecclesiastical institutions and their concern in
the creation of this social emphasis on *misericordia*. He argues that
canonists of the twelfth and thirteenth centuries led the movement
toward a more active life of apostolic poverty and charitable activity. That the vibrant theological academy flourishing in the University of Paris in the twelfth century produced a group of churchmen,
which included the future Pope Innocent III, stressed the importance
of actively engaging in a pious life of communal commitment.[30]

   This perspective denies the primacy of the laity in the creation
of the apostolic charitable movements of the age. As will be illustrated here, the founders of lay and semi-religious groups active in
charitable work were, in fact, grassroots organizations whose popularity forced recognition and reaction by the ecclesiastical powers.[31]
Their independent activity is particularly pronounced in northern
Italy. Many, indeed, began their existence branded as heretical
movements. Innocent III recognized the popular support for these
groups and moved church policy toward one of accommodation
rather than suppression.[32] The founding of hospitals, apostolic lay
activity, ecclesiastical reform, and intellectual revival were all part
of a fundamental shift in religious culture throughout Europe that
emanated from the highest circles of power but also, importantly,
from a newly active urban population.

   In fact, the move toward greater secular involvement in social
issues and the shift of control over the alleviation of social ills, as
well as the tension this engendered between church and the state
was at the heart of the revolution that challenged ecclesiastical
supremacy in the late Middle Ages. This revolution contributed to
the rise of secular powers and demand for reform throughout

Europe in the Renaissance era. As he is concerned with the context of Europe more generally, Brodman does not recognize Italian political rivalries among bishops, princes and independent-minded city fathers in particular. However, to understand the nature of charitable activity of the period, it must be placed in the context of developing power struggles among these authorities.

The increased attention to the problem of defining poverty by nearly all members of society is a signal that it had become a growing issue by the twelfth century. The desperately poor but able man; growing numbers of orphans, widows, and beggars, unknown and increasingly active characters in the medieval city such as alien pilgrims and travellers who simply pass through challenged citizens' self-identity and security.[33] The reactions to such insecurity vary but ultimately led to an overall civic response that challenged existing social welfare models and forced ecclesiastical authorities to respond.

From a variety of contemporary sources, one can clearly see concern expressed by lay religious, secular authorities, and even commoners over the social ills of the era; discourse abounds regarding necessary actions to alleviate them. Chronicles commented on the need for charity among urban dwellers and noted the efforts being made to redress the problem. The chronicler Jacques de Vitry, writing around 1220, in addition to his sermons and contemplations on the religiosity of the crusader era, was also interested in observing the impact of these new movements on society. According to de Vitry, at the time of his writing, there were approximately 1200 hospitals for the poor and ill throughout Western Europe.[34] He provides us with many descriptive historical surveys of the urban centres, such as Milan, where charitable institutions such as hospitals flourished. In addition to quantitative descriptions of religious houses and hospitals, he chronicled the needs and concerns of urban inhabitants. His definition of the poor is a clear indication of changes in contemporary perceptions of poverty. For example, in a departure from earlier discourse,[35] he included the deserving labourer in his description of the poor as; 'He who by working with his two hands acquires his meagre daily bread and has nothing left after dining.'[36] De Vitry is laudatory of the lay order of citizens who stepped in to take care of the needy. These lay citizens left very little direct evidence in their words, but the comments of de Vitry about their activity illuminates their active participation.

Another contemporary chronicler who gives us insight into the new charitable ethos, Albertanus of Brescia (*c.*1200–51) was very much a product of his urban environment. Serving the city of Brescia and Cremona in many official capacities, including a stint as legal counsellor, he was learned, well respected, and highly involved in the politics of his community. He became a prolific writer and much of his work contains a good deal of social commentary.[37] In a sermon delivered to a confraternity in Brescia in 1250, he exhorted the members to live a godly life of service. Quoting many relative passages from the scriptures, Albertanus suggested that the first basis for the rule of their congregation was the selfless administration of charity.[38] The many references to Augustine in his sermon included the injunction, 'Whoever gives to a poor person not to refresh the belly of the needy one, but to remove the weariness of the one asking, loses both the deed and the reward.'[39] In addressing the confraternity, he stipulated that they must not stray from this injunction, must keep it central to their rule, and must resist the temptation to allow the process to become self-serving. The popularity of the medieval confraternity in general, whose primary purpose was the incorporation of charitable assistance, illustrates the groundswell of lay response to the needs of the community. All social organizations were grounded in faith and legitimized by their orthodox relation to their local or regional church, but their fervent activism suggests impatience with the traditional institutional response of ecclesiastical institutions. Citizens responded to communal issues such as economic instability, rather than personal ones like tragedy or illness. They created charitable institutions like the hospital in response to these specific communal needs.

Political and social action through charity

At their most basic level, charitable institutions, such as the hospital, gave immediate relief to those who were in need, fulfilling a primary service to the urban community. However, they also provided an opportunity for the expression of piety for those responding to a charitable impulse while at the same time alleviating the crime, indigence, and disease that often arose in the wake of extreme neediness.[40] In addition, such charitable activity provided avenues of access to social and political influence for benefactors and challenged existing economic, social, religious, and political organizations. They forced traditional institutions to react and thus, forever altered the landscape of the medieval city. [41]

Charitable activity created an avenue for pious members of the community not only to help their fellow brethren as dictated by faith, but also to ensure their own salvation. Charity was a dual mechanism; it served to alleviate the poverty of others and the sinfulness of the self. This system provided a mutually beneficial relationship for both the charitable institutions and the individuals. For example, the pope offered indulgences specifically for those who gave to charitable organizations. In 1302 the bishop of Parma issued a decree granting indulgences for forty days to those individuals from Parma (and later extended to those from Cremona), who gave alms to Ospedale Rodolfo Tanzi.[42] Similar indulgences were granted to those who gave to the Consortium of Spirito Santo in Parma, which also operated a hospital, in 1289 and again in 1296.[43] For the wealthy, religious charitable institutions, such as, hospitals provided a safe haven for assets – land, wealth – and female or excess members of the family while also allowing for the expression of piety and love of God through charity.

However, charity also provided an avenue for direct influence of one's community beyond personal religious aspirations. It is essential to understand the relationship of the hospital movement of the age to the growing importance of the *civitas* in northern Italy. Communal government was based on a model of citizen participation that depended on semi-independent social networks and support systems. The concurrent rise of lay religious orders and occupational associations, such as confraternities, helped in governing the city. Charitable institutions, such as hospitals, created by these groups structured management along similar lines as these communal organizations.[44] As a result, hospitals too required citizen participation and independent social networks.

In the independent cities of Italy, political self-identification underwent a profound evolution between the twelfth and fifteenth centuries. There the arena of jurisdictional competition was between individual neighbourhoods, and the local hospital became a mechanism for the appropriation of political power and expression of civic responsibility. It also provided an opportunity for the cities' gradual emancipation from the authority of ecclesiastical powers.

Lay and semi-religious groups who founded and administered hospitals became integral players in the political arena.

Roisin Cossar gives us the most compelling study to date of the intersection of religion, community, social class, and political power within the Italian city-state of the Middle Ages.[45] She emphasizes the importance of understanding the increased participation by the laity in urban society and their expanding influence over all elements of that society as integral to providing a comprehensive picture of medieval Italy.[46] Cossar considers the importance of the hospital as a mechanism of civic activity for the laity in the city of Bergamo and her study of Bergamo stands as a test case against which the experiences of many of the northern Italian city-states can be judged.

Early in the era, in the absence of adequate monastic assistance, the bishops with support from the papacy often coopted the laity in order to assist in alleviating social problems.[47] Church officials cautiously allowed lay groups like confraternities, tertiary mendicant orders, and hospitals to aid religious institutions in providing assistance. The challenge for church authorities was how to avoid losing control over these institutions. The papacy even allowed for the inclusion of women, and their participation in bequests, endowments, and the administration of the hospitals affords us a glimpse into their lives and suggests an active role for women in the creation and evolution of medieval civic life.[48] Lay and semi-religious groups enthusiastically embraced the challenge of assisting their community.

One of the ways to view the increased institutionalization of charity in the twelfth through fifteenth centuries is to understand it as a method of converting religious aspirations of the lay community to active service for the wider community. The lay community was anxious to alleviate the social ills of society and to increase their own security, but they were also acting out of a very conscious desire to lead a religious life.[49] The two impulses converged in the creation of charitable institutions.[50] For those who did not wish to follow a path as drastic as joining a religious order, participation in confraternal organizations, simply giving to charitable institutions, or working to provide charity offered some assuaging of guilt. We can see this increased desire to help the poor specifically in the increase in testamentary donations made to 'the poor' as an independent category as early as the middle of the twelfth century. [51] One of the primary activities of these new lay movements was the foundation of hundreds of local hospitals as a way of institutionalizing their charitable mission.

Such lay and semi-religious organizations became a central mechanism that organized what was the convergence of communal needs, increased moral tension, emergent civic consciousness, and the traditional ecclesiastical body's inability to respond adequately into a collective societal response.[52] Despite their many differences, these groups were committed to remaining in an urban setting and assisting their neighbours. The founding of hospitals represents one of these 'wide range of experiments', which sought to alleviate the many social stressors while providing for acceptable political and social prospects for benefactors.[53]

Charitable organizations, such as hospitals, were also readily embraced as a mechanism for social mobility and political influence because even prominent citizens of the new communes found they lacked the legitimacy conferred by traditional feudal titles and the social validity created by earlier community structures. Charitable organizations that founded hospitals afforded the wealthy an opportunity to create new communities and conferred on them traditional ecclesiastical approval backed by familiar cultural ritual and fervent religious belief.[54] Leadership in a confraternity, the management of a hospital, or even the substantial donation of goods or land, often gave an urban dweller entrée to political participation and influence. In addition, competing powers within the city – that is, the communal government versus the bishop – and opposition between cities and with the Holy Roman emperor often created difficulties for citizen engagement, as well as maintenance of business and family interests. Charitable organizations such as hospitals often provided a safe place to secure one's assets, and even life, and acted as a neutral space in the political arena. For example, in 1264, Guiduccius Beccarius entered, with his entire family, the third order of the *Humiliati*, which was active in the administration of hospitals, and donated all of his worldly goods because he feared for his safety during a period of war. At the end of the war, he left the order and demanded a return of his goods.[55]

Perhaps Rodolfo Tanzi of Parma, for whom the Ospedale Rodolfo Tanzi was named, provides the clearest example of this phenomenon.[56] In 1201, the bishop of Parma granted Tanzi approval to build a new hospital. There is no mention of Tanzi or his family in communal documents prior to the hospital's founding, but for the

subsequent ten to fifteen years, he successfully built and administered the new hospital, which became an important institution in
the city. He was thoroughly engaged in politics of the city and we
can see some of the internal and external political conflicts of the
commune played out through the activities of Tanzi and his hospital. The hospital was part of a neighbourhood association, the
Capodiponte, which was involved in disputes with the city government on numerous occasions. Tanzi spearheaded many of the association's efforts. In addition, as the hospital was under papal
protection, several prominent families such as the Gonduino joined
the hospital and placed their possessions there to protect them from
political threats.[57] Tanzi served as arbiter in public disputes, manager
of public works issues for the neighbourhood, and mediator and
protector of family groups.

The creation of charitable institutions was not only beneficial to
the needy, the state, and the church, but also provided an important
replacement mechanism for lost social networks of rural communities. Confraternities, lay religious orders, and hospitals created 'arti-
ficial family communities' in the city while serving to assist members
in fulfilling their roles as good Christians. Ties of patronage, obligation, service, and neighbourhood bound medieval Italian urban
society tightly. These bonds were as important to citizens as any
feudal structure, but were less clear-cut, more fluid, and very fragile.
Membership in a confraternity, religious order, or guild helped to
define one's place in the social network, protect oneself from exclu-
sion, and articulate one's relationship with others. Providing charity
or participating in a charitable organization not only cemented
one's place in the new social order but also ensured a reciprocity
in case of need, that is a form of insurance against hardship. Sweetinburgh describes the exchange as a form of 'spiritual economy'
within the new urban material economy.[58]

The hospital movement arose with the growth of the communal
government, which also recognized the need for public administration over private authority, particularly in northern Italy in
the twelfth and thirteenth centuries. There, the nascent communal governments desperately tried to wrest sovereignty from both
the imperial throne in the north and the nearer episcopal powers
represented by the local and regional bishoprics. The security of
the citizenry and their economic prosperity were paramount to
such independence. City leaders actively pursued lay alternatives to

charitable relief, and created novel methods of administering them. Lay initiative institutionalized charity in the form of hospitals, alms-houses, and tertiary lay religious orders. Prosperous urban dwellers saw such institutions as means to social acceptance, and even advancement, as well as communal security.[59]

Conclusion

The outcome of this evolution was the creation of novel approaches to the perception of poverty and of communal and personal responsibility. These new perceptions led to the creation of a social welfare system. This complex web of participation and exchange existed in all charitable institutions throughout the Italian city, and the foundation and administration of hospitals provide clear evidence for this relationship. Considering the multifaceted network of charity, we can see that while hospitals and other charitable outlets can be viewed as 'sensitive indicator[s] of contemporary attitudes regarding piety and charity',[60] they also illuminate the evolving attitudes and activities regarding the social, political, and economic system of the medieval Italian city. They did not arise and prosper simply due to renewed religious fervour or ecclesiastical pressure, nor simply in reaction to the new urban milieu, or as an offshoot of urban growth. They were vital cogs in the overall machine of the *civitas*, which affected all members of society to a large degree. However, it would be quite cynical to believe the actions of the participants in providing charity were solely driven by political or economic motive. This was an age of intense piety and a good deal of the charitable activity must be analysed for its pious intent as well. It is the intersection of these factors – religious, personal, political, and social – that gave rise to this novel institution that was the medieval Italian hospital.

Notes

1 K. A. Lynch, *Individuals, Families, and Communities in Europe 1200–1800* (Cambridge, 2003), 106–7.
2 G. Cracco, 'Dalla misericordia della Chiesa alla misericordia del principe', in M. Alberzoni and O. Grassi (eds), *La Carità Milano nei secoli XII–XV, atti del convegno di studi Milano, 6–7 novembre 1987* (Milan, 1989), 31–3, 35. Cracco shows that there are far fewer mentions of *caritas* in writings of the period and many more references to

pietas and *misericordia*, for example, references to *opera misericordiae* are increasingly abundant in ecclesiastical documents.

3 Augustine, *On Christian Doctrine*, D. W. Robertson (trans.) (New York, 1958), book I, chapter 32, 27–8. For more on the role of the early ecclesiastical administration of charity and the institutions see J. Brodman, *Charity and Religion*, 50; P. Brown, *Through the Eye of a Needle: Wealth, the Fall of Rome, and the Making of Christianity in the West, 350–550 AD* (Princeton, NJ, 2012).
4 Brodman, *Charity and Religion*, 3–4.
5 Brown, *Through the Eye of a Needle*. Brown has shown that early medieval charity moved from the civic model of the late Roman era to charity given to the poor through an intermediary mechanism: the Christian church. In S. Holman, *The Hungry Are Dying: Beggars and Bishops in Roman Cappadocia* (Oxford, 2001), Holman also illuminates the civic model of charity in the late Roman world and illustrates how the purpose of charity, while an expression of civic pride, was divorced from the reality of the actual needs of the poor.
6 Morris, *The Papal Monarchy*, 1.
7 For more information on the role of the early church in the administration of charity, and particularly, on the view of the obligation of charity specifically to the poor, see Brown, *Through the Eye of a Needle*, 75–6.
8 For a consideration of earlier hospital foundations see P. Horden, 'The Earliest Hospitals in Byzantium, Western Europe, and Islam', *Journal of Interdisciplinary History*, 35 (2005): 361–89; and *Hospitals and Healing from Antiquity to the Later Middle Ages* (Aldershot, 2008).
9 Brodman, *Charity and Religion*, 43–88; Henderson, *The Renaissance Hospital*, 4–33.
10 Brodman, *Charity and Religion*, 50.
11 *Xenodochio* was the name given to hospices, hostels, and hospitals in the late Roman and early medieval period.
12 A. Ambrosioni, 'Gli Arcivescovi e la Carità nel Secolo XII', in M. Alberzoni and O. Grassi (eds), *La Carità Milano*, 47–9.
13 Ibid., 48; Albini, *Città e ospedali*, 67.
14 E. Rocca, 'Ospedali e canoniche regolari', in *La vita comune del clero dei secoli XI e XII.: Atti della settimana internazionale di studio: Mendola, Settembre 1959* (Milan, 1962), 17. He wrote both a book and an article. This reference is to the article.
15 Lynch, *Individuals, Families and Communities*, 103.
16 For general information on the crusade routes and their impacts on the medieval cities of Italy see D. Glass, *Portals, Pilgrimage, and Crusade in Western Tuscany* (Princeton, NJ, 1997); and M. McCormick, *Origins of the European Economy: Communications and Commerce, A.D. 300–900* (Cambridge, 2001). See also discussion below, Chapter 2.

17 See Little, *Religious, Poverty and the Profit Economy*.
18 Morris, *The Papal Monarchy*, 321.
19 A. Thompson, *Cities of God: The Religion of the Italian Communes 1125–1325* (University Park, PA, 2005), 45.
20 Albini, *Città e ospedali*, 23, 66, 76.
21 Morris, *The Papal Monarchy*, 320.
22 Waley and Dean, *The Italian City-Republics*, 52–6.
23 For a comprehensive perspective on the variations in episcopal governmental relations in Italy see Thompson, *Cities of God*.
24 M. Rubin, *Charity and Community in Medieval Cambridge* (Cambridge, 1987), 6–8. For studies on charity in Europe see also the work of S. Farmer, *Surviving Poverty in Medieval Paris: Gender, Ideology, and the Daily Lives of the Poor* (Ithaca, NY, 2002) and M. Mollat, *Etudes sur l'histoire de la pauvrete: moyen age-XVIe siècles*, 2 vols (Paris, 1974). See also B. Geremek, *The Margins of Society in Late Medieval Paris* (Cambridge, 1987); A. Scott, *Experiences of Charity, 1250–1650* (Farnham, 2015). E. Bressan and G. Rumi, in *L'ospitale e i poveri: la storiografia sull'assistenza: L'Italia e il 'caso Lombardo'* (Milan, 1981), addresses the need to study the poor and poor relief in the Lombard region of Italy in the overall historical, social, economic, and cultural context of the region.
25 B. Tierney, *Medieval Poor Law: A Sketch of Canonical Theory and Its Application in England* (Berkeley, CA, 1959), 72.
26 H. Grundmann's grand monograph, *Religious Movements of the Middle Ages: The Historical Links between Heresy, the Mendicant Orders, and the Women's Religious Movement in the Twelfth and Thirteenth Century, with the Historical Foundations of German Mysticism* (Notre Dame, IN, 1995) still stands as the greatest guide for anyone interested in understanding the pan-European religious movements of the period. For more on the apostolic movements of the period see S. Brasher, *Women of The Humiliati: A Lay Religious Order in Medieval Civic Life* (New York, 2003); W. Simons, *Cities of Ladies: Beguine Communities in the Medieval Low Countries, 1200–1565* (Philadelphia, 2001); A. Vauchez and D. Bornstein (eds), *The Laity in the Middle Ages: Religious Beliefs and Devotional Practices* (Notre Dame, IN, 1993).
27 For further information on the intellectual movement of the Middle Ages see E. Grant, *God and Reason in the Middle Ages* (New York, 2001).
28 Brescia was a regular canon in the city of Brescia. Educated in Paris, he was an intellectual figurehead for the independent commune movement and supporter of lay activism throughout Italy. See G. Greenaway, *Arnold of Brescia* (Cambridge, 1931).
29 For a discussion of the reformed articulation of papal power see Pennington, *Pope and Bishops*, 31–74.

30 Brodman, *Charity and Religion,* 16–18.
31 See also Grundmann, *Religious Movements in the Middle Ages;* Simons, *Cities of Ladies;* Vauchez and Bornstein, *The Laity in the Middle Ages.*
32 See B. Bolton, *Innocent III: Studies on Papal Authority and Pastoral Care* (Aldershot, 1995).
33 Albini, *Città e ospedali,* 63.
34 J. Frederick and J. Hinnebusch, *The Historia Occidentalis of Jacques de Vitry: A Critical Edition* (Freiburg, 1972), 146–51. Also translated in L. Little and S. Buzzetti, *Liberty, Charity, Fraternity: Lay Religious Confraternities at Bergamo in the Age of the Commune* (Bergamo, 1988), 88.
35 For example, in *Summa Theologiae* Thomas Aquinas wrote, 'Spiritual danger comes from poverty when it is not voluntary, because a man falls into many sins through the desire to get rich, which torments those who are involuntarily poor.' This sentiment consigns the involuntary poor into immediate suspicion and elevates the status of the voluntary poor. Aquinas, *Summa Theologiae,* 2a2a, quast. 186, art. 3, resp. ad 2, 47.
36 J. De Vitry and T. Crane, *The Exempla or Illustrative Stories from the Sermones Vulgares of Jacques De Vitry* (London, 1890), 27.
37 Albertanus of Brescia, 'A Sermon to a Confraternity (1250)', introduced by J. Powell and translated from Latin by G. Ahlquist, in K. Jansen, J. Drell and F. Andrews, *Medieval Italy: Texts in Translation* (Philadelphia, PA, 2009), 393–9.
38 Ibid., 394.
39 Ibid., 395.
40 Lynch, *Individuals, Families, Communities,* 103.
41 S. Watson, 'City as Charter: Charity and the Lordship of English Towns', in C. Goodson, A. Lester and C. Symes (eds), *Cities, Texts and Social Networks, 400–1500: Experiences and Perceptions of Medieval Urban Space* (Farnham, 2010), 17. Watson argues that for England the 'hospital was perhaps the most public tool by which the physical environment of the provincial town was transformed from a symbol of regional lordship to its own defined political community'. See also, Geremek, *The Margins of Society,* 175–6; S. Sweetinburgh, *The Role of the Hospital in Medieval England: Gift Giving and the Spiritual Economy* (Dublin, 2004).
42 APSr, RT, b. 8, fasc. 4, 'Quoniam, ut ait apostolus, omnes stabimus ante tribunal Christi recepturi pro ut in corpore gessiumus sive bonum fuerit sive malum oportet nos diem messionis extreme misericordie operibus prevenire et eternorum intuiti seminare in terries quod reddente Domino cum multiplicato fructu recoligere valeamus in celis firmam spem fiduciamque tenentes, quoniam qui parce seminat parce et metet et qui seminar in benedictionibus et metet vitam eternam';

published in G. Albini, 'Dallo sviluppo della comunita ospedaliera alla sua cirisi (secoli XIV e XV)', in R. Creci, *L'ospedale Rodolfo Tanzi di Parma in età medieval* (Bologna, 2004), 33.

43 Ibid., 35.

44 R. Cossar, *Transformation of the Laity in Bergamo, 1260-c.1400* (Leiden, 2008), 11.

45 Ibid.

46 Ibid.

47 The struggle for authority between bishops and the papacy is best exemplified by Innocent III's efforts to strengthen papal claims to divine authority through canon law and reformed doctrine but also reflects Italian territorial political conflicts. See Pennington, *Pope and Bishops;* Waley and Dean, *The Italian City-Republics.* Resistance to the centralizing efforts of the papacy resulted in a particularly northern Italian school of reform exemplified by the teachings of canon regular Arnold of Brescia who supported the idea of a strong lay-backed decentralization of ecclesiastical institutions. See Greenaway, *Arnold of Brescia.* The impact of these jurisdictional disputes will be discussed in depth in Chapter 5.

48 For more on women's role in religious lay movements see S. Brasher, *Women of The Humiliati;* W. Simons, *Cities of Ladies;* Vauchez and Bornstein, *The Laity in the Middle Ages.*

49 Little, *Religion, Poverty and the Profit Economy.*

50 M. Gazzini, *L'ospedale a Parma,* 18–19. Closely related to the rise of a perception of civic responsibility was a rise in the role of what Albini calls 'civic religiosity.' Albini, *Città e ospedali,* 28.

51 Little, *Liberty, Charity, Fraternity,* 89.

52 Grundmann, *Religious Movements,* 3.

53 G. Merlo, 'Religiosita e cultura religiosa dei laici nel secolo XII', in *L'Europa dei secoli XI e XII fra novita e tradizione: sviluppi di una cultura* (Milan, 1989), 201–15.

54 Thompson, *Cities of God,* 141.

55 Brasher, *Women of the Humiliati,* 101.

56 Tanzi, and the hospital named for him, will be considered in depth throughtout the current study.

57 See subsequent chapters for more on Rodolfo Tanzi and also, Gazzini, 'Rodolfo Tanzi', 3–28.

58 Sweetinburgh, *The Role of the Hospital in England,* 36.

59 Little, *Liberty, Charity, Fraternity,* 95–6.

60 Sweetinburgh, *The Role of the Hospital in England,* 36.

2

The foundation of hospitals

The foundation of so many small community hospitals in northern Italy in the twelfth century was more than just a spontaneous, coincidental development; the phenomenon suggests a very specific moment in the history of the area. The impetus to house the sick, the poor, and pilgrims within the community with distinct specifications for the location of the institution, its construction, and management, gives us a very clear insight into the process of urbanization of the period as well as a localized portrait of civic engagement and communal will. It is important to focus particular attention on the foundational moments in the evolution of the hospital because it is necessary to differentiate the founding of the hospital from its later character. Once ecclesiastical, lay, or civic authorities, appropriated the administration of the hospital it could often look very different from the institution its founders intended. This chapter will explore the foundation of various individual hospitals and consider the physical location of the facilities, the identity of the founders, and the motivation of those founders, along with a discussion of the communal context and jurisdictional structures under which they originally operated.

The suggestion that the growth in foundations of hospitals in the high Middle Ages was explosive is not overstated. The thirteenth-century chronicler Bonvesin de la Riva indicated that in the city of Milan there were ten hospitals within the city walls, including the Ospedale Brolo, which could accommodate up to five hundred poor and ill people.[1] Opicino de Canistris described ten hospitals inside the walls of Pavia as well, with an additional seven just outside the city walls.[2] The chronicler Giovanni Villani, at the turn of the fourteenth century, reported that there were thirty hospitals in Florence, with more than a thousand beds between them to house the poor and sick.[3] By the time of the Black Death, this number had increased to nearly forty-one hospitals in a city with a population of just under 100,000.[4] In Como, a much smaller and less important city than Florence, there were between twenty and thirty hospitals in existence, with over six hundred beds at this time.[5] According to John Henderson, there was a spectacular increase in the number of hospitals in Italy between 1100 and 1550. He has calculated that forty-three per cent of that growth occurred between 1250 and 1349.[6]

The precipitous rise of hospital foundations of this era was a result of a confluence of economic stressors and increased mobility among many people in medieval Europe. Initially, the hospitals' main functions were as places of accommodation for pilgrims and travellers as well as providers for the sick and needy within the immediate community. They were typically small communities located within neighbourhoods. By the early part of the fourteenth century economic pressures from overpopulation, climate stress, famine, and disease increased demand on the traditional charitable activities of hospitals and other groups forcing them to grow and evolve.[7]

This era of intense religious activity witnessed the emergence of unprecedented apostolic zeal among the population throughout Europe. While this extreme piety took many forms, the desire to express one's faith through service in this life in the manner of Christ, a *vivere religiose,* meant active participation in charitable giving and administration by laypersons. The hospital was the ready vehicle for this desire.[8] The specific nature of these early institutions, small, community-led, and localized, indicated a major change in the personal as well as institutional response to communal need.[9] Hospitals provided the institutional mechanism for the convergence of social, religious, and communal interests.

Documentary evidence

There is a plethora of notarial documentation from cities in the Lombard region that gives evidence for the foundation of hospitals in the area. These include indirect references to the actual origins of hospitals from subsequent relevant documents and a fair number of foundational charters or foundational testaments for specific hospitals directly noting their institutional inception. Although they were generally consolidated into larger institutions in the fifteenth

century, it is still possible to trace evidence of independent hospitals
in their earlier incarnations. Often, this is due to the record keeping
of the later, larger hospitals. For example, Ospedale Maggiore in
Milan as well as Ospedale Sant'Anna in Como, which are both still
in existence, have records dating back to their founding in the mid-
fifteenth century, but they have also maintained accounts from the
independent hospitals they absorbed or replaced at that time. In
other cases, general notarial records provide the foundation charters of hospitals by year or by notary. Records of foundation
charters frequently list the name of the hospital; the date of its
foundation; the location of the institution; the individual or group
who donated land, money, or buildings for the foundation; stipulations made for the management of the institution; and often, ecclesiastical approval for its establishment.

Testamentary bequests regularly refer to the charters and can be
quite detailed as to the identity of the testator, his family, and the
specifics of his donation, including his stated purpose in leaving the
funds. These bequests provide insight not only into the origins of
the hospitals but also give us information about the testators'
family, wealth, social position, and community affiliation. The
information they supply on building location provides a sense of
neighbourhood and social space as well as a map of the perceived
areas of need in the medieval city.[10]

Specific charters are helpful in not only providing the foundation
date and initial patrons of hospitals but also in indicating the original name and location of the institution which can alleviate the
confusion of more vague references in subsequent documents. One
frequent difficulty encountered in researching these institutions
arises from the confusion and discontinuity of their names. Often
one hospital is referred to by several different names over the course
of its history. This makes tracing it back to its original foundation
difficult. For example, Ospedale di Santa Maria Maddalena in
Como was also known as Ospedale della Canava and Ospedale
della Colombetta at various times. There is still scholarly debate as
to the true provenance of the hospital. One document suggests
Isacco da San Benedetto and 'certain principle persons of the *casa
de'Marini*' established it in 1300.[11] But an eighteenth-century
chronicler of Como suggests that in 1313 heirs of Gigliotto de
Marini gave money for the foundation of a Ospedale di Santa
Maria Maddalena and indicates that it was in fact attached to an

older hospital, also probably founded by the family, called Ospedale da Marini.[12] It is subsequently also referred to as Ospedale Colombetta. Cosmacini suggests this may be because it was attached to a semi-religious order whose symbol was the dove or *colombetta*.[13] There is enough later documentation to indicate one single facility, but its foundation and original religious attachment remain obscure.

In the case of Ospedale Rodolfo Tanzi, its initial connection to another church, Ognissanti, and the order of St Antonio, created some ensuing ambiguity regarding its name. It is alternately listed in the documentary evidence as Tanzi, Ognissanti, or S. Antonio. Marina Gazzini has found that the choice of name for a hospital often reflected the parties involved in the documentation. When the laity – secular authorities, donors, administrators – had dealings with the hospital it was most often referred to as Tanzi or Rodolfo Tanzi. When ecclesiastical authorities were involved in issues with the hospital they frequently called it one of the other names. For example, Archbishop Amizio refers to it as 'l'ospedale beati Antonii qui vulgariter appellatur ospitale Rodulfi' when donating to the institution in 1253.[14]

Frequently, the evidence for the earliest years of the hospital is vague or contradictory. In some cases, the original document is lost; subsequent records refer to the original but are not always in agreement. For example, in Como, according to an eighteenth-century chronicle, Giovanni and Obizzone Cacci and their mother Silvia founded Ospedale San Vitale in 1218 for the poor and infirm.[15] Another document refers to its existence in 1221 and yet another compiler gives this as the year of its foundation.[16] These documents all point to its foundation by the Cacci and subsequent placement under the order of the *Humiliati* in 1239, making it one of the oldest such institutions in Como. However, another eighteenth-century complier of the most comprehensive archival information on hospitals in Como, Ballarini, does not even register its existence.[17] These complications aside, it is still possible to reconstruct the origins of an extensive number of hospitals in the region.

Location of hospitals

While hospitals were located throughout the medieval city, early charters suggest that a common feature of many was their location near the gates of the city, and often along major roads.[18] While there are a few early hospitals located near the city centre,[19] most were located just inside or just outside the city walls and frequently by a major gate. Such a pattern of locations supports the view that the early hospitals were predominantly dedicated to the care of pilgrims and travellers rather than of the poor and the sick, and reflect the concerns of the community with the traffic that flowed through the city.[20] By constructing hospitals at these sites, neighbours could ensure that the many poor pilgrims, foreigners, travellers, and immigrants who passed through were cared for, but also and perhaps more importantly, accounted for.

The region of the Po river valley was one of the most urbanized commercial centres of medieval Europe. Most towns of a medium size or larger would have a city wall encompassing the majority of businesses and dwellings. Usually there were at least four gates leading into the cities with corresponding thoroughfares that often crossed paths in a central *piazza*. It was in this large public space that farmers brought goods from the surrounding *contada* and set up markets. There was, therefore, constant traffic through the gates of the city from the countryside alone. In addition, many of the city dwellers had at least some land outside the city gates, which necessitated their travelling in and out of the city frequently.[21] Merchants, pilgrims, and job seekers would also pass through the city gates.

Urban hospitals

The massive urbanization of the twelfth and thirteenth centuries resulted in a building frenzy in many of the cities. City walls that had stood for centuries could no longer contain the growing population and had to be rebuilt. It was also a constant effort to maintain these walls in light of the incessant warfare of the period. Several cities, such as Lodi, suffered major destruction from wars and floods and had to rebuild more than just their walls.[22] Marina Gazzini has suggested in her research on Ospedale Rodolfo Tanzi, that the activity associated with the founding of the hospital must be seen as an integral part in a general pattern of urban planning of the period. Evidence suggests that the founding and building of a hospital, with the purpose of mitigating the tensions developing within an expanding city, required the institution to be critically involved in issues such as traffic, urban planning, water rights, and water usage, as well as in the care of travellers, indigents, and the sick.[23] The hospitals had to do all of these things within an existing ecclesiastical and civic framework while also altering the landscape of neighbourhoods by introducing such a social service institution in their midst.

Ospedale Rodolfo Tanzi provides an excellent example of the importance of location in the founding and development of the hospital. It was built in Borgo Tascherio, a suburban area *'locus caput de ponte'* by the Parma River along the western part of the city walls, which faced the major intersection of the roads leading to Piacenza, Rome, and Tuscany.[24] Recent evidence has suggested the Rodolfo Tanzi was actually two hospitals of the same name and administration located, literally, across the street from one another. They shared resources and expertise and their services appear to have been in great demand.[25] The fact that two hospitals were needed in such proximity and straddling the major road into Parma indicates the degree to which the institutions were focused on travellers. The importance of the city walls and gates is reflected in the fact that they are frequently specifically referred to in charters. For example, in Treviso, the charter for Ospedale Ognissanti specifies that it was located outside the city walls by the S. Teonisto gate on the southwest road to Pavia, which then connected with major routes south to Rome.[26] In the province of Friuli, in the town of Gemona, a major hospital was constructed inside the city walls in the neighbourhood of the duomo near a major gate for the main road heading south into the Po valley.[27] Merchants and pilgrims followed this route from Germany into the Lombard and Venetian regions.[28]

Foundational documents often list the proximity of a hospital to a road suggesting the primacy of this characteristic. Examples of such designations include one for Ospedale Casale Lupani, originally founded as early as 972 and located outside the old city walls of Lodi along the old Roman road to Cremona.[29] Ospedale S. Michaelis Atastaverne, founded in 1261, was located along the Roman road to Piacenza as was Ospedale de Senna founded in 1152 along the same ancient route. Ospedale S. Blasii was located outside the city gates along the road to Cremona.[30] These are just a few of the hospitals found in Lodi with a clear reference to roads, they provide an indication of the comprehensive attempt by city fathers to cover the passages into and out of the city.

Rural hospitals

While the region was densely populated and travel between cities meant there were generally accommodations nearby, there were stretches of rural areas where hospitals were also located, but they were far fewer in number. Although he does not substantiate this claim with specific evidence, Rocca has suggested that the common pattern was to have a hospital every ten miles or so along the major highways.[31] We do have direct evidence of several rural hospitals in the region around Lodi. However, these generally appear to be either earlier medieval institutions or they were connected to an existing monastery. They do not appear to follow the urban pattern of establishment exactly. For example, Ospedale S. Maria di Arlino, mentioned in documents as early as 885, was located in a small rural village and connected to a religious house of the same name. There is evidence that the lay religious order of the *Humiliati* administered it in the twelfth century. This order was representative of the new movement of lay religious involvement in hospital administration, but it is clear that they did not found this particular hospital and only came to be involved much later in its history.[32] Noble families, whose ancient feudal lands and ties may have provided the motivation and capital for such endeavours, founded several rural hospitals near Lodi. Count Iderado da Comazzo founded Ospedale S. Giovanni in 1039 and attached it to a monastery of San Vito on the road to Cremona. This large compound was originally comprised of around one thousand acres and was already one of the richest monasteries in the Lombard region by the twelfth century. Ospedale S. Giovanni seems to have echoed early monastic models of an isolated institution, separated from society, and, in fact, there is no documentary evidence extant for it after 1158. It was not in existence in the fifteenth century when the consolidation of hospitals of Lodi occurred.[33] The noble family Alboni founded another rural hospital, Ospedale San Michele di Brembio, near an old Roman station on an ancient road. It appears in documentary evidence in 1265. However, at that time the document reports that it was already in decline and so was probably much older. It too appears to reflect an older tradition of monastic control.[34]

We can most clearly see the difference between the rural and urban hospitals with the case of Ospedale di San Pietro in Senna,

which was located in the countryside near the village of Senna
outside of Lodi. Described as an ancient, well-established hospital
by the time it is first mentioned in documents from 1152, it had a
great deal of land, including various farmhouses, stables and shops,
woods and pastureland, and was protected and supported by the
old aristocracy of Milan and Lombardy. In the twelfth century,
the brothers who administered the hospital vowed their obedience
to the bishop of Milan with the stipulation that he not interfere
or change the institution or put it under another jurisdiction. The
hospital was so prosperous under the protection of the nobility of
Milan that it continued to accrue land and wealth and eventually
constructed an abbey and monastery there in the fifteenth century.
At its height, thirty to forty brothers lived in the monastery, as
did youth from some noble families.[35] This arrangement clearly
suggests an older, aristocratic model of monastic life and did not
reflect the urban apostolic vocation of the majority of hospitals
considered.

On occasion, evidence indicates that some hospitals were constructed in areas where they would not occupy valuable or habit-
able land. Several documents list the construction of hospitals in
wetlands, swamps, or other 'inhospitable' areas. Ospedale SS.
Giacomo and Filippo in Lodi was built along the ancient road to
Milan in the 'uninhabited wetlands.' Ospedale S. Blasii, also near
Lodi, was located in a swamp.[36] Frequently, hospitals were located
near a river or other water supply and the need to tap into that
supply required the cooperation and consideration of neighbourhood water concerns.[37]

Caretta's examination of the location of hospitals in Lodi gives
us a glimpse into the implications of the constant rivalry and
warfare among cities for their citizens and their institutions.[38] Lodi
was frequently in conflict with Milan, and in the year 1111 warfare
between the two led to the destruction of much of the old city of
Lodi. The city walls had to be reconstructed, as did much of the
city creating a 'New Lodi'.[39] In fact, the complicated and ever-
changing network of political alliances and enmities in the region
was a constant threat to the stability of the population. In addition
to the area's position as a battlefield between the Hohenstaufen
imperial claims and papal resistance to these claims, regional struggles led to frequent hostilities. The archbishop of Milan, a virtual
aristocratic overlord, challenged the claims of the *cittadini* as well

as those of the bishops of Pavia, Lodi, and Cremona.[40] Hospitals built near the city walls played an integral role in the civic affairs of the city and were much affected by its internal and external struggles. They both suffered destruction and were critical components of revitalization efforts. As we shall see in Chapter 5, they often became a battleground for the jurisdictional disputes between various constituencies.

Whether built close to city gates or repurposed in existing buildings, hospitals became such an integral part of a neighbourhood that they often took on civic tasks outside their purview, such as contributing to the building or repairing of bridges or roads, or the mediation of communal disputes.[41] They had to coexist with their neighbours, many of whom had a role in the founding or administering of the hospital as well. As such, hospitals were always oriented most directly to their immediate vicinity, reflecting local concerns and issues. Frequently, the conflicts that arose over issues of administration reflected this bias.[42]

Apart from locating new entities in cities near walls and roads, testators frequently donated their own property with existing buildings for the foundation of a hospital and these donations often determined the locale. For example, testator Buillemus de Buboi founded Ospedale S. Alessandro in Bergamo in 1352, stipulating that his house be used for the facility. Such donations were often the optimal option as the transitions cost very little. The creation of S. Alessandro cost the confraternity charged with its oversight only 16 lire,[43] requiring little more than the building of beds, adding of locks to the doors, and a placing a roof over the courtyard.[44] It is clear from examples of this type that testators founded these institutions specifically for the care of their own family and local community.

Many of the foundational documents do not overtly specify the exact location of the hospital. However, for some, it is possible to infer their locations from their names. While most of the hospitals were named for a saint, often referring to their association or attachment to a church or parish of the same name, some hospitals' names referenced their location. Ospedale de Senna's name refers to a (then) well-known local landmark along the ancient Roman road Piacenza-Laus Pompeia–Milano. Another Lodi hospital located in the old city along an important ancient route was Ospedale S. Michaelis Atastaverne. Atastaverne is probably the bastardization

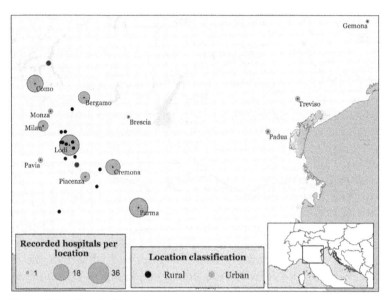

Figure 2.1 Hospital locations

of the name of an ancient Roman stable located along the old Roman road.[45]

At times, owing to confusion with the changing taxonomy of both places and hospitals, it is difficult to establish the locale of an institution. For example, in Como, chroniclers and modern scholars disagree as to the original location of the Ospedale di San Gottardo. Writing in the eighteenth century, Ballarini states that the hospital was located near the ponte di San Giovaninni but subsequent scholars have suggested alternate locations as diverse as 'near the Piazza Popolo' in the centre of Como and 'on the eastern side of the valley in the village of San Giuliano'.[46] These three locations are very different and would have served very different constituents. Despite the difficulties with locating some institutions, it is possible from the anecdotal evidence to map out the location of a great many regional institutions.

Pilgrimage and travel routes

The frequent reference to roads and gates in the documentation of hospital foundations has led some scholars to conclude that the primary purpose of the hospital was simply as a hostel for poorer pilgrims and travellers. The road network in northern Italy was well established by the twelfth century. Main roads as well as the locations of many of the cities dated back to the Roman period. The Po River was a major transportation conduit as well. Milan sat in the central plains of the Po valley and was the historic centre of routes travelled by invading armies from across the Alps, and pilgrims converging on Italy from all over Europe. It was also a major market place for goods from the surrounding countryside and abroad, and eventually the seat of government for much of the region. The Lombard capital of Pavia, an earlier Roman *castrum* site, was located along the Via Emilia, an ancient route that connected northern Italy and thus all of Europe to the coast of the Adriatic. That road in turn was connected to the major southern thoroughfare, Via Flaminia to Rome. Trade, pilgrims, and wayfarers en route to Venice converged on the cities and villages of the Po valley. The Po River itself conducted goods and people throughout the region with tributaries and ports throughout the region.[47] Therefore, any individuals travelling from one place to another would make their way at some point in the journey through the gates of the cities. They would be in need of hospitality.

The surge of hospital foundations in the twelfth and thirteenth centuries was concurrent with the crusader movement of the age. These armed pilgrimages to the Holy Land beginning at the close of the eleventh century did not reflect a new phenomenon, just a much larger, more organized, and much more international movement. In fact, pilgrimage had been an important facet of Christian religious experience since at least the fourth century.[48] The movement of people from all corners of the European continent to religious sites, from the Compostela de Santiago in Spain, to Rome, and to the Holy Land, reached an apogee both in individual pilgrimage and in holy crusades during this period. Traditionally, monasteries and local churches, following the principle that Christians should imitate Christ, provided food and lodging as was necessary for those pilgrims who were too poor to pay their way. As most pilgrims were travelling on foot, practically, this meant providing a place of respite every twenty to thirty kilometres.[49] One of the original purposes of the hospital was to provide this service. Ospedale San Giacomo di Pellegrini was established in Milan in 1332 specifically for the care of pilgrims en route to the sanctuary of Compostela from throughout Europe.[50] The question arises then, to what extent were these early hospitals more than simply hostels for these travellers? Did they serve the poor and the ill as well?

Lombardy and the surrounding area of northern Italy was a major thoroughfare for pilgrimage travel. The Via Francigena pilgrimage route from France passed over S. Bernardo Pass and continued through the Aosta valley, toward Pavia and Piacenza. Pilgrims would then continue along the road to Rome if that was their destination, or board a boat that would sail down the Po River to Venice where they would join a ship bound for the Levant.[51] Caretta believes that the fact that the hospitals were so predominately located along these major routes indicates their main function as pilgrimage hostels in the twelfth century. Although the institutions were frequently listed as being hospitals for the care of the poor, sick, and pilgrims, he believes their primary concern was for the last. He also suggests that the poor or *miserabili* these early facilities cared for were probably more the vagabonds and poor wayfarers who travelled the roads, rather than the *miserabili* living within the city itself.[52]

An examination of the geographic location of the hospitals does indicate a direct correlation between pilgrimage routes and the incidence of some hospital locations. Rome was the destination for much of the pilgrimage traffic throughout Europe at all times, for Europeans from as far north as Ireland and Scandinavia as well as the rest of the continent. Most pilgrims still followed the old Roman roads to Rome, as did most merchants.[53] However, the religious stipulation requiring hospitality for pilgrims stated that such hospitality should only be given for 'one day'. Clearly, ecclesiastical leaders and community members wanted to keep pilgrims from becoming loiterers and desired that pilgrimage traffic be transient. However, evidence from the records indicate that many of inmates of these institutions stayed for long periods of time and were being provided for in ways beyond simple food and a bed for a night.

Significantly, a geographic map of the location of hospitals indicates that, as many of them were located on non-pilgrimage roads and secondary roads as on the primary pilgrimage routes. Pavia was directly on the pilgrimage route, which supports the evidence of pilgrimage hospitals there. Milan, conversely, did not become a major road junction until the development of other major Alpine passes were constructed and utilized in the eleventh and twelfth

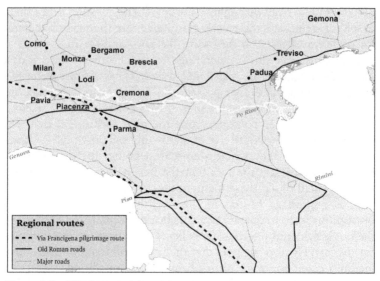

Figure 2.2 Pilgrimage and travel routes

centuries, this junction catered to much more than pilgrimage travel.[54]

It is clear from a thorough examination of documentation from the entire region that hospitals were founded for the purpose of caring for the poor and ill, as well as for pilgrims. The hospital movement may have originated or been founded on the model of the *xenodochia* for poor pilgrims, which gave them a model for poor relief. Yet while hospitals continued to serve this population, their mission developed during the twelfth through fourteenth centuries to providing comprehensive social services to all the communities' needy. The founders of hospitals were often very specific about their desire to have the institutions provide for the welfare and security of their immediate family and community and to provide for the poor and the sick. There is often no mention of pilgrims or travellers in their charters.[55] In fact, as we shall see, most of the testaments by individuals for the foundation of hospitals specifically dictate that they were to serve the poor and the sick. In addition, it is clear from foundation records that many of these hospitals were founded or administered by neighbourhood groups or confraternal orders, which would have had a key interest in alleviating the social ills of a local constituency.

Founders

In order to fully comprehend the nature of the early hospitals in the region it is necessary to examine the identities of the original founders. Bishops, civic and neighbourhood associations, confraternities, lay religious orders, and individuals all took part in creating hospitals. What is clear is that all founders were tied in some way to the specific location of the institution. They were engaging in the welfare of their immediate community. Documentary evidence for the foundation of hospitals in Lodi allows us to observe the development of the hospital movement chronologically and geographically but also illustrates the evolution in the identity and purpose of the founders. In 972 there is evidence of a *xenodochium* that was attached to, and under the jurisdiction of, the abbey of S. Colombano di Bobbio.[56] Documentation refers to S. Sepulchri et S. Crucis, a hospital founded by crusader Giselberto Cainardo in 1096. It was donated to the canons of Church of S. Lorenzo, who possibly followed the rules of order of the Cluny.[57] In 1127 citizen Rogero da Cero founded Ospedale S. Nazarii (later called Leonardi) just outside the city walls on the main road to Milan. It was placed under the jurisdiction of the bishop but allowed self-governance by its administrators, and affiliated with the semi-religious regular canons of S. Nazario di Milano.[58] This progression illuminates the trend toward greater participation in founding and administering hospitals by lay men away from the original dominance of church organizations as founder. However, although its primacy continued to diminish, ecclesiastical entities persisted in playing a role in the origins of many institutions.

Church officials as founders

According to the foundation charters, many of the twelfth- and thirteenth-century founders of hospitals followed an older, ecclesiastical tradition, at least in part. They recognized the regional bishop in his role as 'padre dei poveri' and looked to traditional Benedictine or Augustinian examples, and their rules as models, for their new institutions. Also, there is evidence that the bishopric directly founded some of earliest hospitals from the ninth and tenth centuries. In Milan, for example, Archbishop Ansperto founded Ospedale S. Satiro in 811, and Archbishop Andrea founded the Ospedale S. Celso, among others, in 996.[59] These early institutions followed the traditional monastic model and reflected the urbanization of an older ecclesiastical authority and ideal. As the cities and their communal need grew, local church authorities retained their interest in the foundation of hospitals but found their ability to adequately respond to that need diminished.

At times, the foundation of a hospital followed the natural progression of immediate need and an organized ecclesiastical response. During a famine in the eleventh century, Archbishop Ariberto took charge of general poor relief. Using his recognized authority, he commanded bakers to make eight thousand loaves of bread daily to be distributed to the hungry. He founded the Ospedale San Dionigi next to the monastery of the same name for the purpose of administering this assistance.[60] Ecclesiastical officials, most often those of the bishopric, and the community formed a partnership for alleviating a specific need and attached the hospital to an existing monastery that had the ability to administer such need.

Original founders often stipulated that hospitals be attached to existing monasteries, or they bequeathed to existing monasteries the land, buildings, and goods necessary for the founding of a hospital.[61] Others founded independent hospitals, but frequently still modelled them on Benedictine or Augustinian structures. In general, this reflected a communal appreciation of increased need but also a desire to follow the accepted avenues of authority, protection, and structure. However, lay men initiated many of the charters and this suggests a perception by the public that existing ecclesiastical institutions were not fulfilling this responsibility completely. Also, it is often not clear what being 'attached' to a monastery or church actually meant. It appears that the main benefit to being attached to an existing ecclesiastical institution was that it gave a hospital legitimacy and, it was hoped, the necessary recognition of the bishop. It is not always clear beyond that what benefits such attachment accrued.

The founders did not always solicit protection from the local bishop. Several hospitals went directly to the papacy for approval. A sanction by the Holy See gave an institution protection in times of economic or political strife, strife that frequently meant excessive intrusion from the local bishop![62] The papacy would assure, for an annual fee, its support and protection of the hospital.[63] However, the degree to which any ecclesiastical entity was actually involved in the administration of the hospitals varied greatly and, as we shall see, led to a good deal of controversy.

A number of documents do specifically list the bishop, archbishop, cleric, or a monastic group as founder. However, these documents are generally not direct charters or testamentary records and thus could just refer to the fact that church officials had approved the foundation after its initiation. The eighteenth-century chronicler Francesco Ballarini attributes the archbishop of Como with the founding of many hospitals there. However, subsequent scholars challenge many of his assertions. Ballarini also attaches most hospitals to a noble individual or family from Como.[64] This attribution probably belies more of the interests of the author and the politics of northern Italy in the eighteenth century than of the specifics of the hospital institutionalization.

A few of the charters and other documents indicate an original tie between a monastic order and the hospital but it is often difficult to determine which preceded which. For example, letters issued by the archbishop of Milan to the Curia in Rome in 1288 refer to Ospedale Colombetta in Milan as having been founded by the Augustinian brothers in that year. However, other testamentary evidence suggests it existed prior to 1279, but do not refer to the founders.[65] Documents refer to the founder of Ospedale S. Dionigi in Milan as Archbishop Ariberto, but they also indicate that it was at least affiliated with a monastery of the same name. However, a lack of additional information leaves room for doubt.[66] The process of legitimization and appropriation of administration by the bishopric (a process to be discussed in depth in a later chapter) makes one wary of taking evidence for episcopal foundation of hospitals without corroborating proof. In one case, Ospedale di San Pietro di Senna outside of Lodi, the hospital clearly preceded the monastery to which it was later attached. We have evidence of the hospital in existence from as early as 1152, but the monastery, one of the Order of St Jerome, was established there in the fifteenth century. Confusingly, subsequent documents refer to its 'founding' by the Order of St Jerome.[67]

Other documents clearly suggest the foundation of the hospital by an ecclesiastical official, but indicate that its construction was dependent upon bequests from individuals. For example, Ospedale di S. Simpliciano in Milan was attached to an ancient monastery of the same name. An episcopal document suggests that Archbishop Ariberto d'Intimiano founded, or at least approved the creation of, a hospital administered by brothers from the Benedictine order there. However, we also have documentary evidence that several important legacies from individual citizens were critical in creating the institution. There is some debate as to whether husband and wife citizens Azzone and Rienza, who made a major donation of houses, buildings, and land in 1039, did so with the intent of creating the hospital or whether they were simply donating to an initiative started by the archbishop.[68]

There is almost always a church listed as 'attached' to a hospital and in some instances it is clear that the hospital was erected near an existing church. As the purpose of the hospitals was as religious (the care of one's soul), as medical or hospitable (the care of one's body), the church was necessary to ensure the observation of offices by workers and availability of religious offices for the inmates. However, frequently the attached church was built after the foundation of the hospital. For example, Ospedale Rodolfo Tanzi was constructed prior to the church to which it was later attached. In 1202 the bishop of Parma gave approval for a church to be built adjacent to the hospital to 'serve the needs of the community hospital'.[69]

The continued ties between local and regional churches and charitable institutions reflect the sustained power of religious institutions within the city and the persistence of a religious role for all communal associations. Yet the parallel increased participation by the lay community suggests a diminished capacity of the ecclesiastical organization to meet all needs. Church authorities recognized the increasing need for urban institutional orders to address social need and cautiously welcomed lay contribution.[70] Active participation by the laity in the form of testamentary charity was not novel. However, lay citizens began to dictate the management and organization of the facility, even attempting to bypass the authority of the church officials altogether by the twelfth century. This shift in authority indicates a significant shift in the relationship between the religious authority, the citizenry, and charity.

The causes for this shift are many and will be addressed in depth in Chapter 5 but some of the origins can be traced to internal strife within the ecclesiastical institutions themselves in the era of the flourishing of foundations. Several of the early charters suggest divisiveness within the religious community, and even opposition to the traditional orders. In 1096, in response to increased corruption within the Milanese bishopric, Pope Urban II urged the laity to take a more active role in the election of the rectors and other church officers.[71] It appears that these were welcome words to the lay community in Milan. Frustration with the bishop, antagonism toward some of the monasteries, and a desire to create innovative religious experiences, compelled Milanese constituents to rally around the pope's invective. We see this impatience with the bishop's unethical political machinations in the increased independent founding of hospitals and demand for institutional autonomy.

Neighbourhood associations as founders

Often founders linked the new hospital and its administration to a specific neighbourhood within the city and attached it to the corresponding civic association. These *comunità vicinali*, or neighbourhood associations, were organized around a parish church and fulfilled the needs for community and mutual support that was frequently lost in an urban environment.[72] For example, Ospedale S. Simpliciano in Milan was founded in 1091 by a citizen, Lanfranco della Pila, and his wife Frasia. The della Pilas, of whom we know very little, donated a rather substantial plot of land near the monastery of S. Simpliciano and by the gate of Comasina for the specified purpose of establishing a hospital there to care for the poor and ill. They stipulated the *boni homines* of the neighbourhood of Porta Comasina should manage the facility.[73]

Neighbourhood associations engaged in much more than just charity. The massive population growth of the period fostered a need for urban planning and development. Hospital building was part of a larger program that included the extension of city walls, creation of housing, rebuilding and fortifying of bridges and roads for heavier traffic, and the extension of older city walls. The neighbourhood association of *Capodiponte* in Parma was engaged in decades-long negotiations with constituents, civic authorities, and church officials over various issues with regards to urban planning, including such considerations as water rights for Ospedale Rodolfo Tanzi.[74]

Neighbourhood associations were an integral part of the city-scape. Often they provided militia and elected representatives to the communal government. They usually also maintained a religious character and organized and conducted religious rituals and festivals in their neighbourhood. They regularly provided candles for weekly mass and oversaw the funerals of constituents. In addition, they organized and managed city property, including the rebuilding of walls and oversight of some farmland outside the city walls.[75] Essentially, they became the village within the city. Their many responsibilities included the founding or administration of local hospitals.

By the fourteenth century, neighbourhood associations replaced many of the old family patriciate alliances and patronage systems, which often included not just secular but ecclesiastical elites. These alliances were politically, economically, and socially, beneficial particularly to those middle-class *cittadini* with social aspirations.[76] Charitable activity, such as the founding and administering of hospitals, served to provide social assistance to association members as well as an avenue for participation in the new civic landscape. The hospitals became integral components of the local community, and as such where they were located was important to the founder, the patrons, and the surrounding neighbours.[77]

Lay and semi-religious organizations as founders

As will be shown in subsequent chapters the administration of hospitals was most often turned over to groups of men and women who were part of a specifically late medieval phenomenon of semi-religious orders and groups or confraternal organizations. It is clear that these organizations were also very active in the foundation of hospitals and their involvement illuminates the overall trend of lay piety and civic activity.[78] Citizens seeking an active religious life had a plethora of options to choose from in the late twelfth and early thirteenth centuries. Tertiary membership of traditional monastic groups, penitent orders, and mendicant movements allowed individuals to remain in their communities and to work toward alleviating the ills caused by urbanization. Merlo has referred to this activity as a variety of 'experiments in social welfare'.[79]

Independent groups, such as the Beguines in northern Europe and the *Humiliati* in Italy, not attached to traditional orders, sought to create a unique response to the needs of their fellow citizens.[80] Initially, the papacy felt threatened by the spread of such unortho- dox religiosity. It branded groups such as the *Humiliati* as heretical. However, their extreme popularity as well as their usefulness to society eventually led to their acceptance by the pope. In 1203 Innocent III recognized the *Humiliati* as an official order, allowing for its survival but also thereby exerting some institutional control over its existence.[81]

Mendicant groups followed these early examples in subsequent decades and sought similar legitimization by the papacy. Honorius III granted formal approval to the Franciscan and Dominican men- dicant orders.[82] These most familiar manifestations of this medieval religious phenomenon represented the institutionally approved expression of this popular lay movement. Lay religious sought to respond to very specific needs within their community. Their popu- larity illustrates a great change from the symbolic *caritas* of the generic 'poor' of an earlier age. These novel religious sought out recognizable needy individuals within their midst in order to provide specific assistance, or *misericordia*.

The Ospedale S. Spiritus del la Caritate in Lodi, originally called Domus Fratris Facii, was most probably founded by the fraternal order of Spirito Santo, which also founded hospitals in Verona, Cremona, Como, and Gemona.[83] Spirito Santo was a fraternal religious order that originated in France in the 1170s and spread to Italy by the late twelfth century. They specifically focused on the administration of hospitals and were recognized enthusiastically by Pope Innocent III.[84] A similar semi-religious fraternal organization, the Società della Croce, were powerful players in the politics of Parma in the mid-thirteenth century; they founded Ospedale S. Ilario there in 1266.[85]

Lay penitent groups also became increasingly active in both the religious and political life of the city. Their activity in Parma in the mid-thirteenth century illustrates the convergence of charitable and communal services increasingly appropriated by such lay religious organizations. As the members of the group were lay men with access to public life, penitent notaries, judges, and other notable citizens were active in civic government. In Parma in 1288 peni- tents serving on civic committees oversaw the regulation of bread and wine sales during a famine, ensuring that prices would be held to a point that no one would starve due to poverty.[86] Penitents, both

in formalized groups and as individuals, founded a number of hospitals in the region. For example, penitent Ranieri of Pisa, who was
later beatified in part for his service to the needy, founded a hospital
in Pisa.[87] Church officials recognized communal work of individual
penitents toward the poor and the sick as an increasingly necessary
and beneficial social service. In return, they provided money and
recognition to penitents, which led to institutionalization of such
charity, often in the creation of hospitals.[88]

Individual founders

As early as the middle of the twelfth century there was increased
participation in the patronage of hospitals by individual citizens.
In a few instances, the entire act of charitable impulse played
out through the extreme piety and charity of one person. For
example, Ospedale Bertramus de Brolo, named after its founder,
was established in Bergamo in 1304. Brolo stipulated in his will
that, should he die without heirs, his bequest go toward the establishment of a hospital created from two of his existing properties.[89]
We know he was a notary and it is clear from other documentation that he had some wealth and social distinction. In Piacenza, in
1178, a poor man by the name of Raymond 'the Palmer' founded
a hospital that tended the needs of pilgrims and the poor.[90] In
Milan, lay man Gerardo Tintore founded Ospedale San Gerardo
di Monza in 1175.[91] We know of both Tintore and Raymond's
stories because they both became lay saints, individuals whose piety
and work with the sick and needy became a common archetype
of medieval sainthood. The ecclesiastical authorities and the community appreciated and needed their contributions. Their beatifica-
tion legitimized and sanctioned such activity and allowed church
officials to maintain a level of control over this enthusiastic lay
religiosity.[92] Their biographies were recorded in *vitae* that give
us an unprecedented glimpse at the lives of medieval individuals.
If used carefully, considering the bias of the *vitae*'s purpose, this
hagiography does shed light on the charitable and civic activity of
these men.

The *vitae* of Raymond illuminates the experience of a typical
urban inhabitant of the late twelfth century. Raymond was born to
parents who were not, 'illustrious in origin or completely lowborn.
They were private citizens who were neither rich nor poor in

domestic terms.'[93] He was a trained shoemaker who went on a pilgrimage to the Holy Land with his mother when he was a young man and later on another religious journey to Rome. Although he had no formal schooling, he was a self-taught scholar of the scriptures and felt compelled to 'share' his beliefs through preaching from his workshop on holy days. While in Rome, Raymond claimed that Jesus came to him and asked him to return to Piacenza,

> ... where you will dress in a garment the colour of the sky that extends down to the middle of your legs, with loose sleeves and hood. You will always carry my cross over your shoulder, executing every act of piety in its name and under its power. You will establish through your own effort a pious place for the indigent and for pilgrims.[94]

When he returned to Piacenza he found a building next to the Canonry of the Twelve Apostles that was adequate for 'collecting alms and well suited for offering hospitality to the poor of both sexes, whether pilgrims or sick people'.[95] He then set out with his cross to seek alms from citizens for his new hospital. The institution that he founded took in the poor, pilgrims, orphans, widows, and prostitutes. Raymond's personality and personal endeavour attracted support from a wide segment of the population so that upon his death in 1200, such an 'abundance of things, of money, of images that were offered there [the site of the hospital] day after day was astounding' and the city fathers decreed that a 'Hospice of Saint Raymond' be established.[96]

What is not clear is what the earlier institution founded by Raymond was called and whether the city fathers were simply institutionalizing the existing hospital or appropriating its governance. What is clear is that in the entire account of Raymond's activities there is no presence of the bishop, priest, or any other traditional ecclesiastical authority in the earliest days of the hospital's foundation. Raymond's hospital seems a firmly grassroots-based, communal organization, founded by extremely pious citizens and ratified by the city government.

From a less complete account of the life of Gerardo Tintore, we know he was from the artisanal class, possibly a dyer, and was well known during his life for his pious acts of charity to the poor. Documents do support his role in the early life of the hospital he founded. He is referred to as minister (leader or governor) of the hospital in 1174, then listed as minister again in 1198 and yet again at the time of his death in 1207.[97]

While we find no mention of Rodolfo Tanzi or his family prior to the founding of the eponymous hospital, it appears he was of a middle-class family who were not active in the political life of Parma at the time. Tanzi did far more than dedicate land or wealth to the establishment of the facility, taking on the role of minster and overseeing the facility for many years. This lay hospital became successful and an integral part of the community.[98] Tanzi himself became a representative to the commune in the interests of the hospital and the surrounding neighbourhood. His leadership led to his own personal success, as he became ambassador of the *popolo* in Parma in 1282.[99]

Individual bequests

The majority of documents that reference the foundation of hospitals mention many individual donations. These may have been from individuals who become involved in the administration or staffing of the facility or they may have been one-time bequests with no further activity. There was generally an original foundational bequest and then often multiple references to additional bequests from families and individuals in support of the hospital. For example, Ospedale S. Maria della Pieta in Cremona benefitted from at least sixty-five small testamentary bequests between 1266 and 1339.[100] In addition, it is possible to infer the importance of a family's status and patronage by their association with, or bequests to, the hospital. In Como, Ospedale Santa Maria Nuova del Borgo Vico was popularly known as the 'Maronesa', referring to the Maroni family who were listed in the documents as 'patrons' of the hospital.[101] It is probable that this is the same family, known in other documents as da Marini, who established Ospedale Santa Maria Maddalena, also in Como in 1313.[102] In Bergamo, Ospedale San Vincenzo was founded in 1323 by a cathedral canon, Castelinus de Rapazeltis, who left 600 lire for its establishment. His will clearly indicated that this institution was intended to help his immediate family as well another, the family of Rogerius de La Sale, who were possibly his mother's relatives.[103]

A rather obscure reference to Ospedale di San'Antonio Abate in Lodi suggests that it was founded by a testamentary bequest from *Guidono* dei Riccardi in 1212, and then a *Giacomo* Riccardi who was listed as 'president of the city of Milan' began a later restoration of the facility.[104] This illustrates the foundation and continued patronage of a hospital by a prestigious family. Anselmo Temacoldo, father of Pietro Temacoldo, 'padrone' of the city of Lodi, founded Ospedale di San Giacomo in Vallicella, also in Lodi, in 1347 and the illustrious family dei Cadamosto founded the Ospedale di Santa Elisabetta in Lodi.[105] The Ospedale S. Nazarii was established in 1127 by the will of Ruggerio da Cerro listed as the son of Alberto; the will further stipulated that his 'vassals' were to erect the facility.[106] We do not know much about the da Cerros but this reference to vassals suggests an aristocratic lineage. Of course the clearest indication of the status of a founder from the Milan region during this era is when he was a Visconti. The Visconti of Milan rose to become the strongmen, or ruling family, in 1277[107] but they were an influential family well before that. Giovanni Visconti founded the Ospedale S. Ambrogio as well as others in the region of Milan.[108] As we shall see in subsequent chapters, the church officials challenged the family's administrative control on several occasions but Visconti's continued involvement suggests the level of commitment by these important citizens in the foundation and administration of hospitals.[109]

Men, women, spouses, and whole families made individual bequests. In Como, brothers Giovanni and Obizzone Cacci along with their mother established the Ospedale San Vitale.[110] When Moderno Caccialepre founded Ospedale Santa Caterina in Pavia his will clearly not only indicated his interest in providing capital for the building of the hospital, but also his stipulation regarding its purpose, size, and leadership. He indicated that it should originally feature six beds, with another six added later with the purchase of additional buildings for one thousand florins.[111]

Women were also active in bequeathing land, money, and buildings for the foundation of hospitals. In fact, a survey of the testamentary bequests to hospitals in Lodi indicates a virtual parity in charitable giving to hospitals by men and women.[112] While women's bequests were frequently for small amounts and often directed to established institutions, we do have evidence of them founding some hospitals. For example, an unknown woman founded the Ospedale Nuovo (also called Donna Buona) in Milan in 1260.[113] A hospital in Cremona called Ospedale Donna Berlenda suggests a female founder, as well.[114]

While we do have references in a number of documents to the social standing or at least notoriety of a founder or family, it is difficult to ascertain much about the socio-economic status of the majority of individuals who founded hospitals or left donations to help in the foundation. Usually we have little more than a name and perhaps the amount of the bequest and there is little reference elsewhere regarding these individuals, which makes understanding their status difficult. However, the very fact that we have so many references to the founding of hospitals by lay persons of 'obscure origins' itself illustrates how widespread was the phenomenon of lay religious charitable activity. We can conclude that these individuals owned enough to donate at least part of their estate to the establishment of a hospital, suggesting something about the level of their social standing and reflecting the reality of a growing middle class with disposable income.

This model of individual or family patronage insured the growth and prosperity of the hospital, and the fact that we can see this process followed in many cities across the region suggests the popularity of supporting hospitals as a method of charitable assistance. In fact, by looking at the pattern of bequests one can ascertain some idea of the localized nature of charitable relief and the parameters of communal activity in charity. Samuel Cohn has suggested that after the Black Death there was an increased personalization of piety in which individuals sought to memorialize themselves through their charitable foundations.[115] Yet in fact, such activity may have commenced even earlier, in the thirteenth through fourteenth centuries. The plethora of documents recording testamentary bequests from this era suggests the foundation of hospitals was a common manifestation of the desire to memorialize oneself, as well as to contribute to the continued maintenance and security family and community.[116]

In several instances, it is very clear from the foundational charters that the individuals were specifically seeking to keep control of the hospital away from the local church. Lanfranco della Pila in his will founding Ospedale S. Simpliciano in Milan stipulated that authority should rest with the *boni homines* of the neighbourhood of Porta Comasina: '*et nullus episcopus seu abbas, vel qui'ibet alius nomo sive clericus sive saicus habeat et regat ipsum hospitale*', that no bishop or abbot, or any other man or a cleric or a layman may have and govern the hospital. He also stipulated in his will that his desire was to give lay Christians more power in church life.[117] One citizen named Rodolone founded Ospedale San Michele in Gemona in 1259 as a house for the poor, indicating it was to be open to the all who were in need. Its name derived, as many did, from the adjacent church of the same name, but the founder stipulated that the hospital remain independent from control by church authorities and retain the right to appoint its own prior.[118]

An example of one individual's attempt to establish a hospital within the parameters of ecclesiastical hierarchy while assuring its independence is illustrated in documents from 1170 indicating the testamentary request of Oldrado Mondalino. He founded Ospedale de Guado in Lodi. He gave jurisdiction directly to the archbishop of Milan, along with a promised sum of 20 lire annually. However, he required that in return the archbishop would promise never to attach the hospital to any other monastery or church. The archbishop would also not require any further annual fees or impose any priest, cleric, or lay member on the hospital. The hospital was to be allowed to elect a director by a majority decision of all of those who served the hospital. However, the bishop was given the right to approve this selection and to act as arbiter in disputes within the facility.[119]

While founders of the hospitals may have wanted to keep control out of the hands of ecclesiastical powers, the reality was that formalization by a bishop or papal authorization was useful in ensuring the success of the institution. Beyond the original bequest or even subsequent bequests, the hospital needed to build a facility, to hire administrators, to create a formula for administration, and to ensure the continued activity of the facility. Religious institutions had a ready-made model of such charitable organization and were often already locally placed to assist in the implementation of this model. In addition, in order to secure future donations and to assure the institution's reputation and continuance of operation, the hospital needed the legitimacy the religious reputation could offer. Eventually, as we shall see, the civic authorities took on this role, but in the early years of the communal period the bishop and members of the local clergy were still recognized as the moral authority of the community. Clearly, the move to wrest control from the ecclesiastical authorities indicates that citizens were looking for alternatives to this authority but were, for the time, still forced to recognize the ecclesiastedal power. Church officials, in turn, fought continually to assert control and authority over the hospitals once established. The tension caused by this symbiotic relationship is played out in the jurisdictional disputes that arose over the subsequent centuries.[120]

Conclusion

In cities throughout the Lombard region from the late twelfth through the early fourteenth centuries, small community-based hospitals dotted the civic landscape. Frequently located near major thoroughfares, often under the protection of the city walls, these institutions were communal responses to the increased needs of the poor and the sick as well as to the perceived insecurity posed by a transient population. That lay individuals or communal organizations founded these institutions more frequently than did the ecclesiastical groups suggests the increase demand for this social welfare initiative. While the papacy and regional bishoprics found this assistance valuable, they struggled to ensure control over this expression of civic piety and charitable impulse.

Individuals, neighbourhood associations, confraternal, and semi-religious groups, were all active in founding hospitals. Their participation illustrates the convergence of the recognition of increased social need of the immediate community, popular desire to lead a religious life of service, and participation in civic government by a larger, more diverse segment of the urban population. *Misericordia* charitable activity became an avenue for personal piety, social status, civic participation, and familial and neighbourhood security. Hundreds of these facilities emerged across the region and flourished as models of civic engagement and novel models of social welfare.

Notes

1 Bonvesin de la Riva, *De Magnalibus Mediolani*, ed. M. Corti (Milan, 1974), 56–7.
2 Racine, 'Il sistema ospedaliero', 360.
3 G. Cosmacini, *L'Ospedale Sant'Anna di Como; nella storia della città* (Como, 2005), 57.
4 Henderson, *The Renaissance Hospital*, 7.

5 Cosmacini, *L'Ospedale Sant'Anna*, 57.
6 Henderson, *The Renaissance Hospital*, 7.
7 Ibid.
8 Albini, *Città e ospedali*, 20.; Gazzini, 'Rodolfo Tanzi', 20–1.
9 Orme and Webster, *The English Hospital*, 37.
10 A. Caretta, *L'assistenza Diocesi di Lodi* (Lodi, 1967), 290–2.
11 There is great variation within the documentation as to the use of the abbreviation for Saint or Saints (San, S., Santa, S.S., s.s.) in hospital names. In this text I have tried to stay true to the variation found in most of the original documentation where available or in the majority of references in printed or secondary sources.
12 Copy of original document which suggests its foundation in 1300 in, F. Ballarini, *Compendio della croniche della città di Como* (Bologna, 1968), 405–6; the controversy over naming of the hospital is discussed in Cosmacini, *L'Ospedale Sant'Anna*, 52; and G. Rovelli, *Storia di Como descritta dal marchese Giuseppe Rovelli patrizio comasco e divisa in tre parti* (Milan, 1794), parte II, 313–14.
13 Cosmacini, *L'Ospedale Sant'Anna*, 53.
14 Gazzini, *L'ospedale di Parma nei secoli XII–XIII*, 5.
15 Rovelli, *Storia di Como*, 312.
16 Secondo Galli, *Gli archivi storici degli ospedali lombardi* (Como, 1982), 205.
17 Cosmacini, *L'Ospedale Sant'Anna*, 55.
18 Caretta, *L'assistenza Diocesi di Lodi*, 11.
19 For example, Ospedale S. Vincenzo in Bergamo, see R. Cossar, *Transformation of the Laity in Bergamo, 1260–c.1400* (Leiden, 2008), 63 (original description, ASBg, Notarile, G. Soyarius, bust. 7 (1331–32), 349).
20 This debate will be discussed at length below.
21 A. Londero, *Per l'amor di Deu: pietà e profitto in un ospedale friulano del Quattrocento: (San Michele di Gemona)* (Udine, 1994), 12–13; for a general discussion of the regional networks and importance of public space within the medieval city see David Nicholas, *Urban Europe 1100–1700* (Basingstoke, 2003).
22 A. Bassi, *Storia di Lodi* (Lodi, 1977), 24–38.
23 Gazzini, *L'ospedale a Parma*, 6–7.
24 Albini, *Città e ospedali*, 41.
25 Gazzini, *L'ospedale a Parma*, 4–5.
26 D. Rando, 'Laicus Religiosus' tra strutture civili ed ecclesiastiche: L'ospedale di Ognissanti in Treviso (sec. XIII)', in ed. G. Merlo, *Esperienze religiose religiose e opera assistenziali nei secoli XII e XIII* (Torino, 1987), 44.
27 While Gemona is located outside of the province of Lombardy it was a major trade centre in the Middle Ages and was located along

the trade and pilgrimage routes that led into the heart of Lombard territory. The founding and administration of Ospedale San Michele followed a similar pattern to that of the others discussed in this chapter. For information on Ospedale San Michele and its founding see Londero, *Per l'amor.*

28 Ibid., 13.
29 Caretta, *L'assistenza Diocesi di Lodi,* 290.
30 Ibid., 290–2.
31 Rocca, 'Ospedali e canoniche regolari', 24–5.
32 G. Agnelli, *Ospedale di Lodi: Monografia Stoica* (Lodi, 1950), 21.
33 Ibid.
34 Ibid.
35 Ibid., 23.
36 Caretta, *L'assistenza Diocesi di Lodi,* 290–2.
37 Gazzini, 'Rodolfo Tanzi', 14.
38 For more on the rivalry between constituents in political landscape of Northern Italy see J. D. Hyde, *Society and Politics in Medieval Civil Life, 1000–1300* (New York, 1973), and L. Martines, *Violence and Civil Disorder in Italian Cities, 1200–1500* (Berkeley, CA, 1972).
39 Caretta has done an extensive analysis of the exact geographical location of the hospitals of Lodi. He indicates that there were three major areas of development in the twelfth century. First, several hospitals were constructed with a clear emphasis on covering the ancient routes near the 'old city.' Inside the walls of the old city of Lodi there were no hospitals, but there were two located just outside the city walls along the old roads to Milan and Pavia. After the rebuilding of Lodi's city walls in 1158 newer hospitals were constructed outside them along the major roads. Caretta, *L'assistenza Diocesi di Lodi,* 290.
40 Nicholas, *Urban Europe,* 52–3. See also V. D'Alessandro, *Le pergamene degli Umiliati di Cremona* (Palermo, 1964), 6–8.
41 Albini, *Città e ospedali,* 21.
42 These conflicts will be discussed in depth in Chapter 5.
43 For comparison, in 1372 a shop owner made approximately 400 lire annually, a construction worker would make an average of around one half lire per day. R. Marshall, *The Local Merchants of Prato* (Baltimore, MD, 1999).
44 Cossar, *The Transformation of the Laity,* 61.
45 Caretta, 'Gli ospedali altomedievali', 4–5.
46 Cosmacini, *L'Ospedale Sant'Anna,* 54.
47 C. Wickham, *Early Medieval Italy: Central Power and Local Society, 400–1000* (Princeton, NJ, 1981), 141.
48 Brown, *Through the Eye of a Needle,* 277–8.

49 Racine, *Il sistema ospedaliero*, 356.
50 ASMi, AOM, Consiglio degli orfanotrofio, Ospedale S. Giacomo dei Pellegrini, cart. 5, n. 5.
51 Glass, *Portals, Pilgrimage, and Crusade* ; and McCormick, *Origins of the European Economy.*
52 Caretta, 'Gli ospedali altomedievali', 12.
53 Racine, 'Il Sistema ospedaliero'. Other travellers, primarily merchants, might house themselves at taverns or inn. There is, in the statutes of the city of Pavia from the twelfth century, mention of an association of innkeepers. Bonvesin de la Riva counts about 150 hostel keepers who catered to foreigners in Milan, see Jansen et. al., eds, *Medieval Italy: Texts in Translation* (Philadelphia, PA, 2009), 18. In Gemona, in the bordering province of Friuli, merchants who travelled a main road by the city leading from Germany to Venice were obligated to pay a fee for their passage and compelled by an ancient privilege, called *niederlech*, to stay one night in one of the many inns located in the small town. Londero, *Per l'amor*, 13.
54 Racine, 'Il sistema ospedaliero', 357.
55 Cossar, *The Transformation of the Laity*, 61–2.
56 Caretta, 'Gli ospedali altomedievali', 7.
57 Ibid.
58 Ibid., 8.
59 Albini, *Città e ospedali*, 23.
60 Ibid., 65–6.
61 Ibid., 23.
62 Pennington, *Pope and Bishops*, 154–89. The granting of privileges and exemptions to religious institutions became codified in the twelfth century under the move toward greater papal authority.
63 See for example, Ospedale S. Anna in Cedeo, discussed in E. Rocca, *Ospedali e canoniche regolari* (Milan, 1959), 24.
64 F. Ballarini, *Compendio delle*, Ballarini's possible bias and lack of substantiation of his claim is discussed in Cosmacini, *L'Ospedale Sant'Anna*, 50–3.
65 A testamentary bequest by Negro Viola gave money to the hospital in 1279, ASMi, AOM, Colombetta, carta. 39, March, 1279; discussion of bequest and foundation in, P. Pecchiai, *L'ospedale Maggiore di Milano nella storia e nell'arte* (Milan, 1927), 73.
66 Albini, *Città e ospedali*, 66.
67 Agnelli, *Ospedale di Lodi*, 23.
68 Pecchiai, *L'ospedale di Milano*, 17. See Albini, *Città e ospedali*, 22–3, for debate on the question.
69 Gazzini, *L'ospedale a Parma*, 3.
70 Albini, *Città e ospedali*, 76.
71 Ibid., 27. See also Greenaway, *Arnold of Brescia*, 20–4.

72 Albini, *Cittq e ospedali*, 32.
73 Ibid., 24–5.
74 Gazzini, 'Rodolfo Tanzi', 9–15.
75 Thompson, *Cities of God*, 129–36.
76 D. Owen Hughes, 'Kinsmen and Neighbors in Medieval Genoa', in
    H. A. Miskimin (ed.), *The Medieval City* (New Haven, CT, 1977),
    95–111.
77 Sweetinburgh, *The Role of the Hospital in England*, 35.
78 For a discussion of the development of this phenomenon in Italy see
    Thompson, *Cities of God*, 70–8.
79 Merlo, 'Religiosità e cultura', 201–15.
80 F. Andrews, *The Early Humiliati* (Cambridge, 1999); W. Simons,
    Cities of Ladies.
81 Brasher, *Women of the Humiliati*, 3–4.
82 For a discussion of the process of approval and the various levels of
    approval see Grundmann, *Religious Movements*, 54–7.
83 A. Caretta, '*L'assisstenza Diocesi di Lodi*', in *Archivio Storico Lodi-
    giano Ser. II Anno XV.* (Lodi, 1967), 292; and Londero, *Per l'amor*,
    14.
84 The order of Spirito Santo in the administration of hospitals will be
    discussed in depth in Chapter 4.
85 Gazzini, 'Rodolfo Tanzi', 19.
86 Thompson, *Cities of God*, 94.
87 Ibid., 72.
88 Ibid., 81–2.
89 Cossar, *The Transformation of the Laity*, 62.
90 Jansen et. al., *Medieval Italy*, 358.
91 Brodman, *Charity & Religion*, 74.
92 For a discussion of the lay saints see Vauchez, *The Laity in the
    Middle Ages*, 51–72.
93 Jansen et al., *Medieval Italy*, 358.
94 Ibid., 366.
95 Ibid.
96 Ibid., 374.
97 R. Mambretti, 'L'ospedale di San Gerardo nei secoli XIII e XIV', in
    Alberzoni, *La carità a Milano*, 189.
98 Gazzini, 'Rodolfo Tanzi', 3–28. Gazzini makes an interesting point
    that unlike many of the founders of charitable activity from the
    period who became well known as religious figures, even sanctified,
    Tanzi did not become this type of figurehead or model. Instead he was
    more famous for the building and development of water systems of
    the hospital and for his civic leadership than his religious piety.
99 Albini, 'Dallo sviluppo', 40.
100 ASCr, OSM, indice I, busta, 3.

101 Cosmacini, *L'Ospedale Sant'Anna*, 52.
102 Ibid., original printed in, Rovelli, *Storia di Como*, 313–14.
103 Cossar, *The Transformation of the Laity*, 61.
104 Agnelli, *Ospedale di Lodi*, 16–17.
105 Ibid., 16.
106 Caretta, 'Gli ospedali altomedievali', 9–10.
107 The importance of the rise of the strongmen and centralization of the state to the hospital movement will be discussed in Chapter 6.
108 Racine, 'Il sistema ospedaliero', 371.
109 Other examples of the founding of hospitals by important or wealthy individuals include the Ospedale di Santa Maria in Virolo, Ospedale dei SS. Giacomo e Filippo della Misericordia, Ospedali S. Giovanni, see Agnelli, *Ospedale di Lodi*, 15–17; and Ospedale de Quado, see Caretta, 'Gli ospedali altomedievali', 291. Several hospitals bear the name of the donor family suggesting their status within the community. Ospedale di Santa Maria di Tizzoni was named for the family who founded it and who are referred to as an 'ancient' family of Lodi. They maintained an interest in the affairs of the hospital for a century and a half. Also in Lodi, the Ospedale di Santa Maria di Virolo was probably named for a founding family. In Parma, the Ospedale Rodolfo Tanzi bore the name of founder. Also in Parma, the Ospedale di Frate Alberto was founded by the city in honor of one Alberto di Villa d'Ogna who was referred to as a merchant of wine from Bergamo. Gazzini, *L'ospedale a Parma*. 19.
110 Cosmacini, *L'Ospedale Sant'Anna*, 55.
111 Albini, *Città e ospedali*, 74–5.
112 In my research I found a total of thirty-three bequests by men and twenty-six by women.
113 Albini, *Città e ospedali*, 72–4.
114 ASCr, OSM, Indice I. Busta 13.
115 S. Cohen, *The Cult of Remembrance and the Black Death: Six Renaissance Cities in Central Italy* (Baltimore, MD, 1992).
116 See for example, documents from hospitals in Como including, *Archivio di Stato di Como* (ASCO) Archivio Ospedale di S. Anna (ASCOs.a.) Cart 1, 2, 7, 8, 9.
117 Albini, *Città e ospedali*, 24–5.
118 Londero, *Per l'amor*, 14.
119 Caretta, *L'assistenza Diocesi di Lodi*, 291.
120 These tensions and jurisdictional disputes will be the subject of Chapter 5.

3

Hospital management

Once founded, by either bishop, pope, neighbourhood association, individual, or lay order, the hospital needed to be managed and staffed. As the model for charity in the eleventh and twelfth centuries was almost exclusively religious, these institutions were universally organized within some format of religious or semi-religious community that provided housing for staff and administrators as well as, patients, the poor, and pilgrims. However, the very nature of the independent hospital movement of the period was characterized by a wide variety of innovative administrative models, which makes generalization difficult. It is necessary to examine the various types of managerial and organizational arrangements of the community members and their relationship to ecclesiastical and civic oversight in order to gain a greater understanding of the role the hospital played in urban society.

It would appear from a cursory examination that the hospitals existed within the authoritative structure of the diocese and were under direct control of the bishop whose wishes the resident priest would represent. For example, the archbishop of Milan claimed jurisdictional supremacy over all hospitals within his bishopric regardless of who had founded them, including even those founded by individuals or groups whose stated desire was to remain autonomous or under papal rather than bishopric authority.[1] However, the swell of popular piety of the era that witnessed individuals, guilds, confraternities, and other community groups founding churches and hospitals independently of the traditional episcopate also witnessed the autonomous administration of these hospitals by such semi-religious and lay groups.[2] This chapter will examine the operational structure of hospitals, including jurisdictional oversight, management, and operations of these organizations. In the twelfth through the fourteenth centuries religious institutions and an increasingly active lay religious citizenry created a symbiotic yet increasingly competitive relationship in their governance and management of these charitable institutions.

In 1168, the archbishop of Milan issued a '*statuto ad opera*' to the Ospedale Brolo in Milan, one of the region's large, important facilities. This order appears to have been the administrative model followed, at least to some degree, by most hospital organizations until the mid-fifteenth century.[3] The model outlined an idealized partnership between the laity and the clergy in managing hospitals and established rules dictating each group's role. The statute stipu- lated that, at Brolo, the *frati*, or lay brothers, were to live a common life with the poor they served, reside at the hospital, and take meals with the patients. This rule included an injunction to go out among the community, identify those in need of charity, and then determine the appropriate response. For example, if they found someone who had some level of material support from relatives but needed finan- cial aid they were to give them cash or in-kind donations. If they dis- covered ill or incapacitated individuals they were to bring them to the hospital.[4] The *decani,* or deacons[5] were responsible for overall management of economic assets and oversight of the distribution of alms and services. The *frati* and the *decani* together elected a *ministro* as overall leader and a *cellario* to manage funds and goods of the hospital. Together they were required to make an account of the functioning of the hospital once a month to the archbishop, who played a supervisory role. The statute stressed the need to apply all charity to serving the poor, requiring the brothers to distribute all cash donations directly as alms, and indicating that such donations not be used to purchase land or buildings. Donations of buildings or land to the hospital had to be used and maintained usufruct by the hospital, and the rent from such lands redistributed to the poor. Pope Clement III ratified and approved this *opera* in 1190.[6] Not all hospitals had such clearly defined statutes of operation (or at least we have few extent records for them) but most appear from supporting documentary evidence to have followed a similar plan in the execution of their administration.

Jurisdictional oversight

Generally, the laity administered the majority of hospitals in the region. They were usually subject to some formalized rule and were under the management of one individual, variously referred to as *rettore* or *ministro*. As these were semi-religious institutions there was also the need for a resident priest to fulfil the liturgical needs of the lay brothers and sisters who worked and resided in the hospital as well as the internees. These priests, appointed, or at least approved, by the local bishop, saw to the spiritual care of the patients and staff, but also administered all church offices and oversaw the care and maintenance of the hospital's chapel or church and cemetery. In addition to supplying the community with a priest, the bishop also provided his support and protection for the institution from outside political interference. He would frequently act as adjudicator or mediator in disputes within the community, between hospitals, or with larger civic bodies.[7]

In fact, beyond their mention in the foundational documents, the resident priests very rarely make an appearance in documentary records for the institutions and evidence suggests the *ministro* or *rettore* frequently acted independent of, or in opposition to, ecclesiastical oversight. Thus, for church leaders, claiming supremacy and reigning supreme were two different things. As most of the administrative personnel were lay and not canonical, the hospitals had, in fact, a great deal of independence outside the church hierarchy.

What cooperative partnerships did emerge between lay administrators and ecclesiastical authorities reflected a delicate balancing act between the two sides. A large part of the archival evidence is comprised of canonical orders and their reiterations regarding governance of the institutions as well as disputes and compromises over jurisdictional issues within and between these groups. An example of this type of compromise struck between the individual founders and the ecclesiastical authorities over autonomy and control is provided by the case of the Ospedale de Guado in Lodi. When founder and Lodi citizen Oldrado Mondalino placed it under the jurisdiction of the bishop of Lodi, the bishop promised in return never to attach the hospital to another church or order, not to ask for additional duties in any form, and finally, not to impose on the community a priest, a cleric, or a lay person without the will of the majority of the *servitores* of the hospital. He also confirmed that a majority of the community would elect a *ministro* but that the bishop had the right to confirm that choice. Finally, the decree stipulated that the bishop would act as arbiter for the hospital in

all contested issues.[8] Over the course of the thirteenth and fourteenth centuries a general pattern emerged of the ecclesiastical
officials making compromises and allowances with founders and
administrators and attempting to find the right balance between
maintaining some control and allowing free reign over the rapid
proliferation of these popular charitable institutions.

While much of the documentary evidence records frequent
attempts to assert ecclesiastical control over a hospital, there are
also many examples of the church leaders' concern with at least
profiting from the hospital's revenues. In most cases, the bishops
retained control over lands owned and leased by the hospitals,
including those obtained directly from bequests. The episcopate
then granted a tenth of this income back to the hospital community.
This often created tension between the hospital and the bishop's
office. Archbishop Oberto's statute of 1161 issued to Ospedale
Brolo defining the required distribution of all bequests back to the
poor was frequently challenged by the hospital because it was often
difficult to separate lands or goods intended for direct use by the
hospital from those that produced income, which would go to the
church.[9] Properties controlled by hospitals were not insignificant
and control over these assets would have been a major interest
of the church leaders, the city and the communities. Ospedale
Rodolfo Tanzi, by 1330, had acquired property of an estimated
230–3 hectares.[10]

An additional area of fiscal interest for religious leadership was
the collection of traditional fees. In return for granting protection
and legitimacy to the hospital, church officials often required the
institution to pay an annual duty. In Lodi, for example, the laity
administered all hospitals except those directly affiliated with a
monastery. These lay brothers and sisters answered directly to the
bishop of Lodi who received two types of annual duties from them:
the *censo,* an annual payment in cash given to the bishop by the
hospital on their saint's day; and the *fodro,* a feudal tribute traditionally paid in kind but which evolved into a cash payment over
time.[11] These fees ensured the bishopric at least a modicum of
control over income received by the hospitals from bequests and
donations as well as ensuring the need for their oversight and
annual observance of the fiscal activities of the hospitals.

Clearly church leaders appreciated the delicate balance needed
to maintain influence within these hospitals. The contribution of a

vibrant, active laity who wished to assist the spiritual and physical needs of its congregants helped to alleviate the increasing strain on the episcopate's resources and labour supply caused by massive urbanization and increased social ills. Yet this enthusiasm had to be weighed against the challenge of controlling the development of an independent social institution that would no longer need ecclesiastical support. The jurisdictional disputes and administrative wrangling of the thirteenth and early fourteenth centuries are a manifestation of this tension. There was much more at stake for church officials than loss of control of a few small, localized hospitals. If communities discovered that they could take care of their own, socially, in one area what was to stop them from discovering sovereignty in a number of other areas? This phenomenon challenged the very base of ecclesiastical support within the cities. Increasingly, the church leadership was forced to cede power and authority, first to the hospitals and then ultimately to the city governments.

Hospital management

While the ecclesiastical powers continually attempted to maintain a supervisory or proprietary role over the hospitals, the lay or semi-lay leaders who were attached to each individual institution had a great deal of power over day-to-day issues. According to the majority of documentary references, the person with the most apparent direct authority over activities *within* the hospital was the *rettore* or *ministro*.[12] It was often this leader who figured most prominently in the communities' external relations. In fact, besides the copious references to bequests to, or purchases by, hospitals the majority of archival material in general deals with the mediation of jurisdictional disputes between the bishop or city governors and these lay administrators.

The archival documents include many disputes that centred on management issues. Jurisdictional conflicts were inevitable when the original founders' desire for shared governance is considered. For example, in 1152 the founders of the Ospedale Senna in Lodi awarded administration of the hospital to twelve lay brothers but granted the bishop of Lodi ultimate authority over the community. However, the founders stipulated that the bishop should not 'interfere with the placement of the brothers; they should be under a different jurisdiction'.[13] While it is clear that the community was concerned with an overreaching episcopate, they were also aware of a need for some level of authority or religious legitimacy. These instances provide evidence that ecclesiastical powers fought a continual battle to retain some control over the hospitals while the communities struggled to establish their own spheres of influence.

The *rettore* or *ministro* of the hospitals usually came from wealthy or notable families and reflected the complex web of social, economic, and political power of individual families within the cities. Leadership of a charitable institution gave an individual and his family status and influence within the community. Their activities provide a microcosm of the overlapping and often conflicting spheres of political and social action of ecclesiastical and civic officials. The family da Marano in Parma, for example, was heavily involved in the management of the Ospedale Rodolfo Tanzi for much of the latter half of the thirteenth century and its members were also key players in the city's political activities. Iacobus da Marano served as a *fratre* (brother) of the hospital starting in 1257. By 1267 he was *procuratore*, and then was elected *rettore* from 1270 to 1288. Two other members of the Marano family also served the chapter from 1292 through 1305. Meanwhile, Andrea Marano was elected captain of the *popolo* in 1267 and served as *podesta* for Modena in 1272. Elected ambassador of the *popolo* in 1282, he was sent to ask the pope for absolution against the excommunication of the city as they were embroiled in the conflict between the Holy Roman Empire and the papacy. Cristoforo Marano and Anselmo da Marano, an influential bishop of the monastery S. Giovanni Evangelista, were involved in local politics in 1295 to the point that they were forced to flee the city when their faction was defeated.[14] Bishops often represented the interests of powerful local families, and political conflicts between various constituencies among the *cittadini* often pitted the bishop's party against the *rettore*'s.

In addition to the tension between civic and episcopal authorities, there was often tension between the papal court and the bishop's palace as both were embroiled in the tug-of-war with the Holy Roman Empire.[15] Conflict frequently played out using charitable institutions such as the hospitals as pawns. In fact, some of the earliest established hospitals such as S. Simpliciano in Milan, founded in 1096, reflect the concern of the founders and papal court over perceived corruption in the powerful Milanese bishopric. The community received a *bolla* from Pope Alessandro III in 1179 aimed at preventing the overreaching of the archbishopric in the hospital's affairs.[16] Urban II's address to Milan on 1096 included an injunction against simony, which was rampant in the episcopate. That so many hospitals were founded on a model of semi-independent administration in the era that followed suggests a receptive laity who also resisted an overarching bishopric.[17] Hospitals became essential tools of civic welfare and were thus intrinsically connected to the politics of the city. The desire by founders and administers to act as independently as possible must be viewed in this light.

Management of assets and resources

In addition to the major responsibility of caring for poor and ill patients and community members, hospital administrators also managed the resources and income accumulated by the hospital. Income came primarily from charitable bequests, land rents and income, and tithes from income.[18] These managers oversaw a very complex economic system that made up the hospital organization. They had to supervise workers, manage expenses, collect rents on lands, and solicit and manage bequests to the hospital.[19] The hospitals were self-sufficient communities whose civic sphere extended well beyond hospital services. The management of lands and other bequests was a crucial financial responsibility and could often entail the oversight of large and numerous tracts of land and include handling relationships with tenants, investing profits, and preventing lost revenue.[20] Hospitals even engaged in commercial activity with local businesses. In 1331 Ospedale San Vincenzo in Bergamo, for example, rented out a shop on the property to a shoemaker named Stephanius.[21] While the bishopric generally retained nominal control of all economic assets of the hospitals, granting a tithe of all income back to the hospital, the reality was that hospital communities had a great deal of leeway in that area.[22]

Revenue from land was essential to the economic success of the charitable institution, but the possibility for abuse of its management was a constant concern of the communities and church officials. Many of the statutes issued by ecclesiastical leaders specified the use of bequests. For example, at Brolo, Milanese Bishop

Oberto stipulated that any donations of money to the hospital had to be used for alms and could not be used to purchase real estate. Also, donations of land or buildings had to be used usufruct as well.[23] In 1340 the bishop of Milan issued a decree for Ospedale San Gerardo in Monza that the entire hospital community was to decide in common the direction of the use of all assets received as donations by the hospital and that any additional resources obtained through begging be added to that.[24] Ecclesiastical authorities were constantly attempting to put checks on the administrators of charity but this was difficult to do given the various layers of jurisdiction involved.

Donations and testamentary bequests made up the bulk of a hospital's income. Regulations from church officials, the requests of the testator, the needs of the institution, and frequently the commune tax office, all had to be considered in the use of such proceeds. Testators frequently stipulated the nature of their bequest and its distribution. A benefactor might ask that alms be given on the anniversary of his death or on particular saints' days. These testaments could be very specific. For example, in 1304 Albertus de Aplano specified in his will that a set amount be given annually to the Ospedale Colombetta in Milan.[25] Also benefitting Colombetta, Obizo Musonus asked that food be distributed as alms at the hospital door, and Prevotus de Cabiate gave a testament of clothing.[26] Bequests of goods could be quite diverse and required a good deal of organization and management to curate. In 1300 Andreas de Archuri gave Colombetta, among other goods, fifteen bushels of wheat annually to be baked into bread by the hospital brothers on the eve of San Quirico's day or the following Sunday.[27] In 1304 a woman testator with the intriguing name Negro Viola asked that Ospedale della Misericordia (Colombetta) receive money from her estate, which was then to be invested by the hospital; if the Misericordia failed, the benefits were to be transferred to a different hospital.[28] In Cremona, a testator left a house, mill, land, and the 'fruits of that house' to the Ospedale S. Maria della Pieta in 1304.[29]

Frequently, the specified donation consisted of real estate and existing buildings. For example, in 1322 Iacobus de Maineriis donated thirty pieces of land to Colombetta and an additional thirty to the Ospedale Nuovo.[30] In 1325 Robertus de Comite gave Colombetta a farm located near the hospital and along the pilgrim road. He stipulated that the hospital could use the farm and call it 'Fattoria di Colombetta' as long as they used it to feed the poor and pilgrims for as long as pilgrims continued to use that road.[31] The holdings of the large Ospedale Rodolfo Tanzi included an estimated 230 acres encompassing farms, vineyards, woods, and meadows.[32] In addition to fulfilling a charitable impulse and ensuring one's place in heaven, donating to a charitable institution, such as the hospital, was a good way to protect a family's assets as those assets were usually held by the hospital for the lifetime of the member, after which they would be returned to the family. In some cases assets could be recovered by the individual if he or she left service to the institutions while alive. This could keep a family's assets out of reach of taxation or loss in war or through personal vendetta.[33] In the volatile political landscape of medieval Italy, such supposedly apolitical institutions could protect economic interests.

The donations to hospitals were frequent and continuous, making accounting and administration of such testaments a fulltime enterprise for a hospital. It is also clear that these communities did not just act as caretakers but as investors, perhaps in defiance of some the ecclesiastically imposed restrictions. The hospitals were actively engaged in using their assets to buy and sell additional properties. For example, the archive documentation for the Ospedale San Vitali in Como includes thirty-one documents from between 1248 and 1352 that record activity dealing with bequests and investment of lands and monies. These include several purchases of land by the hospital.[34] For the Ospedale S. Martino di Zezio in Como, there are at least twenty-three extant documents from between 1255 and 1430 that list extensive activity in the management of land assets for the hospital including six that describe sales of land.[35] One document among the forty-five dealing with financial administration for the Ospedale S. Maria di Nesso, also in Como, illustrates the sophistication of such transactions. The hospital's *procuratore* made an investment of five years in a building and mill with an annual fee of 24 *denari* to be collected for the benefit of the hospital.[36]

City authorities could be involved in the distribution of bequests and were continually attempting to impose taxes and duties on the hospitals or the testators with limited success.[37] For example, Bernardo Visconti made a large bequest of an annual 150 lire from property existing in Lodi that was to be used to purchase goods for the poor in November and December, on San Martin's day and Christmas. He placed oversight of this distribution in the hands of a coalition of civic authorities, the order of San Francesco and the prior of San Eustorgio.[38] The bishop or civic authorities had to intercede on a number of occasions because of perceived abuses of financial administration within the hospital. At Ospedale San Dionigi in Milan, a papal commission was called in to mediate a dispute between the *maestro* and the brothers. The *maestro* was accused of defrauding the poor, acquiring massive debts for the hospital, and using funds for his personal gain. The jurisdictional disputes among these parties will be discussed in depth in Chapter 5, but this example, as well as the cases discussed above, illustrates the complex activity in which the administration and staff were engaged and which went far beyond providing just charitable or medical assistance.

Operations

Beyond the lay leadership, documentation for the majority of hospitals founded during this period indicates the presence of semi-religious or lay men and women actively or even primarily involved in sustaining the day to day functioning of the institutions. The multiplicity of lay groups involved in the founding, administering, and staffing of hospitals reflects not just a popular call to service by civic organizations but an overall change toward lay governance that originated in the monastic reform movements of the period. The vibrant participation of these pious citizens also reflects the greater trend of the period toward active participation in apostolic service within one's community. These were not just jobs for these lay men and women, but vocations. Workers became part of the hospital community and swore vows of chastity and obedience. They frequently donated all worldly possessions to the hospital and usually lived on the property. However, a major obstacle to understanding and generalizing the nature of hospital organization rests in the variety of terminology used to describe these religious and in the ambiguity of their specific roles and responsibilities. Community members are variously described as *fratres, sorores, conversi, converse, familiare, famiglia, servatori, residenti, dedicati, and decani* (frequently within one document!). Often there appears to have been a change in administration and nomenclature over time, but it is difficult to determine if the change is only nominal or reflects actual alterations in the institution's structure. For example, at the Ospedale San Gerardo in Monza, staff are referred to as *sorores* in 1308, *domine seu converse*, in 1335, *domine humiliate* in 1340 and *religiose mulieres sorores* in 1351, but it is impossible to infer any major institutional changes from such shifts in nomenclature.[39] As we shall see, in some instances we have a general indication of the requirements for inclusion in the group staffing the hospital but often the specifics are obscure at best. The fact that there are so many terms used to describe the variety of lay service illustrates its contemporary significance; our inability to accurately distinguish among them suggests our lack of modern equivalents. While there is much variety with regards to the 'type' of lay member as well as requirements for membership and responsibilities, it is clear that ecclesiastical and civic authorities took full advantage of pious desire for service by a very active laity of the age, and that hospitals provided an outlet for these community members to fulfil their vocation.

Regular canons

A common reference to lay staff in the documentation is that of *canoniche regolari*, or regular canons.[40] As opposed to the cathedral canons who were part of the clergy and attached to a cathedral, this broad designation described various groups that generally followed a formalized rule (usually Augustinian) similar to monastic and mendicant orders, but were comprised of a mix of lay and clerical members. Their common denominator was the mandate to help the poor and the sick. The establishment of such orders reflected both the grassroots lay religious movement of the era but, as they were ecclesiastically affiliated, also church leaders' attempt to utilize, yet control, lay enthusiasm. Decrees emanating from reform councils held in 1059 by Pope Nicholas II, and in 1063 by Pope Alexander II, codified the establishment of these semi-religious orders but stipulated that members were required to lead apostolic lives of chastity and service and follow a set rule.[41] Still, these canons were not attached in the same way as the traditional monastic orders to the institutional church. Founded by urban lay men, they were thus more driven by the needs of community and laity than to loyalty to a bishop or pope. Many of the newly created hospitals were given to pre-existing communities of regular canons. Others were directly founded by canons regular.

Examples of hospitals attached to the canons include the Ospedale S. Seplocre and S. Croce in Lodi. A crusader founded the hospital in 1096 and entrusted the administration to the canons of S. Lorenzo.[42] Ospedale S. Nazarii (later called Leonardi) in Milan was founded in 1127 and was affiliated since its inception with the canons of S. Nazario. Nobleman Ruggero da Cerro stipulated in his will that the hospital be placed under the authority of the Milanese bishopric and that half of his bequest was to go to the canons themselves and half directly to lay workers of the hospital. This arrangement worked for quite a few decades but subsequent disputes in the following centuries illustrate the problems caused by the tension between autonomous canons and the ecclesiastical authorities.[43,44]

Confraternities

In addition to the canons, confraternities, consortia, and other lay and semi-religious groups also took part in the administration of hospitals. The specifications of their founders, the various needs of their inmates and the level of involvement of the city and ecclesiastical authorities created unique structures of administration in individual hospitals that make generalization difficult. Confraternities were a common feature of the medieval urban landscape and their mission included protection and provision of jobs, as well as care for their elderly, sick, widows, and children.[45] Confraternities often incorporated to provide institutional services, which included the founding and administering of hospitals.

In Bergamo, the large and powerful confraternity Misericordia Maggiore had ties to many of the charitable institutions in the city, including hospitals, but it was not the only confraternal order to participate in this type of charity in the city.[46] Bergamesque Ospedale S. Maria Magdalena was administered by a confraternity called the *disciplinati* or *battuti*[47] who also operated a hospital, S. Defendente, in Lodi.[48] The influential Misericordia Maggiore illustrates the centrality of the confraternity to social, political, and economic life in the medieval Italian city. The order counted thousands in its membership that included many of the city's most important citizens.[49] Confraternities fulfilled many of the social

welfare needs of a community. They were legitimized by their association with both local churches and the city government, while
assisting both of these entities in providing for and protecting their
common constituents.

Other hospitals founded and staffed by confraternities include
Ospedale SS. Trinita in Lodi, founded by a confraternity of the same
name and Ospedale San Defendente, also in Lodi, administered by
the confraternity *dei discipli*. This latter hospital was specifically
intended to house pilgrims, particularly husband and wife couples
who were going on the journey together.[50] Ospedale S. Crucis,
was also founded by the confraternity *di battuti* in 1387. This
late date suggests the greater participation of communal groups in
hospital administration.[51] In Como, Ospedale San Eutichio (also
known as S. Giorgio) was administered by the confraternity of the
parish of San Eutichio and was known for its care of abandoned
children.[52]

Some documents refer to administration by consortia, and these
groups are often difficult to differentiate from confraternities. Consortia were organized groups of lay men and women who joined
for the common purpose of charitable service. They appear to have
been much more loosely defined than confraternities, with less of
a direct attachment to ecclesiastical authority. Often, the terms are
used interchangeably and it is difficult to determine a difference.
Documents referencing the founding of Ospedale S. Barnaba in
Milan indicate the existence of a consortium of lay brothers, led
by a deacon, and represented by a minister of the *converse*, who
operated the institution.[53] The document stipulates that the consortia were responsible for managing bequests to the hospital and
distributing alms but gives us little information as to their makeup
or other activities.

Converse

Quite a few documents refer to lay staff as *converse(i)* or *familiares*.[54] Roisin Cossar has illuminated the activities of these groups
in Bergamo where there appears to have been some uniformity and
even codification of the designation of hospital workers. In Bergamo,
it is possible to determine the distinction between some of the
various lay workers and their roles by looking at the oblation or
entrance ceremonies and rules of conduct imposed on the members

as they entered the institution. Documentary evidence for hospitals in Bergamo prior to the fifteenth century generally refers to lay administrators as either *familiares* or *converse*.[55] While the ratio between the two types and their duties and prescribed roles varied from hospital to hospital, here were some commonalities, which illuminate much regarding the activities of these lay men and women. Upon entering service to the hospital the *converse* submitted to a semi-religious ceremony, donated all his or her possessions, and pledged to live a simple life within the hospital. Usually, but not always, *converse* were required to lead chaste lives and remain celibate. These *converse* played an active role in administering the internal affairs of the hospital, which frequently included semi-religious activities. The *familiares* in Bergamo often lived outside of the hospital, were not required to be celibate or chaste, and did not have to donate all of their property to the hospital for admission into service. Their welcoming ceremony was much less formal. They were simply received by officials and residents of the hospital. They were required to promise the donation of some property to the institution, but that property remained under their control during their lifetime.[56]

The Ospedale S. Vincenzo, located in the centre of Bergamo, appears to have been an institution that assisted a large population and was administered by both men and women *converse* and *familiares*. At S. Vincenzo the *converse* were not required to live celibate lives. They could marry, and in fact, married couples often acted as administrators of the hospital. This was not true for all hospitals in Bergamo. For example, there is evidence that a *converse* by the name of Zambornus left the hospital S. Antonio in Bergamo once he decided to marry, suggesting perhaps that celibacy was a requirement there.[57] At S. Vincenzo, Albertus de Payerolis and his first wife Bergamina, entered service to the hospital in 1335. They acted as co-ministers and even received payment for their efforts. In return for service to the hospital residents, they earned an annual income of 6 lire. The couple had pledged two pieces of property to the affiliated confraternity Misericordia for which they received an additional 8 lire a year and which they bequeathed to the hospital on their deaths. Albertus outlived his wife and married again, to Domina Bona, who also became a *conversa* and co-administrator of the facility. She in turn outlived Albertus and managed the hospital on her own after his death.[58]

Over the course of the fourteenth century the distinction between *familiares* and *converse* in Bergamesque hospitals blurred, particularly when referring to women. According to Cossar, the female administrators were generally from the middle and upper classes, evidenced by the fact they all had some property to donate upon admission. While they did promise substantial property upon entry into service to the hospital, they were able to use the income from that for the duration of their lifetimes. These women tended to be either unmarried or widowed and the only real distinction between the two groups of women appears to have been that *familiares* tended to be younger women and the *converse*, elderly.[59] For these women then, the hospital offered a safe refuge for themselves and their assets.

Oblation ceremonies give us some insight into the living conditions and expected activities of the *converse*. For example, we learn that female *converse* joining the hospital S. Vincenzo in Bergamo had private rooms and access to a shared kitchen. Women could choose to live separately or with others and often brought much of their home with them. Upon her oblation in 1335, Gisla de Sivernatis brought several pieces of furniture to the hospital, including two chests, a large bed with a wooden *celonum*, a feather mattress, feather pillow, linen sheets, and a lambswool cover. She also brought a servant with her who also had her own bed. We know she was able to keep these objects because she requested that they be given to the poor on her death.[60] Domina Marchisia della Fontano also brought furniture with her, including a painted desk, chests, and a bed. A servant who accompanied her was promised six florins from her estate, suggesting that in life Domina Marchisia was able to control her income as well.[61]

Because of their independence, hospitals had many different models of administration; Ospedale S. Vincenzo represents only one type. There are few such detailed records from other hospitals but enough to draw some conclusions. Other documents indicate that the designation of *converse* was not locale specific. It was not that the Bergamesque groups referred to their lay workers as *converse* while they were called *frati* or canons elsewhere. For example, the administrators of Ospedale Rodolfo Tanzi were also called *converse*. This hospital did have some similarities to S. Vincenzo in Bergamo in that it was staffed by a mixed group of religious men and women. However, we have little information on the degree to which they were able to maintain or manage their own properties and assets and little information on their daily activities. It does appear that, generally, *fratres* lived within the hospital and had donated at least some of their property to the institution upon admission. Gazzini suggests that the term *residenti* may have denoted individuals who were not wholly committed to the institution or who were temporary residents and workers.[62]

Two often-competing groups administered S. Barnaba in Milan, established around 1140. There was a consortia led by the *decani* who represented lay brothers working for the hospital. They oversaw the distribution of alms and managed bequests to the hospital. There was also a group of *converse* who were represented by a *ministro*. The *converse* oversaw the work of the lay brothers, reserving the right to take back money given to the hospital if the brothers did not fulfil their function of caring for the poor and the sick.[63] Evidence points to a number of instances in which the bishop was forced to mediate disputes regarding this policy, suggesting this was not the most functional model of administration.[64] Ospedale Nuovo (or Donna Buona) in Milan also featured a dual administrative structure. The first, the *decani,* were originally composed of thirty lay men. There was also a group of *conversi,* or lay brothers led by a minister. The lay brothers were responsible for administering alms and aid along with help from *servi* and *serve.* The *converse,* who at one point numbered fourteen men and nineteen women, had to follow the rule of S. Augustine, which dictated that they wear the black tunic and cross inscribed with their motto.[65]

Semi-religious orders

This seemingly crowded civic charitable landscape also included a number of semi-religious orders and independent lay groups which became increasingly popular in the twelfth and thirteenth centuries, and which had multiple functions in the charitable and social arenas. For example, the *Humiliati*, formed in the late eleventh century and originally branded as heretical for their penchant for preaching and organizing outside ecclesiastical approval, focused their activity primarily on addressing the inequalities created by the newly capitalist urban society. In addition to economic activities mentioned above,[66] they also founded and administered hospitals for the poor and ill. Innocent III recognized the social utility and religiosity of the group and approved their order in 1203.[67]

Hospitals administered by the *Humiliati* include the very large, prosperous, and important Ospedale Brolo in Milan. In addition, the Ospedale S. Maria dei Tizzoni in Lodi was administered by the group. This hospital, founded in 1296 or 1297, was named after the ancient Lodi family Tizzoni who attached it to a house of *Humiliati* called de' Danari.[68] The *Humiliati* administered the facility with supervision from the family, who retained the right to elect a minister. In Milan, the Ospedale SS. Benedetto and Bernardo was founded by the archbishop of Milan, who placed it under the administration of a group called the 'seven *convenia* of the third order of the *Humiliati*', and instructed them to follow the rule of S. Augustine.[69] In Como, Ospedale S. Antonio Astano[70] was run by the *Humiliati* as were Ospedale Maria di Nesso,[71] Ospedale San Martino (di Zezzio),[72] and Ospedale San Vitale.[73] In Monza, Mambretti has uncovered a document which suggests that Ospedale San Gerardo was located adjacent to a *Humiliati* house called domus de Parazo or alternately Marina Robia. He suggests that the *Humiliati* were probably the *converse* noted in the documents of the elections of ministers of the hospital in 1230 and 1308.[74]

One of the most compelling characteristics of medieval urban piety was the extensive participation of women in all facets of charitable and religious life. Participation in semi-religious activities such as the administration of a hospital gave women an opportunity to engage in their community at a level that would be barred to them in any other arena. Women made up a majority of membership in the *Humiliati* and their activity in the administration of charity including hospitals is well documented.[75] For example, Ospedale San Vitale in Como was given to the sisters of the order of *Humiliati* in 1239.[76] In Lodi, Ospedale S. Maria di Arlino was founded as early as 885, but documents indicated it was administered by a group of women *Humiliati* in the thirteenth century.[77] There is even evidence that women were engaged in managing hospital communities. In Genoa, a sister Iacoba was named to the office of minister of Ospedale Rivarolio. Members of another hospital in Pavia disputed her claim. Iacoba petitioned the papal court for assistance. The pope indeed interceded advising Genoese officials to investigate her claim and if found valid reinstate her with help from secular authorities if necessary.[78] We do not know the outcome of the dispute but the ability of a woman to claim such possible authority all the way to the Vatican says much about women's participation in the religious movements of the age.

Non-affiliated groups

In fact, it is clear from much of the documentation that women worked alongside men in most of the hospital administration. Many of the documents giving evidence of administrative activity simply refer to the lay staff as *fratres* and *sorores*. Similar to their monastic brethren, these 'brothers' and 'sisters' made a vow of obedience and chastity. Some small groups such as the *Antoniani*, the *Crocideri*, and the *Trinitari* were organized into formal 'orders', which flourished in several locations simultaneously. Some were tertiary members of larger organized groups such as the *Humiliati*. Others appear to have been connected only to the individual hospital and to have belonged to no larger group. The *fratres* and *sorores* dedicated themselves specifically to service in the hospital and usually to residing there (there are exceptions to this, which we will examine.) They generally made professional vows and swore an oath of obedience to the minister and the 'rule' of the order. They did not always, however, make the traditional vow of poverty.

Many houses were administered solely by *sorores*. Women were a valuable but vulnerable asset to religious institutions and the community. The city government accepted that this was an appropriate avenue for women's economic and social activity. The ecclesiastical officials welcomed their zeal and dedication but worried over their participation in the public sphere and the implications of their independence.[79] Ospedale San Gerardo di Monza reflected this balancing act by religious officials and city. Hospital statutes of 1175 stipulate that the 'pious women' chosen to administer the hospital were allowed to elect their own minister but they were to be 'protected' by an advocate selected by the commune and invested by the archbishop.[80]

In Treviso, Ospedale Ognissanti was founded in 1204 to care for the sick, poor, and pilgrims. The administration of this hospital followed an unusual model. A mixed group of lay men and women were responsible for the day-to-day running of the institution. According to documents, these groups included a large group of

'*frati e sorores extrinseci*', brothers and sisters who were allowed
to own property and live in the city with their families and children.
In addition, there were a number of '*domine incluse*' who did not
leave the hospital, as well as some clerics, a minister, and *procuratore*.[81] This organizational structure probably reflects a reaction to
very individualized needs of a community. Perhaps the number of
members who would agree to entirely forfeit their civilian life and
reside in the hospital did not adequately meet the hospital's need
for staff. The dual system may have been necessary for maintaining
a constant and effective administration.

Whole families were engaged in charitable activity geared
toward hospitals. There are quite a few references to families taking
up service to a hospital and residing on the hospital grounds. There
is evidence of married couples who pledged a life of chastity, obedience, charity, and service to a hospital. Pledging such ties to the
hospital did not necessarily mean giving up ownership of assets.
For example, in 1349 Giovanni Vivani and his wife Franceschina
dedicated themselves to religious life at Ospedale Rodolfo Tanzi in
Parma. They entered service together, wore the habit, and swore
chastity and obedience to the minister.[82] In response to their vows
the *rettore* uttered the words, '*Acipite iugum, mum suave est et
honus meum leve.*'[83] Statutes for the hospital demanded that *converse* such as the Vivani leave their property as a legacy to the
hospital, under penalty of denial of last sacraments and burial
outside of the cemetery as rebels or the excommunicated. They were
allowed control of their property and assets while alive, but were
required to make an accounting of all their assets upon entrance
and denounce the acquisition of further material gains. The agreement promised the couple continued maintenance and protection
of the pledged legacy by the community.[84]

Such commitment, particularly by families and women, reflects
the insecurity of the urban society in which the hospital functioned.
The institution offered protection during unstable times for both
the individual's soul and material assets. This was a mutually beneficial relationship. In return for a way to serve and facilitate the
salvation of one's soul through service to the ill and needy the
oblates assured the success of the institution through the promise
of their legacy. In addition, the oblates found a way to have that
legacy as well as their current assets protected from outside interests
while the donor was still alive.

Management by civic authorities

Founders occasionally specified the city itself act as administrator of the hospital. City governors appointed lay men to provide the services but often retained oversight. For example, a noble citizen, Gualtiero Garbani, gave land and buildings for the purpose of creating the Ospedale SS. Giacomo (Iacobi) e Filippo della Misericordia in Lodi, founded in 1206. He stipulated that the commune of Lodi was, '*fundatotur, patronus, et advocatus*' of the hospital, which should be staffed by *fratres* and *sorores*. The commune could approve the election of a rector and retained the right to supervise the administration directly without any interference from the bishop.[85] As discussed above, when the della Pila family founded Ospedale San Simpliciano in Milan in 1091, they specifically requested that the hospital be administered by the '*boni homines*' of the neighbourhood of Porta Comasina. These community leaders were to select a minister, and the della Pilas stipulated; 'no bishop, abbot, or any other man or cleric or layman may have and govern the hospital, itself or their property'.[86] The *boni homines* were instructed to elect two people to oversee the administration and management of the hospital.[87]

While ecclesiastical officials administered, or at least supervised most hospitals, frequently there were overlapping jurisdictional functions. For example, records for Ospedale di San Gerardo di Monza from the early fourteenth century indicate that it was governed by capitulary statutes but administered by pious women who elected their own minister and were represented and protected by an advocate selected by communal authorities.[88] Frequently, this led to jurisdictional disputes and competition for control between the commune and the church officials. This was particularly the case when electing a leader.[89] These disputes make it clear that the leadership of an institution was as much a political position as it was administrative.[90]

Conclusion

The hospitals that sprang up around northern Italy in the twelfth and thirteenth centuries were more than functional institutions for the care of the sick, poor, and pilgrims. They were communities of religious and semi-religious men and women who sought to follow the apostolic life of charity, poverty, and service. These communities were self-sustained economic entities that provided care for their inmates as well as community for their staff. They reflect the experience in the medieval Italian city where individuals and families were creating new familial and social networks and responding to the increasingly evident inequities produced by rapid urbanization.

The variety of institutional models for the administration and staffing of the hospital communities reflects the diversity and vibrancy of the urban citizenry's enthusiasm for the possibility of leading a religious life of service as well as the perception of an increased need for such apostolic responses to community problems. Individuals, confraternities, semi-lay orders, and the commune itself, orchestrated new models of management and staffing of hospitals and often operated somewhat independently of ecclesiastical oversight. Church leaders were faced with the challenge of utilizing apostolic zeal among the laity to alleviate growing social pressures while at the same time retaining control over charitable activity and profiting from the revenues and duties of the hospital communities.

For administrators and staff, hospitals provided a mechanization of control in areas of life that were increasingly insecure. The volatile political atmosphere of the Italian city-states as well as the ever-present threat of disease and poverty created unprecedented levels of instability. Hospitals, independent civic organization generally blessed with ecclesiastical legitimacy, allowed for the protection of assets and even family members' well-being. Citizens were able to follow a life of piety and charity while remaining in their community and often retaining their social status and even property. The focus of their pious activity reflected the needs of the city. They catered to the sick and poor among them, directly addressing the new capitalist, urban reality around them.

The hospital also allowed for political families or families of higher social status an opportunity to serve as leaders in the charitable arena. This added avenue of civic ascendency challenged ecclesiastical authority indirectly. Popes and bishops, recognizing the necessity of these creative institutions to help fulfil the increasing needs of social welfare, allowed for the development and partial independence of these facilities while attempting to control them and benefit from their success. Over the course of the fourteenth and early fifteenth centuries church leaders increasingly lost the battle for supremacy, as did the laity, to the communal government.

Notes

1 Albini, *Città e ospedali*, 11; Caretta, 'Gli ospedali altomedievali', 12.
2 Thompson, *Cities of God*, 40.
3 G.C. Bescapé, *Antichi diplomi degli arcivescovi milanesi* (Firenze, 1937), doc. n. 4, 71–4, discussed in Albini, *Città e ospedali*, 69–70; Brodman, *Charity and Religion*, 72; Pecchiai, *L'ospedale di Milano*, 44.
4 Ibid.
5 Deacons are traditionally defined as ordained members of the church hierarchy, below the priests; they were responsible for the more 'secular duties' of the church such as the administration of alms. There is some confusion as to the exact meaning of the term deacon in this period. For hospitals, deacons generally appear to have been lay individuals who did not reside in the hospital but were active in administering financial aspects of the hospital.
6 Bescapé, *Antichi diplomi*, doc. no. 4, 71–4.
7 Caretta, *L'assistenza Diocesi di Lodi*, 291.
8 Caretta, 'Gli ospedali altomedievali', 5.
9 Racine, 'Il sistema ospedaliero', 366.
10 For comparison, the Cathedral chapter of Cremona had a similar acreage, the important Ospedale S. Maria della Scala in Siena held 489 hecters, and the convent of S. Dominico in Bologna counted 135 hecaters in their possession. M. Guenza, 'La formazione della propreita fondiaria dell'ospedale Rodolfo Tanzi', in R. Greci (ed.), *L'ospedale Rodolfo Tanzi di Parma in età Medievale* (Bologna, 2004), 145.
11 For example, the Ospedale de Guado, in Lodi gave twelve Milanese dinari annually in 1170 and Ospedale S. Blasii contributed five soldi in 1163. Caretta, 'Gli ospedali altomedievali', 290–1.
12 In Gemona in the hospital San Michele, the leader had the title of Camera (or Chamira) who, like a rector, had administrative duties over the hospital. In this case the Camera was chosen by the confraternity in charge and was limited to a one year term. Londero, *Per l'amor*, 31.
13 Caretta, *L'assistenza Diocesi di Lodi*, 290.
14 Albini, 'Dallo sviluppo', 40–1.
15 See above, Chapter 1, n. 6.
16 Albini, *Città e ospedali*, 33, 79.
17 Ibid., 27.

18 Racine, 'Il sistema ospedaliero', 366. Racine indicates that the privilege
    to receive tithes was granted by the bishopric during the twelfth and
    thirteenth centuries. For example, from a document dated, 4 August
    1215, Archbishop Enrico granted to the Ospedale S. Abrogio a tenth
    of the income from their land holdings. Bescapé, *Antichi diplomi*, cit.,
    n. XIV, 84.

19 Ibid.

20 Caretta, 'Gli ospedali altomedievali', 290. For example Ospedale S.
    Blasii in Lodi was operated by *conversae* who also accepted and
    managed quite extensive lands bequeathed to the hospital in 1163.

21 ASBg, Notarile, G. Soyarius, busta 7 (1331–32), 48; Cossar, *The Trans-
    formation of the Layity*, 63–4.

22 Racine, 'Il sistema ospedaliero', 366.

23 Bescapé, *Antiche Diplomi*, doc. no. 4, 71–4.

24 Mambretti, 'L'ospedale di San Gerardo', 196.

25 AOM, Aggregazione, Colombetta, cart. 40. 27, November 1304.

26 Ibid., 16 September, 1302; 20 December 1328.

27 Ibid., 15 January, 1323.

28 Ibid., 11 March, 1279.

29 ASCr, Ospedale S. Maria Della Pieta (ASCr, OSM) Indice I, busta 3,
    2 February 1304.

30 AOM, Aggregazione, Colombetta, cart.,3, May 1322.

31 Ibid., 7 October, 1325.

32 Guenza, 'La formazione', 145.

33 For example Guiduccius Beccarius entrance into the *Humiliati* house
    in a time of war for the protection of his assets. See the discussion
    above on page 2. Brasher, *Women of the Humiliati*, 101.

34 ASCO, Archivio Ospedale di S. Anna (ASCOs.a.) cart. 2.

35 Ibid., cart 7.

36 ASCOs.a. cart. 8–9, March 1324.

37 Disputes regarding taxation will be discussed in Chapter 5.

38 ASMi, AOM, Consiglio degli orfanotrofio, Ospedale di S. Giacomo
    dei Pellegrini Cart. 74, no 9. For discussion see R. Cippo, 'Le piu
    antiche carte dell'ospedale di San Giacomo (secolo XIV.)', in M.
    Alberzoni and O. Grassi (eds), *La Carità a Milano nei secoli XII–XV,
    atti del convegno di studi Milano, 6–7 novembre 1987* (Milan, 1989),
    239–72.

39 Mambretti, 'L'ospedale di San Gerardo', 193.

40 Rocca, *Ospedale e canoniche regolari*, 16–17. For the differences
    between regular canons and cathedral canons see Thompson, *Cities
    of God*, 45, n. 153.

41 1059 (IV) Niccolò II (Concilio romano): '*Et praecipientes statu-
    imus, ut ii praedictorum ordinum, qui eidem praedecessori nostro
    obedientes, castitatem servaverunt, juxta ecclesias quibus ordinati*

sunt, sicut oportet religiosos clericos, simul manducent, et dormiant: et quidquid eis ad ecclesiis venit, communiter habeant. Et rogantes momenus, ut ad apostolicam, communem scilicet, vitam summopere pervenire student;' 1063 (IV) Alessandro II (Concilio romano): *Et praecipientes statuimus, ut hi praedictorum ordinum, qui iisdem praedecessoribus nostris obedientes castitatem servaverint juxta ecclesias quibus ordinati sunt, sicut opertet religiosos clericos, simul manducent et dormiant et quidquid eis ab ecclesia competit communiter habeant. et rogantes momenus, ut ad apostolicam communem vitam summopere pervenire studeant, quatenus perfectionem consecuti, cum his qui centesimo fructu ditatur in caelesti patria mereantur adscribi',* Rocca, *Ospedale e canoniche regolari,* 18–19.

42 Caretta, *L'assistenza Diocesi di Lodi,* 290.

43 Ibid.

44 Additional hospitals staffed by canons include Ospedale S. Pietro della Cade, in a rural location near Piacenza, which was founded by individuals in 1100 and assigned to the 'righteous hospitaliers of S. Augustino' – canon regolari. Others in Piacenza include, S. Spirito and S. Misericordia, S. Matteo founded in1106, S. Marco in 1090, S. Vittoria 1110, s. Cristoforo 1164, S. Antonio, 1172, S. Maria di Betlemme (S. Anna) 1172, and S. Raimondo 1170. From Rocca, *Ospedali e canoniche regolari,* 24.

45 Little and Buzzetti, *Liberty, Charity, Fraternity*; G. Meersseman, *Ordo Fraternitatis: Confraternite e Pietà dei Laici nel Medioevo,* Vol. 3 (Rome, 1977).

46 Cossar, *The Transformation of the Laity,* 7.

47 Ibid., 60; Caretta, *L'assistenza Diocesi di Lodi,* 293.

48 Agnelli, *Ospedale di Lodi,* 17.

49 Cossar, *The Transformation of the Laity,* 7.

50 Agnelli, *Ospedali di Lodi,* 17.

51 Caretta, *L'assistenza Diocesi di Lodi,* 293.

52 Cosmacini, *L'Ospedale Sant'Anna,* 54.

53 Albini, *Città e ospedali,* 36–8.

54 For example, the bishop of Lodi placed administration of Ospedale S. Blasii in Lodi in the hands of citizens Arialdo de Goldaniga and Bonatto da Casalta, as well as *conversi* and assistants of the Ospedale S. Biagio. Caretta, *L'assistenza Diocesi di Lodi,* 290.

55 D. Osheim has outlined the evolving meaning of *conversi* in 'Conversion, Conversi, and the Christian life in medieval Tuscany', *Speculum,* 58:2 (1983), 368–90, 371. Before the mid-eleventh century the term *conversus* was generally used to denote an individual who had joined a monastery as an adult but who lacked the education to become a full member. By the late eleventh century the term was used to denote

any adult who was associated in some way with a religious institution. This designation could include lay donors to religious houses who promised goods to the institution and promised to live within the institution, but still maintained some contact with the outside world and often continued to live off their donated income. It also referred to widows who joined religious houses and other lay people who offered a variety of services to the institutions.

56 Cossar, *The Transformation of the Laity*, 78.
57 Ibid., 7.
58 ASBg., Notarile, G. Soyarius, busta 10 (1349–50), ASBg, Notarile, G. Fanconi, busta 117a (1353–54) 634–6.
59 Cossar, *The Transformation of the Laity*, 79- 80.
60 Ibid., 64.
61 Ibid.
62 Gazzini, 'Una comunità', 263.
63 L. Grazlioli, *La cronacca di Goffredo da Bussero in Archivio Storico Lombardo*. s. 4a v (1906), 211–40.
64 Ibid.
65 ASMi, Arch. Osp. Maggiore Milano, perg. 1305.
66 Discussion of economic activity of the *Humiliati,* see above, pages 46 and 47.
67 For information on the Humiliati see Andrews, *The Early Humiliati*; Brasher, *Women of the Humiliati*; L. Zanoni, *Gli Umiliati neilLoro Rapporti con l'eresia, l'industria della Lana ed i Comuni nei Secoli XII e XIII Sulla Scorta di Documenti Inediti.* (Roma, 1970).
68 Agnelli, *Ospedale di Lodi*, 16.
69 Zanoni, *Gli umilitati*, 288.
70 ASCO sa. PFV cart 8–9.
71 Ibid.
72 Cosmacini, *L'Ospedale Sant'Anna*, 56.
73 Ibid., 55.
74 R. Mambretti, *Le Carte dell'ospedale di San Biagio in Monza: (secoli XII–XIII)* (Milan, 1999), 193.
75 See Brasher, *Women of the Humiliati.*
76 Cosmacini, *L'Ospedale Sant'Anna*, 55.
77 Ibid., 21.
78 ASVat Registro Vaticano 21a (a copy from the original made in 1762 by G. Garampi), fo. 317v-8r 640, reprinted in Andrews, *The Early Humiliati*, 275.
79 For women's participation in the apostolic movements see D. Bornstein and R. Rusconi (eds), *Women in Religion in Medieval and Renaissance Italy* (Chicago, IL, 1996); Grundmann, *Religious Movements*, Vauchez and Bornstein, *The Laity in the Middle Ages.*
80 Brodman, *Charity and Religion*, 74.

81 AST, Ognissanti di Treviso, perg., b.2, doc. 11, December, 1204, reprinted in D. Rando, 'Laicu religious' tra stutture civile ed ecclesiastiche: l'ospedale di Ognissanti in Treviso (sec. XII), in *Esperienze religiose*, 43–83.

82 ASPr, RT, b. 17, fasc. 41: Doc. 21 December, 1349.

83 In later oblation records the oath was extended to include the word 'service', see Gazzini, 'Una comunità', 273.

84 Ibid., 279.

85 Caretta, *L'assistenza Diocesi di Lodi*, 292.

86 Albini, *Città e ospedali*, 25.

87 Ibid., 24, 25.

88 Brodman, *Charity and Religion*, 74; Mambretti, 'L'ospedale di San Gerardo', 189–90.

89 Mambretti, 'L'ospedale di San Gerardo', 191–2.

90 Jurisdictional disputes and their implications will be discussed in Chapter 5.

4

Internal life of the hospital

As much of the documentation for various medieval hospitals is fragmentary and obscure, it is difficult to reach broad conclusions regarding the administrative model, physical composition, or daily life of a hospital over the entire course of its existence. However, we do have ample documentation for a few hospitals that must serve anecdotally to illustrate the internal life of these communities. One such facility is Ospedale Brolo in Milan. It is well documented in the archives, primarily because it was located in the heart of the city, received a rule from the archbishop of Milan, and became the largest and most prosperous hospital in the city. Bonvesin de la Riva, a contemporary chronicler who was very interested in the charitable and religious movements of his age, gave a specific description of Brolo. He claimed that the community had beds to accommodate five hundred poor and sick individuals and maintained that no one was turned away except lepers. He reported that the facility cared for three hundred and fifty abandoned children, and that food and alms were given daily to five hundred people outside the hospital doors. He also suggested (at least by the time he was writing in 1288) that members of the third order of the *Humiliati* administered and staffed the hospital.[1] Evidence from 1268 indicates there were a *maestro*, or minister, and thirteen brothers who went about the city collecting for the poor and taking in abandoned children. In addition, nineteen sisters worked inside the hospitals caring for the sick. The brothers wore a distinctive wool tunic with a black cloak and a cross stitched on their chests. The sisters were clothed in similar fashion but had a cross stitched on to the shoulder of their cloak with the words, '*ave, gratia, plena*'.[2] It appears that from a point early in its history, two groups managed Ospedale Brolo, with administrative oversight by the *decani*, and

daily management by the lay brothers. The first, a *consortium pauperum* of the church S. Barnaba, were *decani* and *fratres* who went
out into the city to collect and distribute alms for the poor. The
second were lay members originally affiliated with another, smaller
hospital called S. Stefano who cared for the ill internees.[3]

However, while the documentary evidence is abundant for Brolo,
it is somewhat ambiguous and the various interpretations of the
events of its founding and incorporation illustrate the difficulty with
reading the evidence. This difficulty also illuminates how misinter-
pretation alters some of the fundamental questions of authority and
jurisdiction. For example, even the identification of the founder as
Goffredo da Bussero is perhaps problematic. Albini attributes the
reference to Bussero in early documents in actuality to a relative
of Bussero's and suggests this may have been an attempt to by the
founder to connect the bequest with an illustrious past ancestor.[4]
Some scholars, referring to the bull issued by Archbishop Oberto in
1161 decreeing that it merge with another hospital and follow the
rule of S. Augustine, interpret the archbishop's interference as the
moment when two failing hospitals were consolidated and management appropriated and ordered by the church officials.[5] However,
when one looks at all the documentary evidence for the hospital
it appears the two consortia managing the hospital, the consortia
di San Barnaba and consortia di San Stefano, merged earlier than
1161, probably in 1158.[6] San Stefano probably managed the new
hospital through leadership by a lay administrator and with a staff
of lay brothers.[7] Albini suggests that the two groups decided to
pool their resources, possibly during the war with Milan, in order
to save both hospitals. However, they did retain separate identities
and administrative structures.[8] Then, in 1161 Archbishop Oberto
interceded in the affairs of the hospital in response to a dispute
between the two groups over jurisdictional issues. He imposed a
regulation on their organization and management. He stipulated
the number of brothers required to live and dine in the community
with the poor and the sick. He indicated that the *maestro* was to be
chosen by the *decani* and *frati* and that the *maestro* was to choose
a *cellario* to manage economic aspects of the community.[9] These
managers then, rendered an account of hospital affairs to the office
of the bishop each month. Finally, the bishop claimed a supervisory
role over the entire enterprise. Pope Clement III ratified this statute
in 1190.[10] Despite some inconsistencies, this reading of the evidence

suggests much more original independence and agency by the hospital itself with the imposition of ecclesiastical structure occurring in response to perceived abuses by staff and leaders within the system.

In addition, the administrative structure of the hospital does not appear to have always followed the model imposed by Bishop Oberto even after his intervention. Subsequent documents from the beginning of the thirteenth century refer to the presence of *servi*, lay men who took on many of the original activities of the *fratres*. Albini suggests this indicated the *fratres* had become involved in more important community affairs and had ceded much of the daily assistance activities to these individuals.[11] By the time that Bonvesin was writing, administration of the hospital had been taken over by the third order of the *Humiliati*.[12] In fact, the archbishop's attempts to impose a structure on Brolo suggest the reality of a desire for such order among organizations that arose and prospered independent of ecclesiastical oversight. Often ecclesiastical officials' intercession and imposition of statutes and rules occurred at the behest of a hospital when faced with internal disputes and challenges. Therefore, while Ospedale Brolo is one of the better-documented hospitals of the era the various ambiguity of archival evidence suggests the difficulty with getting a comprehensive picture of the medieval Italian hospital. Still, it is possible to reconstruct, to some degree, life within the walls of the hospital community.

The physical structure of the hospital

One of the features that distinguishes the medieval hospital from its Renaissance successor is the lack of uniformity among the physical structure of the institutions. The proliferation of communities across the region happened at a rapid pace with no unifying concept except the desire to provide adequate shelter and sustenance for the poor and ill. Many hospitals were created using existing structures. At times this was little more than a single family dwelling. For example, Ospedale S. Alessandro in Bergamo was transformed at very little expense (16 lire) from the testator's house. The money went toward a new roof over a courtyard, locks on the door, and beds and bedding.[13] At the other end of the spectrum hospital compounds could be quite substantial comprising many buildings and housing hundreds of individuals.

Ospedale Rodolfo Tanzi became one of the most important institutions in the region. From inventories taken in 1305 and 1330 we know that the complex contained at least six buildings. The most important and largest was the main ward of the hospital, which housed pilgrims, travellers, the sick, and the poor under one roof. This main structure featured separate rooms for men and women internees and included seventy-two beds with mattresses, linens and other bedding, and included additional furniture and several rugs. As beds were generally used for one to two people, the hospital could conceivably accommodate up to 140 individuals.[14]

Two additional large buildings housed the brothers and sisters who worked at the hospital. Men lived together in one building that accommodated fourteen individuals. The men lived simply; the list of their possessions includes only beds, bedding, and a few items of furniture. They lived in common in a large dormitory space on the upper floor of one building. This building also had a small infirmary, kitchen, and refectory located on the first floor. The *rettore* lived with the brothers but had his own, much more luxuriously appointed, room on the second floor with four personal servants. The women appear to have lived less simply than the brothers in a separate, smaller building. They were able to retain some personal property. The inventory lists their name and their belongings, which include such items as mattresses, linens, blankets, and various housewares. These women's individual entries also frequently included servants who entered service with them and had their own beds and linens. From the mention of children's articles in the inventory there is even the suggestion that the women's dormitory housed some children. The descriptions of goods such as furniture and trunks were quite detailed and indicate that some of the women had a good deal of status and wealth. The inventory also listed fifteen service individuals, attached to the hospital who appear to have lived outside of the hospital grounds.[15]

It is possible to ascertain the compound's level of self-sufficiency. The inventory lists several additional small buildings on the property including a wine cellar, stalls for oxen and horses, and a chicken coop. In addition, there was a small vegetable garden with an adjoining building that housed a gardener. The kitchen was apparently fully supplied for feeding a large community storing supplies of butter, cheese, flour, oil, and wine. A list of properties held by the hospital in addition to the actual hospital compound include

Hospitals and charity

more than one hundred and fifty various buildings in the city, eight mills, and over four hundred and fifty plots of land outside the city walls in the surrounding *contado*. Massimo Guenza has estimated the total acquisition of land by the hospital to be between 230 and 233 three hectares. Seventy-seven per cent of this land was arable, nine per cent wooded, seven per cent vineyard and six per cent meadowland.[16] Clearly, this was a large, successful, and prosperous institution, probably among the largest in the region and while perhaps not representative of all the independent hospitals it does give us insight into how these institutions operated.

Anecdotal references to smaller hospitals can give us a glimpse into their physical structure. For example, Ospedale San Vincenzo in Bergamo was a medium-sized facility made up of two buildings with a staircase leading up to two *solari*.[17] This would suggest a similar composition to other hospitals where the patients were housed in a lower building with living quarters for the staff arranged on a higher floor. While often evidence of how existing homes and building were transformed into hospitals for nominal costs suggests the functionality of this civic space, we can also get a glimpse of the origins of the Renaissance impetus toward the beautification of civic space that Henderson calls their concern with '*bellezza*'.[18] While the Ospedale S. Alessandro in Bergamo was built in 1352 in such a cost-effective way for only 16 lire, it was also decorated with 'certain figures' by 'Andrea the painter' who was paid 4 lire.[19] That Andrea was known by his craft and was paid a tidy sum for his work suggests the beginning of the movement of civic art that would be emblematic of the Renaissance. Members of the community believed that the hospital represented more than a functional service provider. The impetus toward charity and community assistance was a reflection of civic pride and articulation of the nascent ideals of civic humanism.

Social composition of the hospital staff

It is possible to ascertain some information regarding the social status and living conditions of lay staff of the hospital community from inventories such as the one for Ospedale Rodolfo Tanzi as well as oblation ceremonies and testamentary bequests. It is clear from documentary references that individuals of means were attached to many of the hospitals and were able to maintain their lifestyle to a certain extent. For example, women working in the Ospedale S. Vincenzo in Bergamo had the choice of rooming together in a dormitory or in separate accommodations. They had access to separate kitchens and were able to retain the service of personal servants.[20] Women brought many personal items with them upon entering the hospital, including substantial items of furniture and bedding. We know that these women retained control over property while working for the hospital as they frequently stipulated that their wealth be donated to the poor upon death.[21]

Cossar has suggested that the private rooms and retention of private property indicates that the women who joined this, and other hospitals in Bergamo, were women of means and that they were basically 'paying' for their accommodation with their bequests. However, there is also evidence that the hospitals did not turn away poor women who wished to serve and that they were usually provided with bedding and linens, but not necessarily private rooms.[22] Some hospitals, such as Rodolfo Tanzi, did not allow women to retain use of their property upon oblation to the community. The hospital's statutes indicate that they were to report their assets upon admission and were not allowed to use them during their lifetime. To avoid any disputes regarding assets, family members were required to renew their oath of dedication of property on each birthday.[23] As we shall see, the requirements regarding personal property could cause disputes among and within the hospital communities but it is clear from the abundance of references to the practice that joining a hospital community gave individuals, particularly women, protection of assets and a safe, protected, environment for their person. It also probably provided them with a replacement kin or community group. Some founders, such as Guillelmus de Buboi, at S. Alessandro in Bergamo, requested that women in his family act as *maestro* and specified that the community provide security for his family, a place for them to go in times of strife.[24] The religious life was always a popular option for widows and single women and this urban model of apostolic service was a novel manifestation of this tradition.

In fact, the family was fundamentally instrumental in the growth, development, and transformation of the hospital movement. Married couples and families often founded, joined, and even administered the facilities. In Lodi, SS. Simonis et Iudae, S. Iacobi, S. Bassiane, S. Mariae, and San Michele di Brembio were all founded by the bequests of important city families.[25] Married couples often joined the communities with varying stipulations regarding their status while there. At S. Vincenzo there were several sets of spouses administering the community in the latter half of the fourteenth century. Albertus de Payerolis and his wife Bona were co-ministers from 1350 until his death in 1361. Bona continued on as administrator until her death in 1384 when she was replaced by another couple, Venderminus de Guascalla and his wife Catlina. [26] There are references to married couples in service to the Ospedale Colombetta in Milan as well. Three separate profession vows from 1292, 1308, and 1338, specify the commitment of husbands and wives to the hospital, but their level of commitment differed. In 1292, Leo Malrestidus and his wife Cecilia dedicated themselves to serving the community but remained in their homes outside of the hospital grounds; while in 1308, Anricus Tessera and his wife Mirana became *converse*, living within the hospital compound. In 1338, Saraminus Garimondus and his wife Simona also committed to live within the community but were called *dedicati*.[27] Wealthy, powerful families could also serve as insurance against threats to the hospital. When the consolidation and elimination of hospitals occurred in the fifteenth century, important families whose fortunes were tied to that of the facility protected some of them. For example, the large Ospedale Santa Maria Maddalena in Como maintained its independence well into the eighteenth century due to the fierce protection of the families Marini and Sambendetto. The Marini family were involved in the founding of the hospital around 1300.[28]

As the civic landscape increasingly gave political and social power to urban individuals and families, these *cittadini* utilized charitable institutions such as hospitals to protect their growing assets. In the ever-insecure political arena, the hospital offered a place of refuge for not only a family's assets but also their vulnerable family members, namely women. Once the families tied up their fortunes and reputations with the hospital they came to demand influence in the affairs of the communities. This often brought them into conflict with religious and civic authorities. As they increasingly became the civic authorities their control over semi-religious orders like hospitals altered the very nature of charity and health care and challenged ecclesiastical pre-eminence in providing these services to the general public.

Rules and statutes

On those occasions when the church officials did intercede in the affairs of the hospital, the outcome was often the imposition or reinforcement of a 'rule' or statute of operation. These detailed instructions give us a glimpse into the prescribed daily routines of the members of the medieval hospital communities. However, there are relatively few of these documents in the archival collections. This might indicate that many of the institutions operated independently of an imposed rule or statute of operations, or it might suggest that the rule was being followed faithfully with little need for ecclesiastical intervention. When mentioned, most frequently there is a reference to a hospital following an existing monastic rule such as those of the Augustinian or Benedictine orders. The Rule of S. Augustine was the generally adopted model, and most innovative religious orders of the twelfth and thirteenth centuries followed that rule, or created their own rule that tended to at least echo the major themes established by Augustine. This suggests the importance of having an articulated, ecclesiastically approved, procedure for the administration of charity. Church officials often stipulated that a group follow such rules in order to regulate the activities of members and retain some form of institutional control. However, there are enough documents referring to the necessity of the ecclesiastical interference in the affairs of a hospital in response to a complaint about their non-compliance with a rule to suggest that the imposed rules may have been more prescriptive than strictly obeyed or enforced.

The focus of any rule imposed on, or created by, a hospital was on the apostolic value of ministering to those in need outside of the community. The Rule of S. Augustine stressed the need to lead a chaste life of voluntary poverty and dedicated service to the community. It regulated behaviour for communal living, and accounted for the distribution of private property. The rule does not directly refer to the running of hospitals but its application would fit nicely with charitable goals of the institutions as it did with the goals of the mendicant groups that arose at this time.[29]

Smaller and more independent communities followed less formalized rules. We know from documents referring to visits from ecclesiastical representatives to the Ospedale San Gerardo in Monza in 1319 and 1340 that the hospital was affiliated with a *Humiliati domus* and that the community followed a general rule that dictated their daily activities.[30] While there are mentions of the activities of *fratres*, it is clear from this document and others that women actually made up the majority of membership in the community. The rule stipulated that these women were to live separately from the lay brothers and were allowed to enter the compound only on approval of the minister. They never left the community without accompaniment, and only went out in groups of three, of whom one had to be elderly. Sisters were not to speak to visitors alone and were to be accompanied when caring for the sick. The minister agreed to provide meals and beverages, including meat two to three times a week, to the sisters, who took them in their own refectory. These sister *converse* observed silence during their meals. They were to give linens and a blanket and adequate meals to their patients, including wine depending on the patient's condition.[31]

The hospital had an oratory and the bishop required it to be 'kept' both day and night. Mass was celebrated twice a week and brothers and sisters were required to observe daily hours and pray for the sick. They were only excused from observing hours if hospital activities required their presence. They went to confession twice a year and observed silence during meals. As the statute recommended that the minister have a direct relationship with the patients, and that he visit with them every day to see to their needs, we can get a sense of the minister's direct involvement in the life of the community.[32] As will be discussed in Chapter 5, church officials' visitations to the hospital on several occasions, and resulting reiteration and specification of the imposed rules, were a result of complaints made by members of the hospital community that some of their members were not following the rules of the order. This tension illustrates the concern by the religious leadership and members of these charitable orders with maintaining the pious life among these semi-religious individuals.

Rule of Santo Spirito

The order of Santo Spirito is one example of a lay order of brothers and sisters dedicated solely to administering hospitals that established well organized, successful, and widely recognized institutions. This order was founded in Montpellier, France in the 1170s by Guy de Montpellier and enjoyed almost immediate and enthusiastic support from the papacy. It then spread quickly to include hospitals in Verona, Lodi, and Cremona as well as its most famous institution in Rome. Innocent III pledged his patronage in 1198, which assured its protection and expansion.[33] In a *breve* granting the order indulgences and privileges Innocent laid out a formula for the administration of charity. He decreed that as:

> At the wedding [at Cana] there are said to have been water pots ... in this hospital as at Cana in Galilee ... are to be found six water pots, that is, the six established works of mercy, feeding the hungry, supplying the thirsty with drink, gathering in the stranger, clothing the naked, visiting the infirm and attending the prisoner.[34]

Innocent issued a rule for the order, an early copy of which still exists and is one of the oldest and most comprehensive documents pertaining to the administration of hospitals, the *Liber Regulae S. Spiritus*.[35]

The extant copy of the *Liber Regulae* (LR) found in the state archives in Rome, contains specific rules that cover everything from the comportment of its administrators to the specific daily feeding and bathing of patients. In addition to the rule itself, sixty-one illustrations provide a unique treasure trove of visual records of life in and around the hospital.

The LR was issued for the Ospedale Santo Spirito in Sassia in Rome, which became, and remained, a prominent and papal favoured institution throughout the Renaissance. Under this order the much smaller hospitals in northern Italy would not have received such recognition nor grown to such proportions and status, but the rule was applied throughout the order and so we can conclude much about these communities through an examination of the LR.[36] In addition, for the Ospedale Santo Spirito in Lodi, there is similar document, *Constitutiones dedicatorum familiarium servitialium et omnium in Hospitali Sancti Spiritus de la caritate Civitatis Laude commoriantum* (CDF),[37] which contains a rule for that hospital which exactly refers to the more comprehensive LR. From these we can gain a very clear picture of daily life inside the hospitals of this order.

Organized into 105 chapters, each with a specific regulation, the original LR requires those of the order be lay men and not clerics; following the Augustinian ideal, the brothers' and sisters' primary concern should be to serve the poor. However, it differs from the

Figure 4.1 Searching out and serving the sick

Augustinian rule in that they are also specifically entrusted with
serving the ill.[38] This difference is intriguing as it challenges the idea
that hospitals of the era were primarily meant to house pilgrims
and provide charity for the poor and for travellers.[39] In the introduction to a 1946 print edition of the rule, Cava argues that as
'care' is mentioned repeatedly in the LR we can deduce evidence of
nascent medical care as a motivating impulse for these hospitals.
He adds that Innocent III heartily approved and supported the
order and was well versed in the ascension of medicine within the
academic community of the period, thus encouraging the practice
of medicine in the order.[40] He goes so far as to conclude that we

Figure 4.2   The election of the maestro

can see the birth of practical medicine in these institutions.[41] However, the idea of 'caring' for the sick in the way he describes is a post-Renaissance conceit. The primacy of spiritual care can be seen in the rule imposed on the Ospedale SS. Giacomo e Filippo della Misericordia in Lodi. The doctors there were instructed to wait for three days after ill patients were admitted into the hospital when they would then be required to confess their sins. If the patients refused to do so, the doctors were instructed to abandon them *'donec penitentiam acceperit'* until they repented.[42] Certainly in the case of San Spirito in Rome, we can see the beginning of the practice of medicine in the hospital and the introduction of the *medico* to the hospital early in its inception. However, this phenomenon, if apparent this early, undoubtedly occurred earlier in the

Figure 4.3 The poor seeking aid

larger, wealthier hospital in Rome than in its northern cousins. It is true that we have evidence for the attachment of surgeons to some of the hospitals such as Brolo in Milan, but their role was extremely limited.[43]

It is not accurate to consider the charitable services provided by the hospitals in the twelfth century as truly attempting to divine the nature and cure of illness, considered first as a sickness of the soul, and increasingly as a sickness of society. Members of medieval society equated care for the ill with care for the poor, pilgrims, and orphans. The emphasis was on the social, rather than on the

Figure 4.4 The hospital receiving the poor

physical, condition. The physical condition was merely a manifestation of the underpinning social and religious ills. Treatment would be that which would protect the patient from descent into death or absolute ruin from a material and spiritual standpoint. Illness might have been an indicator of such a condition and hospital workers would have worked to alleviate suffering and ease pain but hardly with the intention of curing the sickness. That was something only God could do.

However, the variety of services provided by Santo Spirito does indicate a much more comprehensive array of social and health services than many similar institutions, or perhaps at least suggests

Figure 4.5   Brothers fallen into immorality

that we may not have a complete picture of the services rendered by other institutions. There were rules that specified the care of a wide spectrum of society's downtrodden. There were chapters that covered the care and upbringing of abandoned and orphaned children, the care and redemption of repentant prostitutes, the protection and deliverance of poor pregnant women, and the housing of the elderly.

The LR specified the process for the initiation of lay men into service for the order. Once admitted, postulants served as novitiates for three months. Initiates were to give up all property to the hospital, which the hospital could then use, but only for support of the hospital community. The LR required they live a chaste life together

Figure 4.6 Caring for infants

with the other initiates in the hospital.[44] The lay men wore a tunic of dark blue with a black cloak and hood with the sign of the dove on it and carried a short sword.[45] The vow of profession for the postulants stated, '*Ego [name] amore Jesu Christi offero et dedico me in obesquium infirmorum Sancti Spiritus de la Caritàte Civitatis Laudae et promitto obedientiam Ministro ipsius secundum consuetudines dicti hopitalis usque ad mortem*,'[46] promising to love Christ and dedicate their lives to the order and to charity, and pledging obedience to the minister of the hospital unto death.

The rule distinguished between men and women postulants. Women and men lived and worked separately and had distinct duties. Men attended male patients and women attended female

patients.[47] Women washed the patients and changed their linens.
The instructions for care could be highly specific. Sisters were
required to wash the heads of patients on Tuesdays and their feet
on Thursdays.[48] The rule made an allowance for times when the
patients were the brothers or sisters themselves. A special section
of the ward was set aside for each gender. The rule did allow the
sisters to care for the brothers in exceptional cases.[49] Lay brothers
and sisters were required to observe religious hours and services,
which included attendance at daily Mass and lustral blessings.
Brothers served the Eucharist to the bedridden, and the whole community processed through the neighbourhood every four weeks in
the name of St Martino.[50] Meat was provided for the lay workers
three times a week, on Tuesdays, Thursdays, and Saturdays, but was
provided daily to the ill patients.[51] There were admonitions to the
brothers and sisters to always act respectfully and obediently and
transgressions that required punishment included grumbling,
slander, heresy, rebellion, abandonment of the order, quarrels with
fellow postulants, immorality, and taking advantage of the hospital's assets.[52] There is even a chapter in the CDF and LR on the
nature of punishment, at least for female transgressors: they were
punished with either a 'flogging or a swift kick'.[53]

The LR gives clear evidence of the active charity practiced by
these hospitals. They did not simply wait for the poor and the sick
to knock on the doors of the hospital. The rule instructed brothers
to go out into the city and find those who were ill or destitute and,
if necessary, bring them to the hospital using a wheelbarrow.[54] Once
under their care, brothers and sisters provided patients with clothing in accordance with the season. In winter, the *maestro* and two
brothers gave out woolen cloth as needed.[55] Also, patients received
one bed per person.[56] While this may seem obvious, in fact, most
hospitals did not make this distinction and it was common to place
as many in a bed as necessary.[57]

The rule for the order of Santo Spirito suggests that it was a
more comprehensive care institution than some of the other hospitals in the region. The community served and provided free assistance to orphans and abandoned infants; they provided wet nurses
for infants, and service for poor pregnant women and prostitutes.[58]
The attention to the care of women and infants is very instructive
and illuminates some the increasingly pressing social issues of the
day that centred on the growing presence of poor women and poor

and abandoned children. One chapter of the LR required the hospital provide adequate wet nurses for abandoned babies, even allowing for those abandoned by prostitutes. Each infant, particularly children born of a pilgrim en route, were to be given a cot or crib.[59] The LR gives us one of the earliest mentions of the use of the foundling wheel for the abandonment of children.[60] The hospital provided a hinged cradle in the gate of the compound where someone could place an unwanted baby anonymously. Hospital workers retrieved the baby by turning the cradle inward.[61]

The hospital cared for boys and girls until their adolescence if necessary. Once boys became teens their continued care was up to the rector's discretion. If the rector approved, boys could stay and serve the community. For girls, the LR suggested the hospitals should attempt to find them a husband of a 'favourable age' and provide them with a dowry and a ceremony.[62] Any girls who wished to serve the poor and remain chaste could also make the vow of chastity and obedience and join the community. This very interesting segment of the LR provides insight into concern for the continued supply of lay men for the order. Allowing adolescents to join a community who raised them, and for whom they undoubtedly felt an attachment, would ensure a continuation of lay servitors for the hospital. However, the rule stipulated that no child should feel compelled or required to profess vows, and clearly the preference for girls was that they marry. One senses that while recognizing the possibility of a perpetual labour supply the founders were concerned with preventing the compulsion or exploitation of these children by the order. Completing the cycle of cradle-to-grave care the hospitals also provided housing for elderly nobles and the elderly in general. The rule also provided instructions for caring for the dead.[63]

In addition to the information on the Ospedale Spirito Santo in Lodi, we have apparent documentary evidence that additional hospitals in the city were connected to the order. For example, in Cremona a collection of testamentary bequests between the period of 1266–1339 provided the foundation for the Ospedale S. Maria della Pieta. A diverse group of people provided the legacies, 'a favore del consortio Spirito Santo'.[64] The Ospedale di San Biago di Carità in Lodi possibly had an attachment to the order of Santo Spirito but it is difficult to say exactly how that relationship transpired. It appears to have merged, or at least been referred to as 'of

Santo Spirito della Carità' at some point. A deacon, and canons regolari administered it. However, they followed the rule of S. Augustine, not Santo Spirito.[65]

In Friuli, in the town of Gemona,[66] Ospedale San Michele was ceded to the Spirito Santo consortium in 1274.[67] Londero indicates that San Michele, because of its association with the Spirito Santo as well as its location just north of the city and outside the city walls, remained fairly independent of the city and diocese of Gemona. The brotherhood could choose a prior but they had to await confirmation of their decision from Rome. This protection allowed the hospital to prosper. It became very wealthy and possessed a great deal of land, rents from lands, meadows, vineyards, a mill, and various houses.[68] The connection of a hospital to the order of Spirito Santo, however tenuous, could protect it from political interference from the commune and even the bishop. As the order was a particular favourite with the papal court, such a connection could ensure that office's support for the order and could assist a hospital in maintaining its independence, particularly in the north where it was farther away from Vatican oversight.

Statuto ad opera

Outside of a formal organizational rule, ecclesiastical officials, and sometimes the commune, often issued statutes to specific independent hospitals that give us insight into the operation of these facilities. One of the most extensive examples of such '*statuto ad opera*' imposed on a hospital comes from Ospedale Rodolfo Tanzi. There are over 290 extant documents from this active hospital and a number of these are statutes issued by the bishop in an attempt to regulate the activities of the staff and administrators. In 1304, the bishop of Parma placed the hospital under the rule of S. Augustine[69] and recommended that it employ a minimum of twenty men and six women at all times.[70] The limit placed on the number of members was probably suggested in accordance with what the hospital was able to sustain economically. They were not to take in additional individuals unless they lost a member or the assets of the hospital increased.[71] The hospital had been in existence since 1202 and the number of members had actually decreased by 1304. In 1208 there were fourteen or fifteen brothers and unknown number of sisters, in 1365 there were ten brothers and five sisters, and in

1369, nine brothers and four sisters.[72] We can get a sense of the responsibilities proportioned to each group from various further statutes issued by the bishopric dictating acceptable conduct of community members.

In 1306 the bishop issued a statute reiterating the command first delivered in 1202 that brother and sister workers were to live in the hospital and that a *rettore* should be chosen from someone who was already in residence and who was at least thirty years old.[73] This requirement was continually challenged by the hospital, as they often desired to choose leaders from outside the hospital,[74] causing tension between the bishopric and the institution on many occasions. The hospital had an interest in obtaining outside leadership that tied it to the powerful families of the city, and the bishop had an interest in restraining this external influence.

Statutes issued in 1365 by Bishop Ugolino appear to be concerned to a great degree with the behaviour of brothers and sisters within the hospital, and it must be assumed that they were imposed in reaction to perceived or real trespasses against earlier rules. The decree insisted that the brothers and sisters live in chastity and be obedient to the *rettore*. They were admonished not to wear fur or coloured clothing, and were, instead, told to wear 'robes of humble cloth with a hood and cap' at all times outside of the hospital. They were forbidden to leave the city without the permission of the *rettore*.[75] Men and women lived separately with each group having its own buildings, including a dormitory, refectory, and kitchen. They were only to come together for specific work or worship and then only in groups. The punishments for transgressions against this rule were clearly articulated and included public shaming, private penance, and flagellation. The statute stated that members of the community, except in the case of violent crimes, would impose these punishments, or if the *rettore* was the accused, cases which should then be brought before the bishop's court.[76] The daily life of the sisters and brothers was also described in detail. They were to attend mass three times a day and recite the daily prayers on the canonical hours and at meals as well as in honour of the souls of dead members of the community. They were told to fast on holy days and go to confession at least two times a year. Brothers and sisters cared for the sick and poor in gender-separate wards, and also took part in general maintenance and agricultural responsibilities for the institution.[77]

Members did not take a vow of poverty but were required to leave their property as a legacy to the hospital under penalty of the denial of last sacraments and refusal of burial in consecrated land; instead, they were buried outside the cemetery with rebels, suicides, and the excommunicated.[78] They were to report their assets upon admission, and while they did not have to give them up, they were not allowed to profit from them during their lifetimes. The strict stipulation that they leave the legacy to the hospital insured the eventual gain of income by the hospital. This was beneficial to both parties. The community was assured an income from the oblates and the oblates received protection for their assets from taxation, confiscation, and other losses, as well as salvation for their soul upon their death. It was an excellent way for families to protect the interests of their children and women as well.[79] Members had to renew an oath of dedication on their birthday each year.

Similar statutes imposed on other independent hospitals suggest the repetition of the process of attempted control and codification of communal life by the religious officials as well as evolution away from that control by the hospital staff and administration. Citizen Gerardo Tintore founded Ospedale San Gerardo in Monza in 1174. He and his family wrestled with the church and civic authorities for administrative control of the facility over the next century. While details of this struggle will be discussed in the following chapter, documentary evidence of the ecclesiastical representatives recurring attempt to impose structure on the hospital gives us evidence for this desired model of governance and daily life of the community.

Statutes imposed in 1319 and reiterated in 1340 stipulated that sisters and brothers who staffed the facility live separately and never enter the other compound, even to make beds, without the direction of the *maestro*. Women were not to go out of the hospital grounds in groups smaller than three. One of these three was to be elderly. In addition, anyone speaking with visitors to the facility had to be accompanied and would only take care of the ill if required. The *maestro* was to provide food and drink for meals, including meat three times a week, and these were to be taken in the separate gendered refectories. The *maestro* was instructed to have a direct relationship with the patients; he was to approach their bed every day to 'learn of their needs and satisfy them'.[80]

Ecclesiastical visitations that prompted these statutes were made in response to complaints and from these we can obtain some sense of the physical space and other characteristics of this hospital. The *maestro* was asked to attend to the roof and walls of one dilapidated building that was used as laundry room by the sisters. There was also a building on the grounds, an oratory dedicated to the founder of the hospital that was apparently being neglected. The *maestro* was instructed to 'keep' it day and night and they were to celebrate mass there two times a week. This document also gives us insight into the religious observances made by staff. They were to observe daily hours except in the morning or when exempt by hospital duties. They were to make confession two times a year and observe silence during meals. The difficulty with enforcing these rules is clear from the repeated visits by church official. In 1352 someone brought allegations of mismanagement and misconduct by the hospital staff to the attention of the bishop's office. Church officials responded by questioning community members about the regularity of worship, obedience to the *maestro*, their suitability to serve at the hospital, the administration of assets by the *maestro*, the number of beds made available, and the care and feeding of children to name a few. This document gives us an intriguing glimpse into the difficulties with managing facilities, and in particular with dealing with the nature of the dual gendered living arrangements. A *fratre* named Molus was brought before officials and accused (apparently not for the first time) of transgressions of a carnal nature with one sister Franzina.[81]

Again, the fact that religious officials were forced repeatedly to intercede and mediate in the affairs of this facility suggests a crisis in management and jurisdiction that will be discussed in depth in Chapter 5.

Conclusion

The medieval Italian hospital was a vibrant, active, community that functioned both as a mechanism for providing socials services to the public as well as a refuge for the protection of security and stability to the *cittadini* and their families. The grassroots organization and rapid expansion of the hospital movement resulted in a wide variety of institutional experiences that, coupled with a lack of direct documentation of daily life, make it difficult to generalize about the internal life of these facilities. However, through a thorough examination of documentation such as rules, statutes of operation, oblation ceremonies, inventories, wills and bequests it is possible to illuminate some aspects of the physical structure, living conditions, internal and external relations of members, and relationships between the hospitals and ecclesiastical and civic authorities.

A reconstruction of evidence for the physical structure of the hospital indicates that, whether large or small, the communities were largely self-sufficient units that provided a standard of care for patients, poor, and travellers that reflected the apostolic ideal of an equitable charity regardless of station or condition. Staff were intimately engaged with all aspects of the institution, living, eating, and working within the compound. Their housing was gendered, but there was a great deal of difference from institution to institution regarding their ability to retain property or control over their assets. However, clearly the hospital could be seen as a mechanism for the protection of family members and assets in an insecure political climate.

The largest body of evidence for the daily workings of a hospital comes from the recorded imposition of a rule or statute of operation. The rules imposed on a hospital generally followed a model that was intended to give hospital staff a guide for living a life of pious service and were often articulated by the ecclesiastical officials upon approval of the hospital foundation. Rules such as the Rule of S. Augustine or the LR of Santo Spirito give us a very detailed, but prescriptive, description of activity within those hospitals. Statutes of operation were frequently imposed later in a hospital's existence, often in reaction to perceived abuses by management or staff in a facility and thus, these documents give us evidence of the operation and daily life of the hospital but also, frequently illustrate problems with compliance with rules and statutes. The necessity for church officials to intercede in hospital affairs, mediate disputes within the community, and repeatedly issue reiteration of rules and statutes gives us a picture of the challenges faced by members living in close proximity and their attempts at living a pious life of service. Many of these tensions led to or were caused by jurisdictional disputes between management, staff, church leaders, and civic authorities. Charting these disputes over time provides a picture of the evolution of this hospital movement from a grassroots lay movement, to the assertion of ecclesiastical authority, and finally, to appropriation and consolidation of civic service by the city-state authorities. These jurisdictional disputes will be the focus of Chapter 5.

Notes

1 De la Riva, *De magnalibus Mediolani*, 54–6.
2 ASMi, Anitche Diplomi, cit. n. XIV, 84, Racine, 'Il sistema ospe-daliero', 367.
3 Racine, 'Il sistema ospedaliero', 366.
4 Albini, *Città e ospedali*, 36.
5 ASMi, *antiche diplomatica*, doc. no. 5, 72–4; Brodman, *Charity and Religion*, 72.
6 ASMi, *antiche diplomatica*, doc. 4. 71; Albini, *Città e ospedali*, 70.
7 Albini, *Città e ospedali*, 69–70; Pecchiai, *L'ospedale di Milano*, 44.
8 Albini, *Città e ospedali*, 37.
9 ASMI, *antiche diplomatica*, doc. no. 4, 71–4, Albini, *Città e ospedali*, 72.
10 ASMI, *antiche diplomatica* doc. no. 4, 71–4.
11 Albini, *Città e ospedali*, 72.
12 De la Riva, *De Magnalibus*, capt. III, p. V; Albini, *Città e ospedali*, 70.
13 BCBg, AB 229, 76v and 77r; Cossar, *The Transformation of the Laity*, 62.
14 Albini, 'Dallo sviluppo', 48–50. Original document, ASPr, RT b. 7. n. 12, 11 July, 1305; Guenza, 'La formazione', 135–8. Original document, ASPr, RT, b. 38. no 2.
15 Albini, 'Dallo sviluppo', 48–50.
16 Guenza, 'La formazione', 145.
17 Cossar, *The Transformation of the Laity*, 6l; BCBg, AB 229, 76r and 77r.
18 Henderson, *The Renaissance Hospital*, 70–1.
19 Cossar, *The Transformation of the Laity*, 62; BCBg, AB 229, 76r and 77r.
20 Ibid., 64.
21 Ibid., 64–5.
22 Ibid., 66.
23 ASPr, RT, b. 7, fasc. 27. See Gazzini, 'Una comunità', for discussion of the usefulness of the hospital in protecting family assets.
24 Ibid., 62.
25 Caretta, *L'assistenza Diocesi di Lodi*, 293; Agnelli, *Ospedali di Lodi*, 21.
26 Cossar, *The Transformation of the Laity*, 74–5.
27 AOM, Aggregazione, Colombetta, cart. 39, 13 July, 1292; 10 January, 1308; 2 October, 1338.
28 Rovelli, *Storia di Como* 313–14.
29 Rocca, *Ospedali e canoniche regolari*, 24.
30 Renato Mambretti, 'L'ospedale di San Gerardo', 193–4.

31 Ibid.

32 Ibid.

33 In 1352 Innocent VI initiated the construction of a hospital by the order in Rome that would have 300 beds and be capable of providing assistance to 1,000 poor individuals. Cosmacini, *L'Ospedale Sant'Anna in Como*, 34.

34 Jansen et. al., *Medieval Italy*, 281. The six works of corporal mercy originate from the biblical injunctions to help the needy found in, Mathew, 25:41, 18:15, 6:14. The seventh was added later and comes from The Book of Tobit, 1:17–19. See discussion in R. N. Swanson, *Religion and Devotion in Europe, c.1215-c.1515* (Cambridge, 1995), 29.

35 A. F. Cava, *Liber regulae S. Spiritus. Regola dell'Ordine Ospitaliero di S. Spirito. Testo e commento a cura di A. Francesco La Cava* (Milan, 1947) (LR).

36 Ibid., 83.

37 *Constitutiones dedicatorum familiarium servitialium et omnium in Hospitali Sancti Spiritus del la caritate Civitatis Laude commoriantum*. (CDR), in Agnelli, *Ospedale di Lodi*, 28.

38 *Et eorum cura diligentissime habeatur*, LR, chapt. XIII; Cava, *Liber Regulae*, 81.

39 See discussion above, Chapter 2.

40 Innocent stated in his approval that the order should only be concerned with hospital care: '… omnesque homines, preter tria solemnia vota religiosa, etiam ad regendam specialem curam egrotorum stringuntur.' P. Migne, *Patrologia Latina*, database 1995, CCXVIII 1137.

41 Cava, *Liber Regulae*, 84.

42 Agnelli, *Ospedali di Lodi*, 15.

43 For a discussion on the medicalization of the hospital in the fourteenth century see Henderson, *The Renaissance Hospital*, 25–6. This will also be covered here in Chapter 6.

44 LR, chapt. XV.

45 Ibid.

46 Agnelli, *Ospedale di Lodi*, 28.

47 LR, chapt. LXXX.

48 LR, chapt. LXII.

49 LR, chapt. LXXX.

50 LR, chapt. XVIII.

51 LR, chapt. XII. Many of the specified rules, such as the provision of meat, reflect earlier models such as the Augustinian or even older Benedictine model of formal monastic rules. This suggests the continuity in the monastic model of religious life in the midst of the dynamism of the apostolic reforms. For a discussion of the role of the older rules and charitable institutions see Brodman, *Charity & Religion*, 224–5.

52 CDR, 90.
53 LR, chapt. XXXIV.
54 LR, chapt. XL, and fig. 30.
55 LR, chapt. XXXIII.
56 LR, chapt. XII, and fig. 6.
57 See for example, Ospedale Rodolfo Tanzi, in Albini, 'Dallo sviluppo', 48–50.
58 'orphani infates protecti … paupers femine pregnantes gratanter suscipianturet eis charitative ministretur', LR, chapt. XLI.
59 'ad opus infantium pergrinarum mulierum, qui in domibus Sancti Spiritus, nascuntur, parva cun abula fiant ut seorsum soli iacentes ne aliquid incommode infantibus posit evenive', LR, chapt. LIX.
60 This challenges some scholars' contention that orphanages and 'foundling wheels' originated in the fifteenth century. See for example, F. Bianchi, *La Ca' di Dio di Padova nel Quattrocento: riforma e governo di un ospedale per l'infanzia abbandonata* (Venice, 2005).
61 LR, fig. 30.
62 LR, chapt. LXXXVI.
63 LR, chapt. LVIII.
64 ASCr, OSM, Indice I, Busta 3.
65 Agnelli, *Ospedali di Lodi*, 14.
66 On the relevance of Gemona to the research see n. 27.
67 Londero, *Per l'amor*, 31.
68 Ibid.
69 ASPr, RT, b. 8, fasc. 5: doc. 12 May, 1304.
70 ASPr, RT, b. 8, fasc. 5: doc. 13 August, 1304.
71 Albini, 'Dallo sviluppo', 36.
72 Gazzini, 'Una comunità', 267.
73 Albini, 'Dallo sviluppo', 37.
74 Ibid., 38.
75 Gazzini, 'Una comunità', 273.
76 ASPr, RT, b. 7., fasc. 27.
77 Ibid.
78 Ibid.
79 Mambretti, 'L'ospedale di San Gerardo', 194–6.
80 BCM, P, cart. 11, n. 161a, in Mambretti, 'l'ospedale di San Gerardo', 195.
81 Ibid., 197.

5

Jurisdictional disputes

Hospitals reflected a model of attempted shared governance between the active laity, church establishment – most often in the form of local bishop or archbishop – and communal government. This alliance was intended to safeguard the interests of all involved and reflects a very early experiment in cooperation between the various constituencies of the medieval city. Documents from Ospedale San Gerardo in Monza provide an example of this complex web of authority and cooperation. San Gerardo was founded by an individual lay man and run by a consortium of *conversi*. These lay men and women elected their own *maestro* but an advocate, selected by the commune and invested by the bishop, protected their interests in the public arena.[1] When they worked, such alliances illustrate a very effective mechanism for the balance of power and a way of dealing will the variety of competing interests in running the hospital.

In the twelfth and thirteenth centuries these relationships did work to a large degree, as well as any such alliance forged between competing political players could. However, over the course of the late thirteenth through fifteenth centuries the balance of power shifted. After having been founded as a result of the pious impulse by a wide variety of lay individuals and groups, over the succeeding years administrators became much more oriented to civic and economic concerns which often elicited a reaction from the church officials in the form of a greater attempt to assert ecclesiastical authority. Finally, in reaction to ecclesiastical intercession, as well as a consequence of greater civic institutionalization of the period, the city increasingly moved to consolidate, control, and professionalize the hospital movement. This transition was gradual but not always smooth. In fact, much of the documentary evidence for administrative activity in the hospitals of northern Italy includes letters of complaint regarding mismanagement, visitation records by church officials responding to complaints, or official responses to proceedings. This chapter will examine the jurisdictional disputes which reflect the transition in hospital governance from the lay initiative of individuals founders, through the assertion of ecclesiastical oversight and finally to oversight by an increasingly centralized communal government.

Twelfth- and thirteenth-century lay dominance

The power of grassroots demand on the part of the lay community of the twelfth and early thirteenth centuries ensured their predominance in the leadership of early hospital administration. Conflict between independent bishops, the papacy, and imperial authority drove demand by lay reformers like Arnold of Brescia for control of charitable institutions.[2] The laity, searching for avenues in which to express their civic piety, believed that their ability to retain authority over the hospitals was a way to maintain some religious autonomy and create options for pious living outside traditional ecclesiastical institutions. Albini goes so far as to say that, 'lay Christians understood how assistance to poor and sick could be used as an instrument of power against church domination'.[3] The overextended clergy and ecclesiastical officials, who were themselves locked in internal conflict, warily welcomed the zealous impulses of these citizens. In the beginning, as long as the growing religious institutions needed the lay groups, the coalitions tended to work. However, church leaders feared a lack of sustained commitment and the perceived inevitability of corruption from groups of semi-organized and semi-ordained lay men and women and so sought to impose controls and authority whenever possible. The tension caused by this imposition of outside authority, internal conflict, and accusations of mismanagement, increasingly led to disputes, and challenged the ideal of shared governance.

Internal tensions

Mirroring tensions found among many of the lay religious orders of the period, the *frati* and *sorores* administering the hospitals in the twelfth and thirteenth centuries found their desire to adopt a new and innovative religious life constantly in conflict with a nostalgia and need for the order and structure of older religious models. They frequently organized their communities around the model of monastic discipline and worldly withdrawal espoused by traditional religious.[4] However, their involvement in communal issues in their neighbourhoods, the interests and demands of their secular benefactors, and needs of their constituents, all forced these semi-religious into contact with, and influence by, secular urban society. Often, internal tensions resulting from these competing influences and interests required the intervention of church authorities.

At Ospedale San Gerardo in Monza, the model of shared governance seems to have worked from the hospital's inception in 1174 until 1308. *Conversa* elected a minister with approval from representatives of both the commune and the church. However, in July of 1308, a minister was elected for the second time, after the first election was declared illegal because representatives attended it from the commune but not the church.[5] While one cannot be certain why the church officials did not participate in the original election one might assume that they were purposely closed out by a community that wished to operate with greater autonomy. Evidence suggests that this the became a recurrent problem, as is illustrated in documents from 1319 in which, canon Graziano de Arona, representing the archbishop's office, had to issue the first recorded statute for the hospital, and it reflected strongly worded ecclesiastical demands for structure, obedience, and compliance with a larger religious model of governance.[6]

One of the earliest examples of these internal jurisdictional disputes is illuminated in documents from Ospedale S. Simpliciano in Milan.[7] It appears there were many groups with a stake in the hospital. First, there were the original founders who stipulated it be run independent of the ecclesiastical jurisdiction by the '*boni homines*' of the surrounding community. Second, a monastery of the same name and built there before the hospital, shared property with the hospital and based on this property arrangement, always claimed to have some jurisdictional right to the hospital. Next, the lay brothers who ran the community continually aimed to follow the founders' wishes, which demanded autonomy from any authority. Finally, the church authorities – from the archbishop to the pope – had an interest in its affairs and claimed ultimate authority.

The first documented conflict between these constituencies arose over the right to appoint a provost to serve the hospital. The founders of the hospital had stipulated that the *boni homines* or *vicini* of the neighbourhood were to choose the leader of the hospital, which they did accordingly for several years after its founding in 1091. The abbot of the monastery of S. Simpliciano challenged this right in 1097 and took his case to the archbishop of Milan who decided in favour of the abbot.[8] It appears that for the rest of the twelfth century and well into the thirteenth century, despite the demands of the original founders, the archbishop's office kept a tight rein on the administration of the hospital. There is very little documentary evidence for S. Simplicano for the fifty years after 1097 so it is difficult to determine what, exactly, was its relationship with the church authorities. There is one document from 1147 signed by the archbishop of Milan that includes the hospital among ecclesiastical properties. This indicates continued control by the episcopal office.[9] Evidence suggests however, that the question was not permanently settled. On 5 June 1170 Archbishop Galdino reiterated the ecclesiastical position, placing the hospital under his protection, but also recognizing the autonomy of the *fratres* who administered it and effectively removing jurisdictional control from the monastery of S. Simpliciano. In 1179 monks were able to obtain a *bolla* from Pope Alexander III restoring their authority over the institution.[10] This suggests that the lay brothers and the monastery were fighting over control of the institute and had appealed to ecclesiastical justice. However, as this case illustrates, it is also clear that religious officials did not always provide a united front. On several occasions supplicants took their issue directly to the papacy in order to circumvent the local bishop. In 1196 the increasingly united and influential *vicini* of Porto Comasina petitioned Pope Innocent III, reasserting their jurisdictional rights as stipulated by the founders, in opposition to the monastery.[11]

The re-emergence of the *vicini* into the conflict in 1196 reflects the growing importance of such civic associations in community affairs. Although the original founder had desired governance by this group in 1091, it would appear that they did not have the influence to do so until a century later.[12] This date coincides with the emergence of powerful citizen groups in Milanese political life, such as, the elite la Motta familial civic organization and the more egalitarian *credential sancti Ambrosia.*[13] The second half of the

thirteenth century witnessed an era in which the affairs of the hospital reflected a greater trend toward civic participation of the citizenry of the urban Italian commune. Members of family networks
were attempting to consolidate power and utilized governance and
financial support of the neighbourhood hospital as a way of gaining
and maintaining social status, economic, and political power.[14] The
unrelenting conflict between emperor and pope that characterized
much of the twelfth and thirteenth centuries resulted in the crystal-
lization of a highly politicized, deeply divided, urban citizenry
throughout much of northern and central Italy and fostered active
civic engagement in all areas of society.

External conflicts

It is impossible to consider the affairs of the civic-centred hospitals
without viewing them within the context of the wider political and
social universe in which they existed. Often, evidence of how external political strife adversely affected charitable institutions is illustrated through the jurisdictional disputes in which the communities
became involved. Daniel Waley and Trevor Dean suggest that the
political landscape of the late twelfth century in northern Italy can
be viewed as a chessboard with the city-states being used by
Emperor Frederick I and the papacy to play out or resist imperial
aims. Frederick made six military expeditions into northern Italy
between 1154 and 1184 in an attempt to subdue those lands he
claimed were part of his imperial domain but who had thus far
escaped imperial taxation and subjugation to a large degree.[15] From
a local level, the growing bourgeoisie in the cities increasingly
actively resisted local aristocratic interests as well as the emperor
and the bishops.[16]

The communal movement that grew as a result of cities pitting
their imperial suitor against their papal suitor and purchasing their
independence as a result also forced the cities into competition with
one another. In the Lombard region, Pavia, Como, Lodi, and others
found an alliance with the emperor gave them an edge against their
rival cities, Milan and Cremona. The papacy was also engaged in a
continual effort to bolster the power of local bishops, although not
at the expense of its own authority, and backed any effort to thwart
imperial expansion. Eventually, increased imperial pressure forced
an active alliance among communes who formed the first Lombard

League in 1164. Verona, Vicenza, Padua, Treviso, Brescia, Bergamo, Mantua, Cremona, and Milan, set aside their individual differences to oppose imperial advances. This alliance was tenuous and broke down almost as soon as it was formed.[17] Smaller cities such as Lodi, frequently found themselves caught in the middle of these conflicts. Citizens within the communes were not always (if ever) in agreement as to which side they favoured as the Guelf/Ghibelline political rivalries of the ages illustrate. As civic charitable organizations, hospitals could not escape the political disputes among the various layers of authority represented by these constituencies.[18] As American politician Tip O'Neal said, 'all politics are local' and this is nowhere truer than northern Italy in the twelfth century.

An example of an institution embroiled in the geopolitical disputes of the time can be seen in the Ospedale S. Nazarii (later Leonardi) in Lodi.[19] Citizen Roggero da Cerro founded this hospital in 1127. Da Cerro's will divided his estate between the lay community staffing the hospital and the canons of S. Nazarii who were instructed to manage the institution but he also stipulated that the Church of Milan (in other words the bishop of Milan) have ultimate authority over the hospital. His wishes appear to have been followed faithfully up until 1158. At that time (according to subsequent documents from 1174) Bishop Lanfranco of Lodi, rededicated the hospital and placed it under the sole authority of his bishopric, he expelled the current provost and transferred the hospital's governance to the provost of the church and Ospedale S. Leonardo. From 1158 to 1174 the canons of S. Lorenzo contested this usurpation repeatedly. In 1174 the matter was brought before Pope Alexander III's regional delegate, the bishop of Bergamo. Representatives of the canons gave evidence from da Cerro's original bequest for their claim of jurisdiction. The representative of the bishop of Lodi protested that the original will did not provide a legitimate basis for the claim as, 'It is not possible to build hospitals, churches, and oratories, to place them under the juridical of other religious bodies of another diocese without the consent of the diocesan bishop.'[20] The papal legate proposed a compromise; in order to respect the wishes of the original testator, the canons of S. Nazarii were given the right to choose the provost, but their chosen candidate had to be confirmed by the bishop of Lodi.[21]

This jurisdictional tug of war reflected the larger tensions between the cities of Milan and Lodi. In 1158 the war between them destroyed part of the old city of Lodi. This was the second such defeat in a century for Lodi. Lodi allied its interests with that of emperor and was thus attacked by the opposing Milanese army. Lodi was also involved in a dispute with the papacy concerning jurisdictional rights over property within the city. After the battle, on 3 August 1158, Frederick entered the city at the head of a great procession and consecrated the ground for the establishment of a 'New Lodi'.[22] The contentious bishops were representing both the political and ecclesiastical interests of their political overlords. Ospedale S. Nazarii was caught in the middle.

Ospedale SS. Sepolcro and Croce in Lodi was also involved in a jurisdictional conflict due to these external political conflicts. A crusader founded the hospital in 1096. His will placed the construction and management of the hospital and adjoining Church of S. Lorenzo under the authority of the canons of S. Lorenzo. Before the first war between Lodi and Milan, which occurred from 1107 to 1111, a dispute arose over administration of the hospital between the bishop, the canons of S. Lorenzo and the elected minister of the hospital. The *maestro*, Anselmo da Vicodardo was elected in 1107. However, there appears to have been a dispute with the canons over leadership during the war. Led by Anselmo, the pilgrims and patients in the hospital rose up against the canons of S. Lorenzo. They claimed that the provost and other canons had been making themselves wealthy from donations to the hospital. They elected their own leader, but Arderico, Bishop of Lodi denied him divine offices. However, Bishop Arderico and his followers were ousted during the hostilities with Milan. It is possible that the uprising led by Anselmo was as much a part of this general disfavour with the bishop and one component of a larger popular uprising and regional war as it was about the mismanagement of the hospital.[23]

Much of the city of Lodi, and the hospital, were destroyed in the subsequent hostilities. At the end of the war, a Milanese citizen, Bellencio de Beccaria, tried to revive the dispute over leadership of SS. Sepolcro and Croce that had commenced before the war but the bishop of Milan prevailed and returned the community to the provost from S. Lorenzo and had the hospital and church rebuilt in stone. Soon, people displaced by the war populated the hospital. From 1115 to 1124 no one contested the canons of S. Lorenzo's right to choose their provost. However, after the death of Bishop Arderico in 1127 the dispute was revived. Once again, the church

officials sent an outsider, Berardodi of Pavia, to mediate. His judgment favoured the canons of S. Lorenzo once again and the matter
was finally put to rest.[24]

In Milan, Ospedale Brolo, was supported by powerful constituents within communal government and, during the political conflicts of the twelfth century became more and more important as
an institution, which represented the economic, social, and political
influence of many powerful families.[25] The hospital figured in
another violent conflict in 1256 between the cities of Milan and
Lodi over territory held by Brolo and its access to the river Muzza.
In this case Brolo again benefitted from support of important Milanese citizens.[26] Brolo became a large, prosperous facility throughout the thirteenth century not only because it provided services to
the poor and ill, but also because it also served as an avenue for
the expression of political power and social status for family
members attached to the community.

Communal tensions

Relations between Ospedale Rodolfo Tanzi, the bishop of Parma,
and the city of Parma, illustrate how frustrated citizenry increasingly
organized in response to the political meddling of ecclesiastical and
imperial powers in civic life. Evidence of these disputes also illuminates the complex relationship the hospital had with its surrounding
community. Medieval hospitals existed within a complex network of
existing communities and neighbourhoods. They provided needed
services for the neighbourhoods but also created some ambivalence
within the community as well. Housing poor, indigent, and unfamil-
iar travellers created some tensions with their neighbours that led to
disputes. In addition, those territorial strains that exist in any community affected hospital community relations as well.

Documentation for Ospedale Rodolfo Tanzi over its long history
is peppered with instances of confrontation with local authorities. The local neighbourhood association, the *Capodiponte,* was
actively engaged in many civic projects that affected the hospital.
Intervention by this neighbourhood association grew over the late
twelfth and the thirteenth centuries as the burgeoning urban population demanded an increasing number of services. Parma suffered
from a great flood in 1177 and neighbourhood groups such as
these orchestrated a large bit of the subsequent rebuilding.[27] At the

beginning of the thirteenth century the *Capodiponte* oversaw the building of both residential housing and churches, were engaged in the excavation of a new canal system and the subsequent repositioning of roads and buildings, and were also instrumental in all aspects of building their neighbourhood's section of a newly constructed city wall.[28] The hospital had numerous dealings with the association over a variety of infrastructural questions. For example, in 1209 and again in 1214 the *Capodiponte* brought a complaint against the hospital over water rights. A channel of the river Cinghio passed right through Rodolfo Tanzi's property and the hospital claimed free access to water directly from the river to the institution. The neighbourhood association believed the hospital was exceeding its rights and probably expected at least some fee or tariff on the access. The matter was brought before the communal government. The tribunal decided in favour of the hospital and charged that anyone blocking the hospital's access would be fined 100 Parmese soldi.[29] The commune codified this judgment in statues from 1266 and 1310 and gave permanent power to the *podesta* to oversee and protect the hospital's free access to the river.[30] In fact, it is clear that in the majority of disputes brought before the judicial council of the commune, Ospedale Rodolfo Tanzi prevailed.[31]

Beyond the issue over water rights, Ospedale Rodolfo Tanzi became embroiled in a number of other local disputes including one with another hospital, Ospedale S. Giovanni and neighbours in the S. Maria di Taschieri district, over jurisdictional and administrative issues having to do with an endowment of land granted to the hospital by the bishop in 1228. A member of an important local family, the Gonduini, who had originally backed Ospedale Rodolfo Tanzi, broke with the community over this dispute.[32] While the Rodolfo Tanzi prevailed once again in this clash, it illustrates the growing importance of civilians in the affairs of the hospital community and larger civic powers. Leaders and leadership of the hospital became increasingly politicized and much of the original founding pious impulse was lost. This occurred all over northern Italy and illuminates a growing trend toward secular management.

Fourteenth-century crisis

A crisis in the administration of the Italian hospital occurred in the early to mid-fourteenth century and mirrored the general crisis of the age. Widespread famine, overpopulation, corruption throughout the church, and, finally, the ravages of the plague caused stress on all institutions, perhaps none so severely as that very institution created to manage such crisis – the hospital. However, it was not just the pressure placed on the hospital community from the increased needs of their constituency that caused hospitals to undergo such a challenge in the period. Within the institutional communities themselves there was widespread degeneration of standards, management practices, and piety. There is evidence of concern over such issues by both ecclesiastical and the civic authorities, and for a time the church leaders initiated an attempt at reform, but ultimately it was the civic powers that most effectively stepped in to reform and reorganize the hospital system to react to both the demands of the time and the deterioration of the institutional structure.

Ecclesiastical reform

Early in the fourteenth century the episcopacy was active in attempting to reform abuses of management and to gain control over the activities of the hospital. This most often took the form of trying to control the election of the minister or rector of the hospital. These efforts frequently were in direct conflict with the intentions of the independent hospitals' desire for self-governance, or represented a challenge to the communal government's attempts at oversight. According to Albini, the attempts by hospitals to control the election of leadership within the hospitals must be seen as much as an attempt to resist ecclesiastical interference from outside the hospital as a desire to protect the wishes of the members of the hospital community.[33]

Papal councils of 1311 and 1312 resulted in decrees that attempted to control the election of leadership of hospitals and thus rein in perceived abuses by management. The Council of Vienne in 1311 was particularly concerned that the leadership of the hospitals was becoming too lax.[34] Church leaders were not suggesting they take over the provision of staff and resources to manage the hospitals; they only wanted to gain greater control over the election of heads of the institutions and also sought to replace looser lay groups running hospitals with established, church approved, mendicant and lay orders such as the Franciscans and the *Humiliati*.[35]

In reaction to increased intervention by the church officials, community leaders, and the lay elected rectors and *maestros* became
more and more political and were often individuals who were
less and less primarily motivated by religious vocation. Retaining control necessitated the talents of men of communal influence
and political ability.[36] For example, the da Marano family were
very active in the affairs of Ospedale Rodolfo Tanzi, starting with
Iacobus da Marano who was a *frater* in 1257, then *procuratore*
in 1267, and finally *rettore* from 1270–88. At this time another
member of the same family was captain of the *popolo*.[37] Also,
among those hospitals able to resist the pressure from episcopal
authority, while lay men and women continued to manage the daily
activities of the hospitals, these groups became more organized and
aligned with 'consorzi caritatevoli' or corporate charitable groups
in the community.

In addition to endeavouring to control leadership of the hospitals, church leaders also actively attempted to standardize the rules
of conduct and internal life of hospitals, particularly those that
were not affiliated with a religious order.[38] This move reflected a
larger effort by the papacy to regulate the proliferation of popular
religious groups and institutions but also reflected growing concerns with reports of abuses and corruption within the management
of hospitals.

Beyond just a general desire to exert ecclesiastical authority over
popular lay religious movements, religious reform efforts must also
be seen as a reaction to increasing reports of mismanagement. In
1319, 1340, and again in 1352, a delegation of canons representing
the bishop of Milan made 'visits' to the hospital of San Gerardo.
They were concerned with the management and upkeep of the
hospital and interrogated the management and staff in depth. In
1319 they issued a statute that required the hospital reaffirm its
commitment to its patients. It called for them to make repairs to
the buildings that housed the patients, to provide sheets and blankets as well as an adequate diet and a portion of wine for the ill.
It recommended that administrators have a greater direct relationship with their patients, including the *maestro* who was to approach
the patients in their beds every day to determine their needs. In
addition, it stipulated that the *frati* were to maintain the oratory,
with someone assigned to 'keep' it day and night. Mass was to be
celebrated there two times a week and all workers were go to

confession two times a year.[39] Clearly the concern of church officials here was to ensure that the administrators maintained their commitment to a religious life while sustaining their obligation to their patients and it suggests that such recommendations were made in reaction to a decline in standards within the hospital. In the visit of 1340 the canons again reaffirmed their findings from the first visit but also compiled an inventory of the goods held by the hospital and directed the whole chapter of *converse* to closely administer all goods and assets of the community. They also stipulated that the chapter should include in total assets all goods obtained through begging and collecting alms.[40] It would appear that the ecclesiastical representatives were concerned with the management of the assets of the hospital, which again suggests that there had again been complaints or suspicions of financial mismanagement.

The final visit by the canons in 1352 appears to have been the most serious and in direct response to complaints, possibly issued from within the community itself, of corruption and mismanagement. The canons interrogated the entire chapter. They questioned the *maestro*, *frati*, and *sorores*, about very specific activities. They asked about regularity of worship and prayer, obedience to the *maestro*, suitability of members to serve, administration of property belonging to the hospital, the number of beds available, the care and feeding of children in their care, and generally the enforcement of rules they had set in earlier visits.[41] The *maestro* reported that donations that were gathered at the church and gate of S. Gerardo and were administered properly (suggesting that a complaint had been lodged that they were not). He also said that the brothers were generally obedient except for one, brother Molus, who had been chastised several times for carnal activities with a sister Franzina. Brother Molus defended himself, saying that it was in fact poor management of the hospital that was to blame for its problems. The sisters all denounced Franzina and said that the beds were not adequate and that attendance at mass was poor.[42]

Such disputes may be viewed as inevitable in an institutional setting where many constituents and many individual personalities are forced to coexist. Add to this the attempt to keep celibate men and women from interacting and it might be possible to write these disputes off to weak management or poor group dynamics. However, they do illustrate the problem lay management had with self-governance. At times of crisis, semi-religious organizations needed a higher authority to mediate and that higher authority, at least throughout the fourteenth century, was usually ecclesiastical. We can also view the increasing number of disputes and instances of the intervention of church officials in hospital affairs over the course of the fourteenth century as a possible escalation in the secularization and mismanagement of the hospitals.

The well-documented history of San Gerardo makes clear the episcopate's increasing attempt to impose on individual communities rules, which were similar to those of orders that were more traditional. The statutes from the visitation of 1352 include the imposition of a rule that looks very similar to the Augustinian rule and which was intended to get the hospital workers to conform to an approved regimen. It limited members' ability to move about in the community alone or at least without the *maestro*'s approval. It commanded them to wear distinctive clothing that would identify them as members of the order. In this particular case the imposition of such rules can also be viewed as an attempt to rein in a negligent hospital, but the fact that the imposition of such rules can be found with increasingly regularity in many hospitals in the fourteenth century suggests an attempt to curtail the individuality of independent organizations much as it did with lay religious orders such as the *Humiliati*.[43]

Evidence of mismanagement

It does appear that the general concern with increasing mismanagement has some basis in reality. Examination of a compilation of documentary evidence from hospitals in the latter half of the fourteenth century clearly points to a crisis of mismanagement. There are frequent accusations in documents to a relaxation of standards of the administrators, laziness and incompetence in the management and following of rules, negligence in the care of the sick, and outright corruption.

Records from Ospedale SS. Giacomo e Filippo della Misericordia in Lodi suggest the presence of malpractice. Founded by an individual in the thirteenth century, lay men administered the institution, and the commune of Lodi oversaw the administration, or at least the accounting of its assets. In 1385 there is a reference in the statues of Lodi to concern over the mismanagement of the hospital. The accusation was that its buildings were dilapidated and its revenues were being misused. The complaint was brought before the podesta of Lodi (its chief judiciary and executive office) who appointed a special commission of communal citizens to oversee the hospital's maintenance and income.[44]

In 1343 a papal legate became involved in an internal dispute with Ospedale Rodolfo Tanzi. The appointed legate requested the intervention of the bishop of Parma to settle a dispute brought before the papal courts. The *procuatore*, Bochacinus Benedictus, acting on behalf of the *fratres*, the chapter and the occupants of the hospital, complained of abuses by *rettore* Beltrame Rane and his wife Lazzarina Rane. They were accused of mismanagement of the assets of the hospital and of abusing the brothers and sisters who were members of the community. Interestingly, a few years prior to this case there were co-rectors, Beltrame Rane and Iohanino Soegnano, running the hospital. The rarity of this dual arrangement alone suggests some internal conflict was present prior to the dispute in 1343. The papal legate asked the bishop to assess the allegations and take action if necessary. There are no records of the outcome of the affair but there is also no further record of the Rane family's involvement in the hospital. The *procuratore* Benedictus did continue in his post for a number of years. This suggests the matter was settled against the couple.[45]

The concern here with the management of a hospital's income reflects an age-old issue that often arose regarding the administration of finances within religious organizations. Monastic and lay religious organizations existed and prospered largely on one-time cash donations as well as annual income from donated properties. Land rents and land revenues played an important role in financing the administration of charity but their consistency was not predictable. In addition, the local bishopric or church often retained most of the income from these streams but generally conceded at least one-tenth back to the hospitals. Disputes inevitably arose between church and hospital administrators over use or misuse of those funds, particularly in times of economic stress.[46] For example, a charge levelled against the minister of Ospedale SS. Sepolcro and Croce in Lodi, was that the he was obtaining 'unjust enrichment' from the hospital's assets.[47] In 1414 the *maestro* of Ospedale San Dionigi, in Milan, was charged with mismanagement and his case was brought before a papal commission. Maestro Antonio da Bornago was elected at the age of fifteen years, which surely reflects that this was a political appointment. He was accused of defrauding the poor of the revenue from the hospital, of refusing assistance to some paupers, of forcing others to work outside the hospital, of having contracted a number of debts on behalf of the hospital, of using income for personal gain, and of leaving some of the hospital's land fallow.[48] He was accused and acquitted of charges twice in his career and it is evident that at least part of the opposition to his leadership was political; still these types of charges were levelled at administrators frequently enough to suggest some grounding in truth.

Church and commune

In the late thirteenth and early fourteenth centuries, the increasing role of the commune in the affairs of its citizens had an effect on the nature of lay life. As cities increased their autonomy from crown and religious oversight, they demanded greater and greater monetary contributions in the form of taxation and military service from their citizens. At the same time, communal governments increasingly granted tax revenue and exemptions to the growing number of mendicant and tertiary groups in the cities.[49] Traditionally, churchmen were exempt from most civic taxation and military service and this extended to *conversi* and other semi-religious. Some contemporary chroniclers viewed the increase in numbers of lay men attached to religious institutions such as the tertiary orders and hospitals with suspicion, suspecting them of being little more than tax evaders.[50] Increasingly, anyone who was attached in any way to a religious house was considered a *converse*. In particular men and women who joined the hospitals and promised property to the community upon their death but retained use of income from those properties during their lifetime profited from ecclesiastical protection.[51]

Religious leaders, once again, were placed in a position of balancing the need to take advantage of this willing labour force and its monetary income, with maintaining control over it and assuring quality of purpose and service to the institutions. In the fourteenth century, church authorities spent much time and effort defending the privileges of the *conversi* to secular officials while clearly dictating their rules and enforcing their restrictions. For example, *conversi* were strictly segregated from the regular brothers and sisters and were prevented by decrees issued by both Innocent III and Boniface VIII from participating in chapter meetings and elections.[52] Bishop Guericio of Lucca specifically stipulated rules as to the segregation of *conversi* from the regular religious throughout his diocese.[53] However, hospitals often operated with far fewer regular clergy and as administrators of these more independent religious institutions, *conversi* were often engaged in chapter meetings and the election of officials.[54] This led to more independent action on the part of hospitals, which led in turn to many of the jurisdictional disputes of the era.

Facing pressure from the communal governments the religious authorities increasingly tried to make a distinction between those *conversi* who were truly committed to a life of religious service and those who were just attempting to evade their communal duties. They began to make distinctions between those *conversi* who had donated all their goods, donned the habit, and moved into the religious house and those who had merely pledged their goods but had not abandoned civic life. They were clearly not going to deny the desire (or the income) from the latter but they were interested in defining the status of the 'true *conversi*'. In synodal statutes from 1308, Bishop Enrico of Lucca outlined his understanding of the threat posed by unscrupulous individuals who took advantage of the prerogatives of the religious claiming:

> Some prelates of churches of the Luccan city and diocese and rectors of venerable and religious places, endangering their souls and defrauding the Luccan commune, receive some as *conversi* who, although they offer themselves and their possessions to God with their lips, remain in their houses and maintain secular businesses and offices just as before; they do this so that they can circumvent punishment when they have committed some offense and so that they can evade the burdens of the Luccan commune both real and personal.[55]

Church officials wanted to avoid the possibility of corruption and scandal and to retain the integrity of the claim of the truly pious to a life of apostolicism. Yet nowhere did any religious directive make an attempt to curtail the ability of the laity to donate goods and pursue a semi-religious life altogether.

Similarly the communes attempted to curtail abuses by individuals claiming to be *conversi*. As early as 1251 and 1254 in Lucca, the communal government set up a special council to review the statutes allowing for the exemption from taxation of individuals labelled '*conversi*'. They increasingly attempted to narrow the definition and impose alternate taxes or *dazio* on the property of some of the *conversi*.[56] In Bologna, statutes were written which stipulated that exemptions were to be given only to those 'who live in the *familia* of a church, wearing the attire and following the customs of the *conversi* working for the good of the church and sustained in the vestments and by the bread of the church'.[57] As early as the 1250s the city of Lucca enacted statues that stipulated that the podesta compose a '*Book of Conversi*' which included all such religious who had promised their property to the institution and who were living under the roof and authority of that institution. Anyone who was not registered by the podesta would lose their exempt status.[58]

We have evidence from Ospedale SS. Giacomo and Filippo della Misericordia in Lodi which illustrates this increased level of communal involvement. The hospital was built in 1206 by the testament of a noble citizen. It was administered by *conversi* with leadership of a *ministro* but it appears that from its inception, the commune of Lodi oversaw its financial concerns. In 1385 a complaint was brought before the commune suggesting that the hospital was being mismanaged. It had become dilapidated and the indictment suggested administrators were using its revenues improperly. The podesta of Lodi appointed special officers who were required to audit the hospitals affairs annually and see to the proper disbursement of funds.[59]

The cost of the constant warfare between the city-states and with other European powers placed considerable pressure on the communal economy, a pressure that it that it tried to alleviate with increased taxation. Religious institutions such as hospitals traditionally claimed exemption from extreme taxation because of their status as religious and because of their role in aiding the poor and ill but the commune increasingly attempted to find ways to levy some funds, usually on land held by the institutions. We can see reaction to this costly conflict in acts of protestation from the hospitals. In 1316 the administrators of Ospedale Rodolfo Tanzi went before the commune to request an exemption from taxation for land held by the hospital. The land had been abandoned during a recent conflict and the hospital asked for an exemption from taxation for five years so that they could entice renters and rebuild the property.[60] The pope interceded on behalf of the hospitals in Parma on several occasion, instructing the bishop to make sure hospitals were not overburdened by taxation from the city.[61]

Hospitals often appealed to the pope to intercede on their behalf, but even the papacy was not immune from pressuring its own religious houses to help pay for its wars. In the early part of the fourteenth century the papacy attempted to enforce a rule that all previously tax-exempt religious institutions that followed the rule of S. Augustine were required to pay a special tax to help with the fight against the Turks. This was debated at the Council of Vienne in 1311 and illustrates the unique status of hospitals. While they were perceived as an ecclesiastical institution, the fact that they were providing a communal service to the poor and the sick of the community made them unique and perceived to be somewhat independent of total ecclesiastical authority.[62]

There is also evidence that suggests both hospitals and ecclesiastical entities resisted the increased attempts by the civic government to impose any taxation on the institutions. There are several documents in the records of the Ospedale Rodolfo Tanzi that illuminate the increased pressure of the civic tax burden and resistance by the hospital. In 1326 and then again in 1328 it appears that the hospital went all the way to the papacy in an attempt to avoid the imposed taxes. At this point in time, relations between the papacy and the increasingly independent commune were strained and the hospital appears to be taking advantage of this fact.[63] The papal curia issued provisions in March of 1327 and again in March of 1328, which granted the hospital immunity from taxation. However, not all taxation appears to have ceased immediately as we see renewed complaints lodged against the city in December of 1327, October of 1328 and again in December of 1328 for the illegal imposition of taxation.[64]

The shift to the commune

In general, the late fourteenth century witnessed a period which, in both the religious and civic sphere, authorities increasingly tried to curtail institutional autonomy and impose greater bureaucratic sanctions on all lay and religious groups. Civic governments and church authorities scrutinized confraternities, monastic and mendicant orders, and hospitals and attempted to inhibit any independent action from groups. This reflected an overall movement in the late Middle Ages toward institutionalization of social organizations as well as a continual attempt to eradicate the political and social systems based strictly on kinship or patronage.

There is much dispute among scholars as to when and to what degree the change in authority from the church to the commune occurred. Brodman, Racine, and Mambretti, have recently suggested the ecclesiastical powers remained in control throughout the period.[65] In fact, while the institutional church was resistant to ceding its power, there is abundant evidence of the civic authorities exerting authority over charitable institutions in the fourteenth century while by 1450 they were appropriating all control over the hospitals and seeking to consolidate them into larger civic institutions. Evidence from the first half of the fifteenth century suggests an overall decline the role of the independent individual and ecclesiastical authority and a shift to civic corporate entities and ultimately the communal government.

This shift is illustrated by the fact that the number of individuals who sought designation as *conversi* declines during this period. While the specific legal definition of who exactly constituted a *conversi* remained blurred, there is evidence of greater and greater attempts by civic authorities to curtail abuses by *conversi* and limit admittance into the category.[66] The continued controversy over the status of *conversi* suggests a laity who were attempting, but increasingly failing, to circumvent some of the centralizing mechanisms of their society.

In addition, there was a shift to corporate organizations such as the confraternity in leading efforts at reorganization. The powerful Misericordia Maggiore confraternity of Bergamo was at the centre of the centralization and re-administration of Bergamese hospitals. Beginning in the 1360s, hospitals such as S. Vincenzo and S. Alessandro were placed under the administrative auspices of the order. Elections for administrative offices of the confraternity also included the election of officials to administer these two hospitals as well as chose legal representatives for the institutions.[67]

As early as the mid-fourteenth century there is evidence of communal authorities using civic regulations to curb perceived mismanagement. In 1351 the commune of Milan demanded that wills be recorded within one month of the death of the testator and gave the podesta authority to ensure compliance by the charitable institutions that administered the wills.[68] As the bishopric claimed to be the ultimate authority in the control of such bequests this could have been perceived by them as a critique of episcopal management as well. In a Milanese statue from 1396, which is a restatement of an earlier one from 1351, the podesta instructed communal authorities to make a survey of the archdiocese in order to discover if the hospitals of the city and countryside had adequate resources to take care of the sick and the poor.[69] The statute also required an appointed committee of six lay and six ecclesiastical representatives to seek out the poor, bring them to the city, and provide for them.[70] This is clearly a rebuke to the autonomy of the hospital laity who had traditionally managed this function. From the inception of most of the hospitals, the responsibility of gathering up the city's poor and ill was squarely the provenance of the lay brothers and sisters who ran the hospitals. These statutes point to an increasing concern with lay administration and a shift from their dominance to a tug of war between church and commune over who was in charge.

In 1420, the commune of Lodi looked into the affairs of the hospital of SS. Simone and Giuda. Apparently the number of religious working in the hospital had decreased to the point that the hospital was accused of offering little service to the poor or ill. The officials who were tasked with looking into this case were called 'deputies of unification.'[71] It is clear from this reference that as early as 1420 the commune was considering consolidating and reforming the hospital system in Lodi. The latter half of the fifteenth century would witness the almost complete subjugation of the small, independent hospital and the creation, throughout Italy, of the *Ospedale Maggiore* – a unified, uniform, medicalized, civic institution that would care for the ill and the poor. This shift will be the subject of Chapter 6.

Conclusion

The evolution of the Italian hospital movement from its inception in the eleventh and twelfth centuries featuring small, neighbourhood facilities intended to house pilgrims, the poor, and the infirm, into the civic social and medical providers of the fifteenth century mirrored many of the social, religious, and political challenges of the era. Caught in the crossfire of the imperial aspirations of the Hohenstaufen and the medieval papacy, northern Italy survived by

establishing independent civic spaces that depended on the involvement of a number of patrons serving a variety of constituencies.
Citizens of the city-states of the in northern Italy created hospital
communities that served both their desire for pious charitable work
as well as meeting the needs of a burgeoning urban landscape. They
operated using the traditional institutional models and legitimization of the ecclesiastical authority, while creating communities that
were quite independent of ecclesiastical control.

The late thirteenth and fourteenth centuries witnessed a greater
secularization in the management of the facilities and attempts by
the church officials to reassert control and authority over these
groups. The endemic conflict between and within cities, and with
the institutional church and imperial powers, resulted in a politicization of all civic organizations, but in particular of the administration of the hospital. Institutional mismanagement and even
corruption resulted as the pious impulse was politicized. Efforts
by the ecclesiastical authorities to combat this degeneration were
frustrated by its own inability keep a clean house. At the same time,
civic authorities, who increasingly needed the social services offered
by the hospital and hoped to profit from the income of the facilities,
worked to appropriate control and authority over the institutions.

Notes

1 Caretta, 'Gli ospedali altomedievali', 187–195; Mambretti, 'L'ospedale
di San Gerardo', 192, 196.
2 Greenaway, *Arnold of Brescia*, 12–26.
3 Albini, *Città e ospedali*, 27–8.
4 Thompson claims, as urban institutions did not have the 'ancient roots
and dignity that made for civil legitimacy' they used religious models
and institutional structures to legitimize their organizations. Thompson, *Cities of God*, 141.
5 ASM, BCM, P, cart 11, n. 157a, 2 July 1308; for a discussion see
Mambretti, 'L'ospedale di San Gerardo', 192.
6 Ibid., 194.
7 Documents for Ospedale S.Simpliciano are collected in the archives
of Ospedale Maggiore di Milano, ASMi, AOM, fondo *Origine e
dotazione, S. Simpliciano;* cf., Albini, *Città e ospedali*, 25, 33, 67–8,
77–78; Pecchiai, *L'ospedale di Milano*, 16–26.
8 Albini, *Città e ospedali*, 25, 33.
9 Ibid.

10 Ibid., 78–9.
11 Ibid.
12 Ibid., 32.
13 Ibid.
14 Albini, 'Dallo sviluppo', 39.
15 For a discussion of the communal movement within a wider political context see Waley and Dean, *The Italian City Republics*, 85–93.
16 Ibid.
17 Waley and Dean, *The Italian City Republics*, 93.
18 For a discussion of the Guelf/Ghibelline conflict's affect on hospitals in Como, see Cosmacini, *L'Ospedale Sant'Anna,* 58.
19 Caretta, 'Gli ospedali altomedievali', 8–10; cf., 133–41.
20 Caretta, 'Gli ospedali altomedievali', 10.
21 Ibid; cf. Albini, *Città e ospedali*, 58.
22 Bassi, *Storia di Lodi,* 25–6.
23 Caretta, 'Gli ospdeali altomedievali', 7.
24 Ibid.
25 Pecchiai, *L'ospedale di Milano*, 46.
26 Ibid., 47–8.
27 Gazzini, 'Una comunità', 282–3.
28 Gazzini, 'Rodolfo Tanzi', 15.
29 Ibid., 16.
30 Ibid., 15.
31 ASPr, RT, b. 11, fasc. 20. docs. 7, 30 August, 1209; 10 June, 1229; 17 April, 1246; 9 October, 1288. All but one of these disputes against Rodolfo Tanzi brought by the neighbours to the tribune of the podesta of Parma were found in favour of the hospital. Gazzini, 'Rodolfo Tanzi', 15.
32 Ibid., 17.
33 Albini, 'Dallo sviluppo', 38.
34 Clement V from the council of Vienna (1311) in J. D. Mansi, *Sacrorum concilorum nova et amplissima collectio* (Venice, 1784), t. XXV, col. 363. See discussion in Racine, *'Il sistema ospedaliero',* 371.
35 This change had an impact on the role of women within hospital administration. Whereas prior to the early fourteenth century, women were actively engaged in all facets of hospital management and staffing, by the early decades of the fourteenth century they were increasingly closed out by the church authorities as the sought to 'professionalize' hospital administration.
36 Albini, 'Dallo sviluppo', 39–40.
37 Ibid.
38 Albini, 'Dallo svilluppo', 62.
39 ASMi, BCM, P, cart. 12, n. 167, 23, April 1352, in Mambretti, 'L'ospedale di San Gerardo', 195.

40 Ibid., 196.

41 Ibid., 196–7.

42 Ibid., 197.

43 For more on church authorities' attempt to regulate popular religious movements see Andrews, *The Early Humiliati;* Bolton, *Innocent III;* Grundmann, *Religious Movements;* Vauchez and Bornstein, *The Laity in the Middle Ages.*

44 Agnelli, *Ospedale di Lodi,* 15.

45 ASPr, RT, b. 7. doc. 5, in Albini, 'dallo sviluppo', 53.

46 Racine, *Il sistema ospedaliero,* 366.

47 Caretta, *L'assistenza Diocesi di Lodi,* 290.

48 Albini, 'La gestione', 160.

49 Thompson, *Cities of God,* 422–3.

50 Osheim, 'Conversion, *Conversi,* and the Christian Life', 371–2.

51 Ibid.

52 Ibid.

53 Ibid., printed in P. Dinelli, *Dei sinodi della diocese di Lucca, Memorie e documenti per la storia di Lucca* (Lucca, 1834), 57.

54 Osheim, 'Conversion, *Conversi,* and the Christian Life', 376.

55 Ibid., 375.

56 Ibid., 374.

57 Ibid., original documents from *Statuti di Bologna dall'anno 1245 all'anno 1267.* Ed. Luigi Frati, ser. 1, statuti 1–3 (Bologna, 1869–77), 1:479–80.

58 Ibid., 372, original documents from *Statuto del commune di Lucca* dell'anno MCCVIII, Memorie e documenti per la storia di Lucca 3.3 (Lucca, 1867), 224–5, Lib. III, rub. Exclv; 258, Lib IV, rub. Xv.

59 Agnelli, *Ospedale di Lodi,* 15.

60 Albini, 'Dallo sviluppo', 42.

61 Ibid., 43, original, ASPr, RT, b. 7, n. 9, n. 14.

62 Ibid., 59.

63 Ibid., 45.

64 Ibid., and Gazzini, 'Una comunità', 274.

65 An earlier perspective finds evidence from early in the period for the incursion of the city government into the process. For example, for the hospital San Gerardo in Monza, eighteenth-century chronicler of the city, A. F. Frisi, suggested that documents from as early as the thirteenth century indicate the role of the city in the appointment of lawyers for the hospital who were utilized in all economic transactions as examples of their growing political control over the institution. Mambretti and others have suggested that this is not necessarily so, as these advocates were in fact involved throughout the history of the institutions, and this was evidence of the continued and constant cooperation between communal and ecclesiastical authorities. However, it is

evident that by the middle of the fourteenth century the city government was becoming more vigilant in their inspection of ecclesiastical properties and the lawyers were pressed for more and more accurate data from the institutions. Mambretti, 'L'ospedale di San Gerardo', 190.

66 Osheim, 'Conversion, *Conversi*, and the Christian Life', 385–6.

67 Cossar, *The Transformation of the Laity,* 87; original document ASBg, Notarile, G. Mozzi, busta 84b, 175.

68 Racine, *Il sistema ospedaliero,* 372, from *Statuta jurisdictionum Mediolani,* in *Historia Patriae Monumenta, Leges Municipales,* Torino 1876, t. 3, *pars prima,* rubr. XCIV, col 1017 and col. 1018.

69 Ibid.

70 Ibid.

71 Agnelli, *Archivio Storico,* 1.

6

Reform and consolidation

On the first of April 1456 Duke Francesco Sforza awarded noted Florentine architect Antonio Averlino, popularly known as Filarete, the contract to build a new Ospedale Maggiore in the city of Milan. Almost exactly one year later, on 4 April 1457, Sforza celebrated the beginning of construction with a large procession through the streets. At the end of the procession he and his wife laid the foundation stone for the new hospital. The inscription on the stone read, 'Francesco Sforza, fourth duke, and his wife Bianca Maria Visconti, who gave this site and building, founded this hospital together with the Milanese people.'[1] Sforza had committed land for the project in a relatively open area within the city walls but not in the city centre. Existing structures were torn down make room for the new building.[2] As part of the plan, most of the small, independent hospitals in the city were closed and their services and staff consolidated into the Maggiore. The hospital was completed on 9 December 1458, and Pope Paul II issued a bull approving the new hospital, codifying the administrative structure, and placing it under a governing configuration of leadership composed of clerical and civic officials.[3] The importance of the papal blessing is represented in a painting hung in the new hospital, which depicts Sforza and Bianca kneeling before the Pope to receive this honour.[4]

The construction of Ospedale Maggiore was the culmination of reform efforts begun decades earlier. In 1359 Bernabo Visconti founded a new hospital, San Paolo, in Milan that was under the direction of lay men but which also connected to four other hospitals, including the large prestigious Ospedale Brolo, which was given administrative oversight of five. Each hospital gave Ospedale Brolo three month's income in rotation, which was used for the aid of the ill, indigent, prisoners, and to provide dowries for poor women, and thus insured that the poor were cared for throughout the year.[5] In 1399, Duke Gian Galeazzo Visconti further pursued the aim of reform by unifying and consolidating hospitals under civic authority, and based his plans on the process of unification already underway in Siena. These plans did not come to fruition at that time due to the death of the duke, but illustrate the earliest example of the centralizing aims of the state in cities in northern Italy.[6] This unification and institutionalization of civic oriented hospital care, duplicated in towns and cities throughout Italy in the mid-fifteenth century, signified the end of the small, independent hospital movement that had so transformed the landscape of urban society earlier in the Middle Ages.

The secularization of health care and poor relief evolved over the early decades of the century and was a gradual response to the evolving needs and challenges of the population and the end of the communal era. The rise of the strongman leadership under the Visconti and the Sforza in Milan, which created a much more overtly centralized government than other Italian city-states and featured less of a professed attachment to the communal republican ideals, might suggest that it was this dictatorial government that was responsible for taking over many social services. However, the fact that a similar process occurred throughout Italy illustrates that this process of centralization that swept hospitals up in its wake was a universal feature of Italian state-formation in the age of the Renaissance. Even under the strongman government the ideals of the *civitas* were preserved and Visconti and Sforza despots took advantage of bodies of civic law and administration that were already developed prior to their ascendency. Individuals and families throughout Italy controlled government, often from behind the scenes, but they preserved the ideals and some of the institutions of the *civitas*. The foundation laid by civic leaders of the communal era continued but was altered to reflect the centralized early modern state.

In the late fourteenth century, the unrelenting crises of war, epidemic disease, and poverty as well the growing power of the city-state and the diminishment of ecclesiastical authority, led to widespread reform of hospitals throughout the region. While reform efforts of the late fourteenth century originated from both ecclesiastical and civic authorities, city government ultimately were the most able to respond. In reaction to the spread of disease and increased poverty and crime, the city focused much attention on standardizing the method of charitable assistance and controlling contagion within the limits of their understanding at the time.[7] Reform efforts and the secularization and politicization of hospital leadership led to medicalization of hospital care and the rise of humanist ideals of civic purpose ultimately resulted in the consolidation of hospital care into the large, secularized municipal institutions like Ospedale Maggiore.[8]

Reform

As we have seen, much of the reform effort of the late fourteenth century was due to the increased need for intervention in disputes among the various constituents, and the endemic problem of mismanagement of facilities. The crisis in management reflects an underlying weakness in the structure of the hospital movement, which was apparent from its inception in the twelfth century. The very desire of the founders to retain at least some autonomy from ecclesiastical and civic authorities ensured the continued competition between interests. Dependence on charitable bequests guaranteed the institutions' survival in an age of extreme charitable impulse, but it also meant that certain individuals and families would have undue influence over hospital affairs. In addition, these assets, which included property and income, had to be managed; this invariably led those in control of assets to become engaged in the politics of the community. Some hospitals became very wealthy. Ospedale di Ceppo in Pistoia was the largest charitable organization in the city by 1428.[9] In addition, assets controlled by hospitals were not always taxable. This frequently led to political conflicts with the civic authorities. Finally, as the leadership of the hospital became more political, leaders often lost some of the pious impulse of the original founders. All of this weakened the hospitals' ability to react to the increased pressures of the age.

The Black Death and reform

We can trace the origins of much civic reform effort to the general public reaction to the demographic disaster of the plague decades. The Black Death of 1348–55 placed unprecedented pressure on all institutions but most specifically on hospitals, which were ill equipped to handle such a massive crisis. In fact, hospitals placed plague victims on a much lower priority than poor constituents and survivors, often refusing to accept those with plague symptoms into the hospital.[10] The Latin Church was devastated as well, not only in terms of constituency but also in its loss of land rents, tenants, staff, and income.[11] Church officials thus conceded more and more agency to the city over the control of ill and needy within the community.

City governments created a variety of public health and safety officials and commissions to deal with the repeated plague outbreaks. This process happened first in the cities of Italy and was followed a century later throughout Europe. These offices were originally intended to be temporary and were not considered a replacement for hospitals or for the charitable initiatives of local religious institutions. By the sixteenth century however, these offices had tended to become more or less permanent, centralized civic offices, at least in the major cities. Their appropriation of some of the public issues dealing with health care, poverty, abandonment, and indigence brought on by the pandemic, aided in the similar process of centralization and the imposition of civic authority experienced by the hospitals.

Initially, action took the form of small committees or 'health boards' to coordinate attempts to deal with plague victims. In Florence in 1378, a magistracy of eight members, '*Otto di Custodia*' was created to police the city in the wake of general communal havoc wreaked by the plague. After another wave of the pestilence in 1448 this commission was given the authority to, 'issue ordinances, preserve public health, keep off the plague and avoid epidemic'.[12] Often, officials were charged with removing all plague victims to outside the city walls or placing them in special leprosy hospitals.[13] In Lucca in 1481, a special committee of three citizens was charged with the oversight of health issues after every plague outbreak. They remained in office for one year.[14]

The first wave of plague in 1348 affected Milan less severely than it did other parts of Italy, but this may be due in great part to measures taken by civic authorities.[15] Subsequent outbreaks did affect the city and led to an institutional reaction by the *signori*. As this government was much more centralized than those of other cities in the region, we can see a greater element of hierarchical

Hospitals and charity

structure in the health boards and more specificity in their response. After hospitals in Milan refused care to plague victims, Duke Gian Galeazzo Visconti created the 'offitium perquirendi et exequendi epedentia circa conservationeri sanitatis nostre Mediolani',[16] an office charged with ensuring the care of plague victims and forcing hospitals to accept them. He also appointed a high-ranking official to oversee these measures taken against the plague.[17] With each new outbreak, the number and responsibilities of these boards increased. These were political officials granted wide powers to deal with the 'preservation of health in the city and suburbs of Milan'.[18] Although intended to be temporary, it is clear from subsequent legislation that this office became a permanent fixture in Milanese government until at least 1527. Johannis de Migino was listed as 'commissioner and head of officer for the preservation of public health' in 1424. Perino de Ferrandi is referred to as 'commissioner of contagion, for the city, suburbs and duchy of Milan, as well as for the city and county of Pavia' in a document from 1437. We see similar officers appointed in 1447, 1448, and 1450.[19]

Cities in the region under the influence, if not outright control, of the Duchy enacted similar measures to ensure public health and attempt to contain the spread of disease. Officials from the Milanese commissioner's office placed both Pavia and Como under their authority on several occasions.[20] In Pavia in 1450, there are references in the documents to a citizen acting as a commissioner for public health during plague outbreaks. Again, it is apparent that this position was intended to be held only during outbreaks. In 1476, two officers were appointed after a recent outbreak. They were instructed to 'visit twice a day all those living in suspect and infected homes, find out about the state of their health and report it to the mayor'.[21] In 1480, the duke appointed G. B. Zentillis to the Office of Public Health in Cremona for 'as long as it will please us with the monthly salary of seven florins to be paid by our treasury'.[22]

While these officials and health boards point the way toward the communalization of health care they were not originally necessarily directly engaged with the hospitals and were not primarily concerned with the disease and its cause or cure. Hospitals still primarily focused on housing the poor and indigent and not treating illness, hence their refusal to admit plague victims. The health boards were more concerned with the prevention and spread of the epidemics. Their attention was directed at issues such as quarantine and sanitation, which were seen as concerns of civic administration not medical care. They saw the issue of containing those who had the disease as a responsibility of the public authorities for the safety of the greater population.[23] They were also concerned with monitoring newcomers to the city who could infect the population. Upon arrival, an impoverished traveller suffering a serious illness was assigned by a magistrate to a hospital where they would be cared for and the populous would be 'spared their loathsome presence'.[24] To be sure, as civic authorities appreciated the need for quarantine and as they attempted to quash the spread of illness by destroying people's belongings and isolating them together, they were beginning the process of understanding the nature of the disease – but this was not their original intent or purpose. They were acting to preserve the social well-being of their citizens through the provision of social services and public authority. Ultimately, hospitals and health boards were working separately toward the same goal: alleviating the social ills of the community and providing relief from this demographic catastrophe. As the city became more efficient and effective at coordinating relief efforts, and the hospital movement became mired in mismanagement and inefficiency, the city governments moved to apply what they learned from the management of the health boards to other areas of social assistance such as hospitals.

Poor reforms

It appears that both the ecclesiastical and civic authorities were becoming increasingly concerned about the plight of the poor and vagrants in their cities at the turn of the fifteenth century. However, the concern seems to be centred on the public safety issues caused by increased vagrancy. While there is little direct numerical evidence that the problem of the vagrant poor increased in the latter part of the fourteenth and first half of the fifteenth centuries, the anecdotal evidence and response by church and state officials do seem to indicate that the social safety net which had provided for these groups was being severely tested or at least perceived to be so.[25] This would suggest that the hospitals were not fulfilling one of their central purposes. It is clear from the writings of the humanist architect Leon Batista Alberti that citizens were becoming less sympathetic to the plight of certain 'underserving poor', and the perceived threat from vagrancy:

> Some princes in Italy have banned from their cities anyone like that, ragged in clothes and limb, and known as tramps, and forbidden them to go begging from door to door: on arrival they were immediately warned that they would not be allowed to remain in the city out of work for more than three days.[26]

Both ecclesiastical authorities and civic governments increasingly intervened in the fifteenth century to attempt to address these issues, and to provide relief for the community from the stresses they caused.

The model of plague relief was increasingly applied to the problem of poverty and indigence. In 1396, Visconti appointed a commission to move about the city of Milan searching out the destitute and finding them accommodations in hospitals. He required hospitals to accept those individuals presented by the commission. By 1405 the *Officium Pietatis Pauperum* committee was codified and was comprised of a mix of clergy and lay citizens.[27] In 1402 the duke appointed a prominent citizen, loyal to the duchy, as *gubanitor et rectore*, who was to oversee the activities of all the hospitals in the duchy.[28] This official was expected to be loyal to the duke, but also answered to the archbishop. The official and his wife were required to reside in Ospedale Brolo and were instructed to go about wearing a coat with a white cross for identification.[29] Brolo was a prosperous, successful, and central hospital and this move can be seen as the predecessor to the consolidation all hospitals under one management.

Upon the death of Gian Galeazzo, Milan was plunged into a period of political instability. Archbishop Pietro Filargo, a close associate of Galeazzo, stepped in to take over reform efforts with the establishment of the 'officium pietatis puaperum Christi', an ecclesiastical body commissioned to collect funds for the poor.[30,31] This Office of the Poor of Christ (OPC) was comprised of the apostolic ideal of twelve clerics and twelve lay men who held life terms. According to Albini, that structure reflects less of a jurisdictional parity than it appears, as many of the clerics would have also been members of the cities' elite political families. However, the office also obtained an agreement from the duke that any disputes brought before this office would be adjudicated by an ecclesiastical representative.[32]

The OPC's foundational charter, illuminates the pressing needs felt by the citizen's at the time:

> How can things go well in this most miserable Milan, full of the poor, famished and pestilent who wander through the city showing spots and sores while so great and even adequate provisions are cruelly embezzled? The souls of the benefactors are being damned, for no one prays for them any longer, no one gives charity any longer and the souls of those who do not respect the wishes of the dead are also damned. And it is for such great impiety that God, with his three whips of hunger, war and plague, has inflicted Milan with these apocalyptic punishments.[33]

This paints a very clear picture of the perception of need in the city.

The OPC was very aggressive in addressing the problem of poverty and vagrancy. Its central aim was to raise funds for poor relief, and to see those funds were distributed appropriately and without corruption. The poor were screened as they were admitted to hospitals for their 'worthiness' of aid and were expelled from care if they did not follow the rules of the institution. A statute issued in 1422 specifically stipulated that poor patients accepting care from the hospital could not leave the hospital at any time without approval from the commission.[34] Clearly this is an institutional alteration of the apostolic ideal of taking care of 'the poor of Christ' regardless of their station, and reflects the culmination of centuries of struggle with defining these categories. While individuals, confraternal groups, ecclesiastical bodies, and hospitals had been individually redefining such categories for a century at least, they had generally continued to provide (or at least claimed to provide) egalitarian care within their membership framework. This church-city office created a delineation of care that was designed less for a poor person's benefit than it was to safeguard the community from the poor.

The OPC became the model for governance of the centralized hospitals. Increasingly in the early fifteenth century, both religious and civic powers gave collegial organizations and commissions authority over social assistance. The ecclesiastical commission for the poor became the very model of efficiency and expediency. They took meticulous minutes and kept intricate records, examples of which provide some of the earliest samples of double-entry bookkeeping.[35] The office did not disappear with the creation of the

Ospedale Maggiore; it became part of the process of unification and was called upon to choose the administrators of the new hospital.[36]

Genoa and Mantua had similar offices. Officials there targeted those poor and ill who were roaming the streets, not those already in hospitals, suggesting that the hospitals were no longer able to adequately provide this service.[37] Intriguingly, the language of these officials' appointments echoes the wording of the foundational charters of the hospital movement back in the thirteenth century. The call to 'go out among the community, find those in need and provide for them what is necessary' was very much what the original founders of the hospital movement had intended. It is clear, then, that they had ceased to fulfil that role adequately. The fragmentation and corruption infecting the hospital movement forced ecclesiastical and city authorities to create a novel response to increased social need. Ultimately, they used the hospital movement's model of poor relief to circumvent them.[38]

Mismanagement and reform

While the plague crisis and perception of increased poverty predicated an immediate communal response, reform efforts which included unification and centralization of hospitals were also implemented in reaction to mismanagement and jurisdictional disputes which became even more pronounced in the aftermath of the plague decades. The view of this crisis by civic leaders is articulated in the foundational charter of the Ospedale Maggiore of San Marco in Bergamo, written in 1457:

> Though both in the city and its suburbs there are many hospitals and religious institutions in which divine worship, the fabric, and the relief of the poor are neglected, and where the revenues are consumed in uses to which they have not been assigned. This arises because of negligence on the part of their staff, because of their lack of funds, and because of the misgovernment of the many men who are necessary to run them. We have therefore decreed that in this great city, which has offered to carry out this holy, pious and praiseworthy work, one single great general hospital with a chapel should be constructed. [39]

The foundational charter echoes the widespread concern with corruption and mismanagement.

Archival evidence provides copious examples that indicate the period was rife with individuals who sought the leadership of hospitals for personal gain. For example, Ospedale San Giovanni Battista di Tavazzano in Lodi was administered by Stefano Sannazzaro who requested permission to pass on his leadership to his son. This was in opposition to the founding charter, and although two papal decrees had been issued denying his request he persisted in pursuing this path and the commissioners for Ospedale Maggiore complained to the papacy for a third time. In this complaint, commissioners claimed that the hospital and its resident staff should be taken away from Sannazzaro due to his mismanagement. Sannazzaro was accused of not taking care of the poor or offering adequate hospitality. A papal delegate found in favour of the Ospedale Maggiore in 1472. Sannazzaro contested this finding again but lost once again. San Giovanni Battista was subsumed into Ospedale Maggiore in April of 1477.[40]

One could also conclude from this evidence that the minister of the hospital was becoming decreasingly attached to the original religious role of leadership, due to a number of factors. In addition to the civic social response, much of the religious centrality of the medieval hospital receded to be replaced by personal, political, and civic interests. The medieval hospital, originally a small, communal, religious community became slowly secularized, first, by the interests of individuals with political aspirations and then, by civic minded confraternities and corporations, and finally by the city governments themselves. The intervention of the church officials in the election of leadership in the fourteenth century (discussed above) created a response from the communities and the neighbourhoods who put forward men who would act politically to preserve the independence of the community, but were perhaps not as piously driven as their predecessors were. The nature of the leadership role became much more divorced from the internal life of the hospital and focused more toward political mediation.[41] Rodolfo Tanzi may have originally intended founding his eponymous hospital with pious intentions focused on the needy, but he increasingly became a civic leader and was embroiled in the politics of his city. Frequently, devout lay men and women working and residing in the hospitals became suspicious of these leaders' motives.

A particularly striking example of the increased secularization of the leadership of hospitals and consequent controversies involved is illustrated by the story of Antonio da Bornago, minister of Ospedale San Dionigi in Milan. Bornago was elected minister at the age of fifteen years in 1414. As mentioned above, one must assume there was political or familial influence behind that appointment. Members of the hospital administration contested his management almost immediately. A papal commission was called to look into the legitimacy of his appointment but found in favour of Bornago. Ten years later a complaint against Bornago was lodged again by a cleric connected to the hospital. In addition to the charge that Bornago had been appointed fraudulently, the complaint accused him of defrauding the poor of the revenues of the hospital, refusing hospitality to the poor, and forcing paupers living in the hospital to make an income outside the hospital. In addition, the complaint stated that Bornago was believed to have accumulated debts for the hospital and had used hospital income for personal gain. He was also said to have mismanaged the land owned by the hospital so that land had gone fallow and buildings were abandoned.[42] Bornago again prevailed and was acquitted. He served as minister of the hospital for another ten years and ultimately was appointed to the hospitals consolidation committee by the duke in 1445.[43]

Ecclesiastical intervention for political purposes in the appointment of leadership of hospitals also caused conflict between parties and led to accusations of abuse and mismanagement. Pope Boniface IX gave leadership of Ospedale Vimercate to an eleven-year-old in 1404, and Nicholas V gave leadership of the wealthy, powerful Ospedale Brolo to an eighteen-year-old in 1450. These political appointments were not uncontested. In 1400, Archbishop Pietro Filargo suffered excommunication when he protested the appointment of an unqualified rector as the head of Ospedale Brolo.[44]

The increased presence in the early part of the century of *decani*, or other lay men and women who resided outside the hospital, in the affairs of administration also predicated a more secular role of administration that often strained relations within the community itself. The role of these individuals in the affairs of the institutions centred increasingly on the accounting and distribution of its assets and less and less on the care of the ill and destitute. Frequently, they competed with the ministers or provosts of the hospital for control. Also, during times of economic stress, they were often accused of placing an unfair burden on the institution. For example, two groups of lay men and women administered Ospedale Ognissanti di

Treviso. One group lived within the compound while the other did not. The *'frati and sorores extrinseci'* who served the hospital but did not reside there were accused by the minister and *procureator* of the hospital of creating a drain on the hospital's resources by eating and drinking at the hospital's expense when they had their own houses within the city.[45] In Monza, Ospedale San Gerardo, was visited on several occasions by representatives of the bishop, probably in response to complaints from within the community of mismanagement and abuse. In 1352, the delegation conducted a thorough examination of the hospital and its staff, reminding the minister and the staff (in written statutes) of their commitment to following a religious life and reinforcing the rule that stipulated the dissemination of all property obtained by the hospital only to the poor.[46] Frequently, the hospital became a community divided between those who were still committed to a life of religious service and those who represented the community's interests in the secular world.[47]

Gian Galeazzo Visconti's attempt at an early reform in 1399 included the convening of a central council of inquiry made up of 'devout Milanese citizens' and the appointment of wealthy Milanese citizen Pagano da Rho as *'gubanator et rectore'* of all Milanese hospitals.[48] While these efforts were never fully realized because of the death of the duke they do illustrate the perception of the problem by the city government and pointed the way for reform measures.[49] In addition to external oversight, early reform efforts included some specific alterations to hospital administration that greatly affected the dissemination of services within the medieval hospital. First, the central role of ministers and *frati* in administration was abandoned. The evolution was gradual, but ministers were pensioned off and gradually not replaced. A trained staff paid in wages or in-kind service, replaced *frati*, *sorores*, and *conversi*. The role of surgeons and doctors increased.[50] Poor inmates still traded service to others within the community for their care, but their importance in the day-to-day services of the facilities decreased.[51]

Families, through their association with the minster of a facility, had traditionally held a great deal of sway over the control and distribution of the communities' assets. In the fifteenth century this function was increasingly taken away from individuals and placed under civic control, thus limiting the political influence of individuals or families.[52] Families often reflected the interests of the neighbourhood or community where the hospital was located, thus traditionally insuring the autonomy and independence of the individual hospitals. While some families channelled their influence in a new direction through their participation in civic government, and many of the same families who were instrumental in the independent influence over hospital administration appear on the rolls of new consortia and the commissions that were responsible for choosing leadership of the consolidated hospitals, they were no longer as tied to individual neighbourhood hospital communities.[53]

In general, over the course of the early fifteenth century there is an increasing disconnect between the wealthy citizens and the poor and the sick. Early in the hospital movement wealthy benefactors would often not only donate their worldly goods but also join the hospital as *conversi* to live among and serve the poor and the sick. The vibrancy of the early hospital movement was dependent upon the service of these individuals. By the fifteenth century, while individuals and families still donated substantial sums and estates, they did not always attach themselves to the bequests. Those who did enter the hospital usually lived separately from the ill and poor and did not always participate in their care. Statutes from this period often require only the healthy poor, *poveri sani*, to serve the ill poor, *poveri infermi*. Hospitals became a refuge for wealthy citizens to live out their last years securely and with medical care in return for a bequest on their death but not necessarily tied to service.[54] Overall, bequests to hospitals in general fell over the first half of the fifteenth century. The rampant mismanagement of funds by administrators could thus be seen as a reaction to their decreased revenue streams.

Confraternity and religious orders and reform

Larger more centralized communal organizations replaced the smaller traditional confraternities and consortia that had been crucial players in the earlier era of foundation and administration of hospitals. The unification commission in 1458 included members from several of these large confraternities: *Consorzio della Misericordia* (founded in 1368), the *Scuola delle Quattro Marie* (1305), *La Scuola della Divinita* (1429), *Il Consorzio del Terzo Ordine Francescano* (1442), *Cosorzio della Carita*, *il Consorzio di Santa Maria dell'Umilita* (1444), and the *Ufficio della Pieta dei Poveri di Cristo* (OPC)[55] (1405).[56] With the exception of the *Misericordia* and

Scuola della Divinita, which were founded in the fourteenth century, these were newer organizations that had organized around the new issues of the fifteenth century.[57]

The *Consorzio della Misericordia,* a confraternal order increasingly active throughout northern Italy, illustrates a good example of this influence. Its membership reflects the coalescing of multiple interests in the city of Milan. For example, the wealthy patrician Biraghi family played a significant role in the administration of Ospedale Brolo. One of the ministers of the hospital, Bernardo Biraghi, was active in the chapter of the new Ospedale Maggiore and also a member of the *Consorzio della Misericordia.*[58] While the consortium had been active in this charitable activity since 1368, its membership had changed over the preceding century, made up more and more of members of the emerging merchant class. These individuals saw participation in such orders as not only avenues to spiritual reward, but also as paths to social and political advancement. Their skills in asset and resource management translated well to the administration of charitable works.[59] These 'new men' found ways to gain political influence and social access in an era when direct communal government was increasingly closed to them.

As a few large confraternal orders had become influential in the collegial consolidation of interest in public assistance, some lay religious orders also continued to play an influential role in the reform movement and the establishment of the new unified hospitals, but usually did so at the behest of civic authorities and did not act independently as they had in an earlier era. In Treviso, the powerful Santa Maria dei *battuti* organized and administered public health and medical assistance for citizens and poor under the direction of civic authorities, the organization of which led to the consolidation and medicalization of much hospital care there.[60] In other cities, the order of Observant Franciscans was instrumental in garnering public and ecclesiastical support for the unification and centralization of hospital administration. Observant friar Alberto of Sarteano solicited public backing for the new central hospital in Brescia in 1442. Michele Carcano promoted the new centralized system to the authorities in Como, Piacenza, and Crema.[61]

In Milan, the OPC acted as a confraternal order and joined the other larger groups tasked with redistributing testamentary giving. The OPC had the advantage of direct access to ecclesiastical records of testamentary giving. OPC officials had the power to seize any legacies that they felt were not being utilized for the poor. They gave control of all funds gained in that way to their own hospital, which was used to house vagrants and others who had been turned away from other hospitals.[62] All, particularly those other confraternities who had been responsible for the distribution of charitable bequests, did not initially welcome this mandate but ultimately the OPC became a stable and efficient institution.

An important leader of the OPC and of the hospital reform movement in general was Francesco della Croce, a cleric who served the OPC for many years and ushered in much of the reform effort, which led to unification and centralization. In 1445 della Croce made official visitations to area hospitals including San Lazzaro, San Dionigi, and San Martino, with the purpose of ensuring their compliance with the new fiscal reforms. Statutes from these visitations stipulate what was to be done with the monies received by the hospital but also codified the treatment of the 'registered poor'. They were to be fed regularly, with a daily allowance of bread and wine, as well as a cooked meal that was to include fish and beans during Lent, meat, and eggs during non-fasting periods. Also included in these statutes was a novel requirement: doctors were instructed to visit the sick daily and to order treatment and diets according to the illness.[63]

The power and influence of some corporate groups increased in the fifteenth century but the nature of their structure and relationship to the community had changed. Earlier confraternal and lay and tertiary religious orders had been oriented to the local, neighbourhood, or parish community. They had been a manifest expression of lay piety and community networking of the high Middle Ages. By the fifteenth century there were far fewer small, independent groups and a few large, civic sanctioned organizations had taken their place. Middle-class families still found an avenue to power and influence in these groups but they were much more closely connected to the city government than in the past. These groups were thus very amenable to unification and consolidation hospital reforms.

Reform in medical care

Part of the reform effort of the first half of the fifteenth century included a move away from the traditional view of the sick and the poor as the 'poor of Christ' and from the view that the central purpose of the hospital was to care for the soul. The care of the body became increasingly important to reformers and while they never abandoned the centrality of religion to the mission of the institutions it certainly became more symbolic and less essential. The process of reimagining the role of medical care and the treatment of disease emerged gradually. One reason for this evolution lay in the professionalization and rehabilitation of the medical profession.

A common quote attributed to the period, '*ubi tres medici, duo athei*', where there are three physicians there are two atheists, sums up the suspicion that plagued the medical field in the Middle Ages. In a letter, contemporary chronicler Jacque de Vitry, complained 'God says keep vigils; the doctors say go to sleep. God says fast; the doctors say eat. God says mortify your flesh: the doctors say be comfortable.'[64] Even the great humanist Petrarch inveighs against physicians in a heated diatribe, 'Indeed. I speak the truth and thousands of people are in danger because they are governed by the factious, divergent and uncertain authority of physicians.'[65] These views reflect the growing ambivalence toward the profession that was viewed by many as a necessary evil.

Small numbers of physicians had been attached to the *xeno-dochia* and monastic hospitals since the Carolingian era. Italian city-states recognized the need for physicians and surgeons, and there are records of communal doctors appointed to care for all ill residents of the city as early as the thirteenth century. In Treviso, for example, physicians were given a yearly salary in return for providing care to rich and poor citizens. In 1327 there were two doctors and one surgeon on the payroll, and in 1396 this had increased to six physicians and eight surgeons. Members of the profession founded a college of physicians, whose statutes from 1426 required members care for the poor for free, respect the activities of fellow members, and meet regularly to discuss new theories and practices. By the early fifteenth century university training and humanist ideals were propelling well-educated men into the medical field backed by civic organizations as well as hospital administrators. [66]

While the demand for these services increased over the course of the late Middle Ages there had always been concern over the nature of medical practice. As most early hospitals were attached to monasteries, physicians tended to be members of those communities. In the earlier era, anxiety over the profession revolved primarily around the potential greed of practitioners. Ecclesiastical discourse admonished the brethren to avoid aiding the bodies of the sick for material gain.[67] Much canonical legislation codified this concern beginning in the twelfth century. In 1139, the Second Lateran Council decreed, 'monks and canons regular are not to study jurisprudence and medicine for the sake of temporal gain'.[68] In 1219, Pope Honorius III issued a decree prohibiting the study of medicine and secular law to many members of the clergy. In addition, the Fourth Lateran Council in 1215 forbade the practice of surgery to clergy in the major monastic orders as well as among priests and deacons but allowed it among members of the lower orders.[69] This latter pronouncement is contained among the body of laws aimed at curtailing the rampant clerical avarice.

Suspicion of the motives of physicians increased in the high Middle Ages both among the church establishment and among society in general. While there was continued concern over greed, an additional emphasis emerged regarding the potential for immoral actions by the physicians when treating patients. It is possible to glimpse the perception that physicians were becoming more concerned with the body than the soul. Episcopal dictums repeatedly reminded physicians of the primacy of the needs of an individual's soul over those of their body. Decrees instructed physicians to be sure to call a confessor prior to attending the sick.[70] This was backed up by civil law in Italy which dictated how many times (three) a lay doctor could visit a patient before summoning a priest for confession and absolution.[71] While this injunction had long been in place, it appears more and more frequently in religious sermons and complaints by the laity in the twelfth through thirteenth centuries. Theologians, canonists and patients were wary not only of the physician who acted solely for material gain, but they were increasingly nervous about the physician who was too interested in curing the body and not attentive enough to caring for the soul.

In the mid-thirteenth century Humbert of Romans, in a sermon to hospital workers, reminded them, 'Above [all] beware of doing aught in their art against God in themselves or in others, lest whilst they heal bodies they kill souls, others or their own. Finally, let them have not as much confidence in their medicines as in their prayers, and let them have most in God.'[72] In urban areas that saw increased public health risks from population pressure, violence, the ravages of poor nutrition, and epidemics, concern over curing the body and preventing the spread of disease moved the concerns of physicians and hospitals more and more into the secular realm. Patients were at the mercy of physicians who might heal them, but might also put their souls in jeopardy.

The changing nature of urban society that included contact with foreigners and foreign practices led many people to seek the aid of Jewish or Islamic physicians. In many circles Arab and Jewish medicine was considered more advanced than Christian medicine. However, these physicians also engendered ambivalent feelings among the needy population. When one was sick he would seek out the best care, but a good Christian would worry about the consequences to his soul. Church authorities worried greatly about this development and enacted legislation forbidding the practice of non-Christians treating Christian patients. The Fourth Lateran Council of 1215 strictly forbade the practice of medicine by anyone other than a Christian physician. In reality, Jewish physicians continued to be very active, serving bishops and popes among others, and civil authorities continued to license them despite episcopal injunctions.[73] These contradictions illuminate the increasing tension between the pragmatic, progressive civil society that was developing and the tradition-bound institutional church that sought to retain its authority.

One of the central concerns over the practices of physicians revolved around the inequities suffered by patients. Episcopal leaders, feeling that charity toward the poor and ill was essential, worried that the appeal of compensation from wealthier patients would drive physicians to neglect the needs of the poor. However, they also worried that poor patients would then seek out the services of 'folk' healers, mainly women and other untrained individuals, whose traditional skills reeked to religious minds of superstition and paganism.[74] As in all areas of life church officials sought to regulate the providers of care to ensure that they were practicing approved care, to approved patients, for approved reasons. In practice, physicians with patients of means generally made house calls, had an independent office, or were even in the permanent employment of some of the wealthier citizens.[75] Therefore, the poor who entered the hospitals as a last resort were necessarily dependent upon the charitable services of physicians who would not expect remuneration or, more likely, were less skilled 'nurses' and surgeons.

A few hospitals were able to employ physicians directly, but this was the exception and not the rule. In the thirteenth century, the civil government of cities in northern Italy started to hire medical practitioners to serve the poor in hospitals. Stipulations for employment often included providing services such as ministering to the poor for free, reporting to the health commission, and reporting on cause of death or injury.[76]

Medical professionals were also suspect by many individuals in society throughout the high Middle Ages because, while medical science was increasingly recognized in the nascent university system, the study was much less prestigious than theology or law in most institutions and the line between medicine and magic was still not clearly drawn. The study of medicine relied mostly on ancient Greek and Roman theory and was considered one of the philosophical schools rather than a practical study.[77] Medieval society made a distinction between the *physician*, a university trained theoretician, and the *medicus*, one who actually practiced medicine.[78] Even with the establishment of medical schools such as that at Salerno, which modernized the subject to some extent by incorporating Arab theories, the interest was primarily in the human body but without necessarily an acknowledged aim at curing sickness.[79] At the level of local practitioner the goal remained that of making the patient comfortable and providing for his spiritual needs, and the *medicus* was little more than an herbalist or barber/surgeon. However, as the university system spread with the founding of schools in Bologna, Padua, and elsewhere throughout Europe, the numbers of individuals with medical knowledge increased. At the university in Bologna, the School of Arts and Medicine became the primary area of study, eclipsing even theology. Also, for those who sought answers other than divine retribution for the devastating plague epidemic these schools became the incubators for attempts at understanding its origin.[80]

In fact, even as observers were still proclaiming the outbreak of pestilences as the wrath of God for man's sins, they were observing and commenting on the vagaries of various outbreaks. Matteo Villani, after blaming a punishing God for a recent outbreak in 1357–58, observed:

> At this time, diseased of tertiary, quartene, and other fevers with long-drawn-out illnesses afflicted our territory, in the Valdelsa,

Valdarno di sotto, and Chianti, somewhat like in the previous year,
from which few died. This baffled the people of the Valdelsa and
Chianti, since they had good and pure air, nonetheless, for two years
they infected one another with similar diseases and no one could
identify any single cause for this occurrence.[81]

The need to understand, in order to prevent, these recurring epidemics from a societal perspective gave rise to increased attention
to the individual elements of disease and possible causes. An inventory of the catalogue of course offerings for Arts and Medicine in
Bologna suggests how specific this interest was becoming. While the
curriculum stayed very close to the traditional Aristotelian and
Galenic studies of theory and metaphysics, a few courses used
applied theory to treat specific illness for example, 'Galen, *On Differences of Fevers*', and '*On accident and disease*'.[82]

As medicine became more professionalized, practitioners sought
distinction based on training and status. They utilized the professional guild system to codify distinctions and gain status. The
highest rank was given to university-trained physicians, next were
learned surgeons, barber surgeons, itinerant specialists, empirics,
midwives, and others who gave informal assistance.[83] The newly
professionalized guilds of physicians became a part of the fabric of
civic governance just as had their brothers in other professions.
Confraternal orders and civic governments regulated membership
and oversaw standards.[84] The increased need for their services
during the plague decades increased their prestige and eased some
of the prejudice against them.

Physicians began to receive recognition as part of the new hospital reforms in 1534 Under Duke Francesco II Sforza. First, he
replaced the commissioner by a board of directors composed of
five officers. Three of the officers had to be administrators elected
by the senate from the three main branches of the administration
while the two other officers had to be physicians elected by the
local college of physicians.[85] While other cities quickly adopted
this model it was not always a changed welcomed by everyone.
Cipolla recounts a dispute in which the two physicians appointed
to the board in Cremona felt the other members did not hold them
in, 'proper consideration. The latter either do not call the two
physicians to meetings or if the two physicians are present, do not
want to take their votes into account.' The Board in Milan wrote

back that they should be held in equal status as the rest of the members.[86]

The professionalization of physicians, culminating in their appointment to the unification and governing commissions begins the process in which the hospitals increasingly become medicalized. Learned men, trained in the philosophical school of medicine but practicing in the reality of plague-ravaged cities, applied their knowledge to practical concerns. They were also influenced by the humanist movement, which focused attention on the human person. The care of the body started to overshadow the care of the soul. Once the consolidation efforts were fully realized the hospital became a medical facility and spiritual concerns were relegated to a more symbolic space.

Consolidation

Ultimately, across Italy, the reform efforts of the early part of the fifteenth century resulted in a movement toward consolidation of small hospitals and usually the construction of one central civic hospital. In Milan and its satellite cities the process enabling consolidation and unification emerged out of the reform efforts of the bishop, the *signori*, and confraternal coalitions in the 1440s. In 1448, a complex system for the management of charitable bequests was created. *The Twelve*, the city's central magistracy office, were given the authority to nominate hospital rectors. They first appointed a commission of two of their own members and representatives of the major confraternal orders who then met as a body to nominate forty-eight nominees. Names of nominees generally came from individuals who were already active in the leadership of the hospitals. The archbishop would then choose twenty-four of these as suitable representatives, maintaining at least the appearance of ecclesiastical oversight.[87] This selection process, which existed for almost three hundred years, represents the ultimate solution to the jurisdictional divisions that had bedevilled the hospital movement from its inception. Individuals and families who were active in the hospital system through either generosity or leadership (or often both) were usually put forth for nomination. It was in their interest to make sure they acted above board so that their names might be chosen. The city, through the office of *The Twelve,* was in control of the process and forwarded names that represented its interest. Finally, the episcopate could still claim its traditional role and retain respect as it had the ultimate say in the selection process. These efforts lay the foundation for further consolidation and centralization of the hospital movement.

As stated before Milan was not alone in centralization efforts; the process was underway in Tuscany and other parts of the northern region as well. As early as 1427, the citizens of Brescia proposed the creation of a new centralized hospital. As articulated in the foundational charter, this new hospital would be created by the unification of eleven smaller hospitals. The plan had the backing of the Bishop of Bergamo as well as the highest civic authorities of the city and had been constructed with support from members of the cathedral chapter and the whole citizen council. The charter gave the bishop some influence in the appointment of hospital officials but the city and ecclesiastical officials would jointly appoint a board of governors to one-year terms.[88] War between Milan and Venice delayed completion of the planned hospital for fourteen years. In 1441 Pope Eugenius IV gave approval for the plan with the stipulation that the governors of Brescia accept his candidate, Pietro del Monte, Bishop of Brescia to oversee the project. Observant friar and prominent citizen Alberto of Sarteano was charged with garnering public support for the plan.[89] While it is clear that ecclesiastical authorities retained an important role in the origins of these new large hospitals, once again impetus for their founding came from the citizenry, and control over organization and management would fall to the civic lay charitable organizations, and ultimately the city government.

In 1451 Pope Nicholas V issued a mandate for the creation of a unified hospital in Cremona.[90] Eighteen smaller hospitals united to create the Ospedale S. Maria della Pieta.[91] The *consiglio generale* of the city were assigned the task of finding 'a proper and convenient place' to build the hospital and insure that it serve 'pilgrims and the ill wherever and whoever' should wish their services.[92] Construction of the large new hospital that was built in the form of a T, benefitted from a large donation from the Consorzio della Dona, a large and prestigious confraternity in the city.[93] Again, we see cooperation of all the fifteenth century governing constituencies. The pope legitimized the concept, city governors planned and constructed the consolidation and building effort, and the powerful citizen confraternal groups provided funding, and one would think, influence in the process.

Much like the earlier proliferation of small hospital foundations, these consolidation efforts took place throughout the region
at roughly the same time. Pavia founded an 'Ospedale Grande' in
1449, Mantua in 1450.[94] In Bergamo, the assets of eleven smaller
hospitals were combined under the authority of the Ospedale
Maggiore San Marco in 1457. San Marco's foundational charter
reflects the coordination of efforts of the various political and
religious interests of the city. The bishop of Bergamo, *vice podesta*
and *capitano*, as well as the civic council and members of the
cathedral chapter were all engaged in creating the new institution.[95] The various constituents made sure their interests were
acknowledged. The bishop laid the first stone, followed by two
Venetian governors of the city, then the abbot of San Faustino
Maggiore a member of the prominent (and probably major donor)
Marcello family, and finally two stones by members of the citizen's council of Brescia.[96] As with the small hospitals, the episcopate appointed a priest to look after the spiritual needs of the
inmates and celebrate Mass daily in the chapel within the new
facility.

Resistance to consolidation

While most cities in the region consolidated hospitals and built
a new central institution, for a variety of reasons, some munici-
palities and some smaller hospitals were able to retain their independence.[97] Ospedale S. Crucis in Lodi was not absorbed into the
Ospedale Maggiore there. It moved locations but was in existence
and administered by a confraternity and only ceased to exist when
that confraternity was suppressed in 1786.[98] Some hospitals lost
their status as independent hospitals but retained some level of
service under the major institutions. For example, Ospedale di San
Giacomo in Vallicella, a small hospital founded by a wealthy family
in Lodi, lost its independent charter under the consolidation efforts
in 1470 but continued to house pilgrims and give alms to the poor
up until 1807. Pilgrims had to first report to Ospedale Maggiore
and they were then given a document to present to San Giacomo
for entrance.[99] A similar arrangement appears to have accorded
some independence to Ospedale S. Iacobi in Lodi, as it is listed as
part of Ospedale Maggiore but was still taking in pilgrims in the
seventeenth century.[100]

The consolidation reform was not always without contention. Hospitals and their patrons frequently fought to retain their independence. There are instances when a family or group was successful in opposing the consolidation. In Como, the powerful family Carcano successfully appealed to protect Ospedale Santa Maria del Borgo Vico di Capua from consolidation. It continued to operate independently until 1596.[101] Also in Como, Ospedale di Santa Maria Maddalena was protected by the patronage of the Marini and Sambenedetto families. It was allowed to remain independent but became a house for prisoners who were sentenced to death. They were provided food and shelter for thirty days prior to their execution. Still later, the hospital served as an orphanage. It was not disbanded until 1764.[102]

The loss of power and influence by individual citizens is illustrated by the fate of Ospedale S. Maria dei Tizzoni in Lodi. An old noble family of Lodi of the same name founded Tizzoni in 1296. The family retained the right to appoint the leadership of the hospital throughout its history. However, the last provost of the hospital, Giuseppi Girardini, gave up his rights to the bishop of Lodi in 1459. Upon his death in 1466, three Tizzoni brothers tried to reassert their hereditary claim over the hospital. They took their claim to the civic commission responsible for the consolidation efforts. The commission found against the brothers, but concluded that in recognition of their poverty, they could rent property owned by the hospital for twenty-three years. The building that had housed the hospital was sold in 1467, but documents record that it had not been used as a hospital for ten years.[103] It would appear that the Tizzoni family had fallen on hard times and were unable to retain the influence and ability to manage the facility. The bishop and then the city took over and placed the hospital under central management.

In at least one case, members of the hospital community argued for consolidation. The fate of Ospedale di San Biago in Lodi was hotly contested over early decades of the fifteenth century. In 1405 Pope Innocent VII granted the hospital to Cardinal Angelo Sommariva who ceded control of it to the Olivetani monastic order. The brothers who administered the hospital protested this action in a letter to the pope in 1429. He denied their claim. Apparently, they so detested the control of Olivetani that they petitioned to have the hospital consolidated into the Ospedale Maggiore but were denied this claim as well. The pope finally declared the hospital independent and under the authority of the Olivetani in 1473.[104]

Many of those hospitals that were able to retain their independence were not the typical, small, urban facilities that exemplify the medieval hospital movement. The very old rural Ospedale di San Pietro di Senna outside of Lodi was connected to a larger monastery and had always benefitted from the patronage of wealthy Milanese families; it was able to survive the consolidation because of its link to families like the Sforza. In particular, Duchess Maria, widow of Francesco Sforza, protected the institution. It was not suppressed until 1801.[105] A number of small hospitals retained their independence but became specialized institutions. In Bergamo, Ospedale de Maddalena, was originally a typical medieval hospital, caring for the poor, pilgrims and travellers and ill and administered by the *disciplinati*. Probably because it was relatively prosperous and had the backing of the powerful confraternity, it was not consolidated into the Ospedale San Marco. It evolved into a specialized institution; by the end of the sixteenth century it was known for treating the 'insane, the senile and the mentally defective'.[106] In Como, Ospedale San Gottardo was consolidated with the Ospedale Maggiore in 1496, but there is a record of its continued existence in 1533 when it was listed as a shelter for orphans. Still later, it was granted to a group of women who established an Ursuline order there.

In a few cities it was not necessary to construct new buildings as early institutions had risen to acceptable levels of sophistication in care or benefitted from the patronage of influential elite within the government. In 1470 citizens of the city of Parma petitioned Duke Francesco Sforza and Pope Sixtus IV for approval of consolidation of Parmese hospitals under one institution, Ospedale Rodolfo Tanzi. Both the duke and the pope agreed, and Sixtus issued a *mandate unionis* in 1471, which subsumed at least fifty smaller institutions and made Tanzi the *Ospedale Grande*.[107] It does not appear that the hospital underwent any significant building changes until a wing was added the middle of the sixteenth century.[108]

Conclusion

Albini suggests we view the unification of hospitals in the fifteenth century as a process that reflected a 'polycentric' effort on the part of many agents who traditionally lay claim to hospital management, although in an altered state.[109] In Milan, the bishop still claimed jurisdiction and some control of resources through the bodies such as the OPC. Ecclesiastical officials retained a role in the appointment of leadership in the new unified hospital and the Papal seal was still needed for the legitimization of the whole plan. Communal groups such as the Consortia Misericordia were still playing the role of communal groups where membership gave access to political and social status and allowed some continued involvement in civic affairs. The Consortia too, retained some influence in hospital management by being part of the Unification Commission. Individual families played a role as well, some protecting the independence of certain hospitals while others abetting the unification efforts through their participation in city government or as members of the major consortia. The city, however, evolved its role. From outsiders in the foundation and early administration of the hospital to competitors for revenues and communal control, the city fathers had coopted membership of the competing entities to serve their goals and eventually replaced them in importance.

City officials were reacting to increased pressures placed on society by demographic catastrophes of the age and an escalation of urban crime and indigence. They were also forced to act because those institutions traditionally charged with providing these services, the hospital and the institutional church, were mired in issues of corruption and mismanagement. The city's efforts must also have been seen as not just reactionary, but creative. The health boards and poor offices were novel bodies of corporate authority that strove, and succeeded, in consolidating the various highly contentious civic entities into a centralized bureaucratic welfare provider at the cost of the independence and pious purpose of the small hospital movements. The reasoned analytical way in which the new commissions determined the deserving and registered the ill and poor was not quite in keeping with the earlier apostolic values and *misericordia*. However, it was in keeping with the Renaissance values of *civitas*. The protection and prosperity of citizens was paramount.

In fact, the unification movement was a cause and consequence of the intellectual ethos of the age. The growth of universities combined with blossoming humanism made medicine a practical as well as philosophical study. Medical practitioners gained respect and authority at the very time they were desperately needed to alleviate rampant pestilence. Care of the body came to be of (almost) equal importance as care of the soul. The governing bodies of the cities used the civic ideals of Humanism to order their world and provide for their citizens. The hospital was recognized as an essential element to the maintenance of civic order and central provider of welfare for the population. They did not eliminate the institution wholesale. They recognized the hospital's important function but brought it under their jurisdictional authority. They did not then, just build utilitarian facilities, but central hospitals throughout the region were constructed based on Renaissance architectural designs that reflected utility as well as physical beauty and religious symbolism. They became a part of the patriotic civic landscape of the Renaissance, an expression of the republican values of the Italian city-state.

Notes

1 E. Welch, *Art and Authority in Renaissance Milan* (New Haven, CT, 1995), 115.
2 ASMi, Carte Miniate, n. 22, see Albini, 'La gestione'; Welch, *Art and Authority*, 115.
3 Albini, 'La gestione', 172.
4 Welch, *Art and Authority*, 124.
5 Ibid., 126.
6 Albini, *Città e ospedali*, 212.
7 Ibid., 210.
8 B. Pullan, *Rich and Poor in Renaissance Venice: The Social Institutions of a Catholic State, to 1620* (Cambridge, MA, 1971), 197–200.
9 Ibid., 201.
10 Albini, 'La gestione', 164.
11 Racine, 'Il sistema ospedaliero', 369.
12 C. Cipolla, *Public Health and the Medical Profession in the Renaissance* (Cambridge, 1976), 12–13.
13 L. Conrad, *The Western Medical Tradition: 800 B.C.–1800 A.D.* (Cambridge, 1995), 196–7.
14 Cipolla, *Public Health*, 14.
15 Milan seems to have escaped the brunt of the initial outbreak. While most modern histories of the 1348 plague suggest that Milan was spared due to the efforts of the city to enact extreme preventative measures such as walling in houses that contained the plague, the documentary evidence to back this up is scarce. In fact, while the mortality rate from the first outbreak may have been lighter than elsewhere records do show that subsequent outbreaks caused a

decline that is estimated to have reduced the population of Milan from around 100,000 to 60,000. Welch, *Art and Authority*, 126.

16 Albini, 'La gestione', 164.

17 Cipolla, *Public Health*, 16; for information on the effects of the plague in Milan see also, F. Borromeo and A. Torno, *La peste di Milano del 1630* (Milan, 1987). 1987

18 Cipolla, *Public Health*, 15.

19 Ibid.

20 Pavia in 1400, 1401, and 1435, and Como in 1428 and 1433. *Public Health*, 16; see ASP, b. 2 (letters dated 23 February, 21 May, 5 August, 1400 and 16 April 1401); and ASC, Lettere Ducali, b. 4, 2 November, 1428 and, b. 6, 19 April and 4 August,1433.

21 Cipolla, *Public Health*, 16. See original, ASPC, b. 443, 6 Dec., 1476.

22 Ibid., 17 from U. Meroni, *'Cremona Fedelissima': Studi di Storia Economica e Amministrativa di Cremona Durante la Dominazione Spagnola* (Cremona, 1951), vol. I, 77.

23 Cipolla, *Public Health*, 23.

24 Welch, *Art and Authority*, 120.

25 Racine, 'Il sistema ospedaliero', 374.

26 Welch, *Art and Authority*, 80.

27 Albini, 'La gestione', 164.

28 Ibid.; Pullan, *Rich and Poor*, 202.

29 Albini, 'La gestione', 163.

30 Albini, *Città e ospedali*, 212; Welch, *Art and Authority*, 125.

31 Following the death of Gian Galeazzo, Milan was plunged for several decades into endemic periods of political turmoil, social instability, bad harvests, and disease, but civic reform efforts were not completely derailed. In 1445, at the death of Fillipo Maria Visconti, Milan briefly reverted to a republic known as the Ambrosian Republic; this citizen government continued to promote the idea of poor relief and created their own committee of 'deputies over the distribution to the poor'. Albini, 'La gestione', 167.

32 Albini, *Città e ospedali*, 212.

33 A. Noto, 'Per la tutela dei legati elemosinieri milanesi nel secolo XV', *Studi in onore di Armando Sapori,* Milan, 1957, II, 734; cf Welch, *Art and Authority*, 129.

34 Albini, *Città e ospedali*, 213.

35 Albini, 'La gestione', 166.

36 Albini, *Città e ospedali*, 213.

37 Albini, 'La gestione', 165–6. Similar reform acts were decreed in Brescia in 1429, Cremona in 1450, Lodi in 1454, Como in 1468, and Piacenza in 1471, just to name a few. Racine, 'Il sistema ospedaliero', 374.

38 Albini, 'La gestione', 167.

39 This is printed in English in Pullan's *Rich and Poor,* from the Italian, original in A. G Roncalli and P. Forno, *Gli atti della visita apostolica di San Carlo Borromeo a Bergamo, 1557,* 2 vols (Florence, 1936–57), I/ii, 218 f.

40 Agnelli, *Ospedale di Lodi,* 22.

41 Albini, 'La gestione', 162–4.

42 ASMi Archivio dell'Ospedale Maggiore di Milano (AOM), Origine e dotazione Ospedale di San Dionigi.

43 Albini, 'La gestione', 160, 166.

44 Welch, *Art and Authority,* 127.

45 App., doc. 4, cap. 2,3,6 c7 in D. Rando ' 'laicus religious' tra strutture civile ed ecclesiastiche: l'ospedale di Ognissanti in Treviso (sec. xiii)', in Merlo, *Esperienze religiose,* 43–83.

46 Mambretti, 'L'ospedale di San Gerardo', 196.

47 Albini, 'La gestione', 162–4.

48 Ibid., and Welch, *Art and Authority,* 138.

49 Albini, 'La gestione', 164–5.

50 For more on the role of medical professionals see pages 151 and 152.

51 Albini, 'La gestione', 168–9.

52 Ibid.

53 Albini, *Città e ospedali,* 215.

54 Welch, *Art and Authority,* 126.

55 See page 142 for OPC.

56 Albini, *Città e ospedali,* 214.

57 Ibid.

58 Albini, 'La gestione', 170.

59 Ibid., 169.

60 D'Andrea, *Civic Christianity,* 39–40, 85–90.

61 Pullan, *Rich and Poor,* 203–6.

62 Welch, *Art and Authority,* 130.

63 Ibid.

64 R. Numbers and D. Amundsen, *Caring and Curing: Health and Medicine in the Western Religious Traditions* (New York, 1986), 91. (NY is correct)

65 F. Wallis, *Medieval Medicine: A Reader* (Toronto, 2010), 532.

66 D'Andrea, *Civic Christianity,* 86–8.

67 V. Nutton, 'Medicine in Medieval Europe, 100–1500', in L. Conrad (ed.), *The Western Medical Tradition: 800 B.C.-1800 A.D.* (Cambridge, 1995), 147; Numbers and Amundsen, *Caring and Curing,* 84–91.

68 Numbers and Amundsen, *Caring and Curing,* 83.

69 Ibid., and Nutton, 'Medicine in Medieval Europe', 147.

70 Numbers and Amundsen, *Caring and Curing,* 90–1.

71 Nutton, 'Medicine in Medieval Europe', 147.

72 Numbers and Amundsen, *Caring and Curing*, 93.
73 Ibid.
74 Ibid.
75 N. Siraisi, *Medieval and Early Renaissance Medicine: An Introduction to Knowledge and Practice* (Chicago, IL, 1990), 38.
76 Ibid. Henderson traces the medicalization of Ospedale S. Maria Nuova in Florence in the fourteenth and fifteenth centuries. The hospital evolved from a small facility of seventeen beds in the early part of the century to a facility that housed 220 'sick poor' by the mid-century. During this period the hospital increasingly used the services of trained physicians and surgeons and the professionals gained acceptance into the governing guilds of the city. Henderson believes that the expansion of hospitals during this period was due as much to an increased medicalization of charity as to an increase in need. Henderson, *The Renaissance Hospital*, 27–8.
77 Cosmacini, *L'Ospedale Sant'Anna*, 58, 63.
78 Jansen et al., *Medieval Italy*, 333.
79 Cosmacini, *L'Ospedale Sant'Anna,* 63.
80 Ibid.
81 Matteo Villani, 'Cronica con la continuazione di Filippo Villani', ed. Giuseppe Porta, translated by S. K. Cohn, and printed in Jansen et al., *Medieval Italy*, 32.
82 'The Curriculum in Arts and Medicine at Bologna', translated by M. Michele Mulchahey, printed in Jansen et al., *Medieval Italy*, 328–30.
83 Wallis, *Medieval Reader*, 361.
84 D'Andrea, *Civic Christianity*, 88–9.
85 Cipolla, *Public Health*, 21.
86 Ibid., 22–3.
87 Welch, *Art and Authority,* 132.
88 Pullan, *Rich and Poor*, 204.
89 Ibid., 203.
90 ASCr, Arch. Osp. S.M.d.P., sez 1, b,2; 6 May, 1451.
91 Hospitals in or around Cremona that were consolidated include Casa del Consorzio dello Spirito Santo detto del beato Facio; S. Maria Molinaria detto 'dei prete;' S. Creato, S. Sepolcro, dell'Incarnata, Ognissanti; SS. Maria e Ambrogio, *domus dei*; Donna Berlenda; SS. Simone e Giuda, della Misericordia; S. Alberto, S. Bartolomea in Romanengo; Rebecco, S. Maria in Gabbioneta; S. Cataldo in Motta Baluffe, Martinana; SS. Maria e Balmazio in Paderno. See A. Cavalcabó and U. Gualazzini, 'Nuovi contributi sulle fasi costruitile dell'ospedale di Santa Maria del Pietà nel Quattrocento', in A. Cavalcabo and U. Gualazzini (eds), *Bollettino storico Cremonese: miscellanea di scritti originali* (Cremona, 1965), 77.
92 Ricci, 'Nuovi contributi sulle fasi costruttire', 82.

 93 Ibid.
 94 Ibid., 72.
 95 Pullan, *Rich and Poor*, 204.
 96 Ibid.
 97 Verona, Vicenza, and Padua all retained independent hospitals into the sixteenth century Pullan, *Rich and Poor*, 206.
 98 Caretta, 'Gli ospedali altomedievali', 293.
 99 Agnelli, *Ospedale di Lodi*, 16.
100 Caretta, 'Gli ospedali altomedievali', 293.
101 Cosmacini, *L'Ospedale Sant'Anna*, 52–3.
102 Ibid., 52, 56–7.
103 Agnelli, *Ospedali di Lodi*, 16.
104 Agnelli, *Ospedale di Lodi*, 14.
105 Ibid., 23.
106 Pullan, *Rich and Poor*, 205.
107 A. Ricci, 'La Realizzazione della riforma e la sorte degli ospedali minori', in R. Greci (ed.), *L'ospedale Rodolfo Tanzi di Parma in età medieval* (Bologna, 2004), 79–136.
108 Cosmacini, *L'Ospedale Sant'Anna*, 54.
109 Albini, 'La gestione', 216.

Conclusion

The hospital movement of the thirteenth through fifteenth centuries in northern Italy provides a lens through which to view the transformation of political power, religious life, and the social agency of urban citizens of the region. Traditional definitions of poverty and need, as well as suggestions of a Christian's responsibility to such need, no longer satisfied city-dwellers who saw a much greater demand and variety of suffering in their community than ever before. In addition, they felt vulnerable in the face of such need. Security for their persons and property was threatened by the insecurity of society. Guilt and dread of failure coloured their actions as they went about the inequitable business of capitalism. The rapid spread of disease among people living in extremely close quarters threatened their very health.

Demands for assistance made by this increasingly urbanized population forced a reaction from both the ecclesiastical and secular imperial authorities. As these two entities were locked in a larger political wrestling match, cities and citizens were often left to create their own novel responses to challenges posed by social stressors of the era. The communal movement that saw the creation of citizen-based representative governments also saw the creation of citizen-based religious and charitable organizations. The piety of the age that witnessed the Crusades and the rise of mendicant orders encouraged urban *cittadini* to embrace a life of charity and service. Modelling religious men and women like Francis of Assisi, the greatest exemplar of this impulse and one of their own, *a cittadini*, they did not envision a traditional life of prayer and contemplation far from society, but a life of apostolic service within society.

Initially, church leadership begrudgingly welcomed the increased participation of an active laity in alleviating ills such as poverty, indigence, and epidemics. While constantly trying to at least place ecclesiastical controls on this civic activism, papal policy unintentionally allowed for a wide variety of religious charitable experimentation. Communal need and institutional neglect led to the emergence of the medieval hospital as a widespread institutional phenomenon that served as a nexus of charitable activity, religious life, political access and social mobility.

As a result of the pious impulse of an emerging class of *cittadini*, the focus of such religious charitable activity was targeted on specific localized communities. Hospitals provided a nascent social security system for the medieval city. They protected the citizenry from those who posed a threat to their security: the indigent who might become criminals, the vagrant traveller who might spread disease, the involuntary poor who might challenge their sense of comfort and prosperity. These middle-class merchants reacted to the needs of marginalized groups in a way that reflected civic values and beliefs. Civic charitable organizations provided money, clothes, and a safe place to rest within the heart of their own communities, in buildings next door to their own homes. At the same time, service to such charitable institutions as the hospital gave an outlet for the intense piousness and desire for religious service that characterized the age. Donating time, money, one's life, to a hospital community afforded prestige, social access, and political prestige for families.

We can tell a great deal about the nature of the hospital movement by the foundation and location of these institutions. While their construction near city gates suggests the continued importance of an early concept of the *xenodochia*, or hospice, intended to house pilgrims, a closer examination reveals the motivation to house pilgrims provided an institutional precedent that was combined with a desire to care for the ill and indigent of the community. There is also a very specific difference between urban and rural hospitals that reflects the particular needs of that population. Rural hospitals reflected an older, ecclesiastical model of charity and religious life. Urban hospitals were more lay oriented and communal. Individuals, families, and community groups founded the earliest hospitals of this period. Foundational charters and bequests give great insight into the motives behind this institutionalization of charity and religious life.

This lay initiative must be viewed as part of a general criticism of ecclesiastical institutions' inability or unwillingness to meet the charitable demands of these communities. While the universal desire for legitimization of hospital foundations by ecclesiastical authority indicates the still active perception of the all-powerful institutional church, the specifications for lay control by founders indicates the suspicion and declining respect for this institution's actual ability to provide these social services. Still, once hospitals were founded and approved they tended to follow a method of administration that was modelled, often officially, to older ecclesiastical models of monastic governance. Rules and statutes were imposed that closely followed an ideal of *vita apostolica*. Lay fervour originated a wide variety of institutional responses of which the hospital is one, but while creative, confraternities, semi-religious orders, and lay groups all fell back on ecclesiastical models of acceptable administration and communal life. As happened frequently in older religious institutions it became difficult to maintain such rigour and commitment over the course of a community's existence.

The jurisdictional disputes of the thirteenth century reflect the difficulty of shared governance and the evolution of civic participation and governance. Individual and group piety gave way to greater attention to civic and economic concerns. Increased attempts at the assertion of ecclesiastical oversight often resulted in resistance from institutions and groups. Leadership of hospital management became politicized, as did membership for some in the hospital staffing community. Urban citizens became more engaged in the civic government but as members of competing networks of familial and social patronage and power. The hospital, as it always did, reflected the issues of the community. As civic power became more centralized and neighbourhood and community less localized, and as the local and regional church leadership lost much governing authority, institutions of governance and the administration of charity became more centralized and secular.

In addition, in the fourteenth century, multiple crises led to a further challenge to the ability of the laity to continue their control of hospital leadership. Demographic crises, institutional mismanagement, and corruption led both ecclesiastical and civic authorities to step in and attempt to reign in perceived abuses. The civic response to the plague epidemic was to initiate health boards or magisterial commissions to deal with social welfare aspects of demographic catastrophe. The model for these social welfare providers was applied to hospital management by the end of the fourteenth century. The need to curtail contagion was originally perceived as a social issue but an increasingly professionalized medical profession began to redefine medical care and move hospital care away from primarily spiritual assistance to more corporeal care.

These institutional changes, which took place throughout the civic landscape of urban Italy in the fifteenth century, reflect the emergence of a Renaissance ideal articulated by civic humanists and city governments. The unification and consolidation of hospitals in the 1450s and the creation of the Ospedale Maggiore all over Italy illustrate the culmination of a process begun in earlier centuries. In the thirteenth century citizens of the burgeoning commercial centres of northern Italy, frustrated by perceived inaction and inequity in the providence of social services in the cities, founded the hospital movement to provide *caritas*, charity for those in need within their immediate communities. Over three very eventful centuries ecclesiastical authorities and emerging city-state governments alternately condoned, condemned, appropriated, or emulated the model of social welfare set up by this grassroots semi-religious movement. As the great central hospitals were being built in the 1450s the smaller community institutions were closed. The need for such services had not disappeared but the emergent state structures of the Renaissance city-states were finally able to wrest complete control and take on the responsibility of providing for their neediest citizens.

Appendix

The following is a list of hospitals by city that were examined in the course of this research. Where possible I have listed the location, foundation date, founder, basic administration, and consolidation information for each hospital

Bergamo

Hospital: Osp. S. Antonio
Founded: 1357

Hospital: Osp. Bertramus de Brolo
Founded: 1304
Founder: Bertramus de Brolo stipulated in his will of 1304, that if his heirs died without legitimate successors then his estate should be used to found a hospital named after him and be based in two places: his house in Bergamo and his house in Curno

Hospital: Osp. S. Caterina

Hospital: S. Grata inter Vites
Founded: Twelfth century

Hospital: Osp. S. Lazzaro
Founded   Twelfth century

Bergamo continued

Hospital:	Osp. S. Leonardo
Administration:	Connected to church of same name. Also housed abandoned infants

Hospital:	Osp. S. Lorenzo

Hospital:	Osp. S. Maria della Caritate
Founded:	End of fourteenth century

Hospital:	Osp. S. Maria Magdalena
Administration:	Confraternity *disciplinati*
Consolidation:	Did not merge in fifteenth century. Moved from general care to care for the insane in the last quarter of the sixteenth century

Hospital:	Osp. S. Maria Maggiore
Founded:	End of fourteenth century

Hospital:	San Sepolcro
Founded:	1159
Administration:	1305 *consortium of San Sepolcro* ceded all rights and administration to the confraternity *Misericordia* in 1305

Hospital:	Osp. S. Spirito

Hospital:	Osp. S. Tomaso
Administration:	By a small flagellant community

Hospital:	Osp. San Vincenzo
Founded:	1323
Founder:	Castelinus Rapazeltis, a cathedral canon, left 600 L to found San Vincenzo in 1323
Location:	Substantially large walled compound located in the centre of city beside the canonry San Vincenzo in the neighbourhood of S. Cassiano

Brescia

Hospital:	Osp. S. Giovanni di Bresco

Como

Hospital:	Osp. S. Anna
Founded:	1468 when several other hospitals came together. Probably S. Lazzaro, S. Vitali, S. Martino di Zezio, S. Maria di Nesso

Hospital:	Osp. di Sant'Antonio (also called San Silvestro)
Founded:	1200
Founders:	Archbishop of Como and given to the monks of S. Benedict
Administrators:	Administered by monks of S. Benedict, also known as the friars of S. Antony
Consolidation:	1468 placed under Osp. Maggiore

Hospital:	Osp. S. Bartolomeo del Comasco (possibly later S. Lazzaro)
Founded:	14 October 1163
Founders:	Giovanni Ficani made a donation to the Congregation of Crusaders
Administration:	Followed rule of S. Augustine but also possibly *Humiliati*
Consolidation:	1481 with Osp. Maggiore

Hospital:	Osp. San Berardo
Location:	Sits near the river Cosia not far from the monastery de Pedemonte

Hospital:	Osp San Biagio di San Michele
Founded:	1426 for pilgrims but probably around since 1295
Consolidation:	Consolidated with Osp. Maggiore on 1468

Hospital:	Osp. San Clemente di Zeno
Founded:	1159
Founders:	Giovanni Meda
Administrators:	A leper hospital administered by *Humiliati*

Hospital:	Osp. San Eutichio
Location:	Near the Church of San Giorgio
Founded:	First reference was 1293, but existed earlier

Como continued

Administrators:	Administered from at least 1292–97 by the confraternity of the parish of S. Eutichio. Possibly a safe haven for exposed infants
Hospital:	Osp. San Fedele
Founders:	Founded or extended by bishop Anselmo
Hospital:	Osp. San Gottardo
Location:	Unclear, there are several references: near Ponte di San Giovanni; but also possibly near *piazza popolo*; or on eastern side of valley in village of San Giuliano
Consolidation:	1406, but in 1533 building was used as a shelter for orphans. It was later granted to some pious women who founded an Ursuline community
Hospital:	Osp. San Leonardo
Founded:	First reference in 1409 was for poor and prisoners
Hospital:	Osp. Santa Maria (Nuova) del Borgo Vico
Founded:	Turn of twelfth century
Founder:	Named for church it was attached to, patronage of the family Maroni, popularly called 'Maronesa.'
Administration:	It was run perhaps by the family Carcano who opposed its merger with Osp Maggiore in 1468
Consolidation:	Successfully opposed. Continued to operate independently until 1596
Hospital:	Osp. di Santa Maria Annunciatia
Founded:	1331 or possibly 1236
Administrators:	In 1331 it was given to monks of the order of San Pietro Celestino. Possibly operated under the canons of *collegiati* and church of San Feidel in 1236

Hospital:	Osp. di Santa Maria Maddalena (also called della Canova or della Colombetta)
Founded:	1300 (possibly as early as 1283 under a different name)
Founders:	Isacco dei San Benedetto and 'certain people' from the house of Marina
Administration:	The widow had the executer of the will entrust the hospital to the *frati della Colombetta* to build a hospital di Santa Maria Maddalena which was attached to Osp. de Marina, built in 1313. Thus probably S. M. Maddalena was unified with Osp. de Marina
Consolidation:	They escaped consolidation with Osp Maggiore in fifteenth century because the families of Marina and Sampenedetto were patrons and opposed it strongly. It yielded finally in 1764. In later years it was used for prisoners sentenced to death and also orphans at one time

Hospital:	Osp. S. Maria di Nesso
Founded:	26 March 1275
Founders:	Unknown bequest to the *Humiliati*
Administrators:	*Humiliati* connected to church of same name

Hospital:	Osp. San Martino di Zezzio
Administration:	Prior to 1219 it was governed by two ministers, Arialdo Pinula and brother Giovanni Balesterio. Managed by *Humiliati*. It became hospital for pilgrims and lepers

Hospital:	Osp. San Pantaleone
Location:	Near the bridge of San Giovanni
Founders:	Contradictory evidence for founding date. Probably founded between 1294 and 1325 by the Lambertenghi family which included an archbishop of Lodi in 1313

Hospital:	Osp. San Vitele
Founded:	Probably 1221

Como continued

Founders: Donation by Giovanni and Obizzone Cacci and
                   their mother
Administration: In 1356 it joined the Sisters of the *Humiliati* of
                   San Sisto
Consolidation: Possibly merged with Osp. Sant'Anna in
                   fifteenth century

Other hospitals
  S. Antonio
  S. Martino
  S. Guliano
  S. Genesco (1312)
  S. Vitale
  S. Bartolonieo
  S. Lazzaro
  S. Giorgio

Cremona

Hospital: Osp. S. Maria
Location: In town near the gate of S. Luca
Founded: 1283
Founders: Noble family Bardolana

Hospital: Osp. S. Maria della Pieta
Founded: Earliest mention 1246
Administration: Administered by the Consortia dello Spirito Santo
Consolidation: Many hospitals in Cremona were consolidated
                   under S. Maria della Pieta in 1451

Hospital: Osp. S. Maria Vecchio
Founded: 1245
Founders: Noble family Alepranda (Alaprandi)

Hospitals that are listed as united under S. Maria della Pieta in
  1451
  S. Alberto
  Casa del Consorzio della Spirito Santo
  Domus Dei
  Donna Berlenda

S. Creato
Dell'Incornata
S. Maria Molinaria detto 'dei preti'
Della Misericordia
Ognissanti
SS. Marta e Ambrogio
S. Sepolcro
SS. Simone e Guida
S. Bartolomea in Romanengo
S. Cataldo in Motta Baluffe
S. Maria e Dalmazio in Paderno
S. Maria in Gabbioneta
Di Martignana
Di Rebecco

Gemona

Hospital:	Osp. San Michele
Location:	Inside city walls in the area of the duomo but also near a major gate that lead south
Founded:	15 April 1259
Founder:	Rodolone
Administration:	Became part of order of Santo Spirito in Sassia in 1274
Consolidation:	Never consolidated. Was administered by a confraternity until 1784

Lodi

Hospital:	Osp. S. Alberti
Location:	Castiglione d'Adda
Founded:	1189
Administration:	Absorbed into S. Bassiano in 1337

Hospital:	Osp. di Sant'Antonio Abate (S. Antonii)
Location:	In the countryside on a road of the same name
Founders:	Guidono dei Riccardi
Founded:	10 July 1212
Administrators:	Given to the *Padre Ospedalieri* to administer

Lodi continued

Consolidation: It was never consolidated and on 10 March
                        1618 it was given to the third order of the
                        Franciscans

Hospital: Osp. S. Bassiano
Location: Located outside the walls but on the moat (?)
Founder: By the family of Tressano. Merges with S.
                        Alberto Castiglione to become SS. Bassiani et
                        Alberti, served brothers and sisters, merged
                        with Osp. Maggiore
Founded: 1352

Hospital: Osp. S. Bartolomaei
Location: Located outside walls
Founder: Family of Bishop of Lodi
Founded: 1206

Hospital: Osp. di San Biago
Location: Along the Adda River, suburb of Porta Cremonese
Founded: 1163 – Originally called Osp. di San Biago della
                        Carita. Merged with Santo Spirito della Carita
Administrators: Administered by deans, *canons regolari*, *frati*
                        and minister, follow rule of S. Augustine
Consolidation: Lost independence in 1473

Hospital: Osp. S. Blasii
Location: Located in a swamp 700 metres outside the city
                        gates along the road to Cremona
Founded: 1163 earliest reference but it was already
                        established and had a church, so probably
                        dates back at least to the founding of the
                        new city (1158)
Administrators: *Conversi* of S. Biago under bishop's authority

Hospital: Osp. Casale Lupani (also called sancti Viti)
Location: Outside city walls attached to the Abbey di S.
                        Colombano di Bobbio, along the old Roman
                        road, along the river, near the marshes on the

	road to Cremona. Evidence of a *xenodochia* there as early as 972
Founded:	1039

Hospital:	Osp. di Santa Croce
Location:	Near the gate Cremona in the borgo of Cabianello on the road to San Colombano. It was demolished along with the neighbourhood by Margus Federico Gonzaga in1523 in order to build new fortifications for the city. Administrators moved the hospital to *Grande Contrada* (the street is now named via Paolo Gorini). Building still stands
Founded:	Earliest reference is 1340
Administration:	Confraternity *di Santa Croce*
Consolidation:	Hospital and confraternity were suppressed 10 May 1786

Hospital:	Osp. S. Crucis
Location:	In neighbourhood of *Porta Cremonese*
Founder:	Confraternity S. Croce
Founded:	Documentation from 1387 (possibly as early as 1350)
Consolidation:	Was not absorbed into Osp. Maggiore due to affiliation with the hospital S. Croce existed until the confraternity and church were suppressed in 1786

Hospital:	Osp. San Defendente (Defendetis)
Location:	To the right of via Lodina
Founded:	No mention until 1339
Administrators:	Confraternity *dei Disciplini (Battuti)*
Purpose:	Solely for pilgrims and particularly for husbands and wives who travelled jointly
Consolidated:	Was not incorporated into Osp. Maggiore until 1775 when the confraternity was suppressed but the building was put to other use

Hospital:	Osp. di Santa Elisabetta (Elizabethae)
Location:	Situated in east part of city overlooking a marsh, attached to a small church

Lodi continued

Founder:	Founded by a famous Lodi family dei Cadamosto
Consolidation:	Combined with Osp. Santo Spirito in 1457

Hospital:	Osp. de la Galbera
Location:	Inside walls of the new city but away from centre
Founded:	1160

Hospital:	Osp. dei Santi Giacomo e Filippo delle Misericordia
Location:	One kilometre from the city along the ancient road to Milan and for the use of voyagers in wetlands – unsafe road due to the continual warfare between Lodi and Milan – attached to small church
Founders:	Founded by noble citizen Gualtiero dei Garbagni
Founded:	1224
Administrators:	In 1206 eight acres of land given by Garbagni to *Credenza di san Bassiano* in the Commune of Lodi who would administer the budget
Consolidation:	6 November 1459, management was consolidated with Osp. Maggiore. Still operating at time of plague of 1485–1586

Hospital:	Osp. di San Giacomo in Vallicella
Location:	Called Vallicella for the low part of the city near Adda. It was built opposite the church San Giacomo Maggiore
Founder:	Founded by Anselino Temacoldo, parent of Pietro Temacoldo who was '*padrone*' of Lodi from 1328 to 1335
Founded:	29 August 1347
Administrators:	Maintained four beds for pilgrims and gave alms to poor
Consolidation:	In 1470 management consolidated into Osp. Maggiore. Building continued to

function for pilgrims and travellers until
1807

Hospital: Osp. S. Giovanni
Location: It was a rural hospital along a road to
                 Cremona to serve travellers
Founded: 1039
Founder: It was founded by Count Iderado da Comazzo
                 on 1000 acres of land with the Monastery of
                 San Vito, one of the richest in Lombardy. No
                 mention after 1158

Hospital: Osp. San Giovanni Battista di Tavazzano
Location: Edge of the ancient village of Tavazzano at the
                 part where the road to Milan surpassed
                 Sillaro
Founded: It seems to have been built at the same time as
                 the 'new' Lodi
Administration: Tied to the tenth-century Order of the
                 Monastery San Pietro di Lodi vecchio

Hospital: Osp. S. Iacobi
Founded: Earliest documentation 1347. Probably founded
                 earlier
Founder: Founded by the will of the family de
                 Temacoldo
Consolidation: Was consolidated into Maggiore but continued
                 as a hospice into seventeenth century

Hospital: Osp. SS. Iacobi et Philippi de la Misericordia
Location: On suitable ground outside *Porta Regale*
Founders: Gualtiero Garbani
Founded: 30 April 1206
Administrators: The commune was the *patronus et advocatus*
                 of the hospital, sanctioning and approving
                 election of a rector and retaining the right
                 to supervise the administration directly in
                 general without interference from the bishop

Hospital: Osp. S. Ioannis
Founding: Earliest references, 25 May 1189; 28 May 1191

Lodi continued

Hospital:　　　　　Osp. San Mamerte di Castenuovo
Location:　　　　　150 *pertichi* land with buildings near Castelnuovo
Founded:　　　　　Prior to 1261
Administrators:　　There was a dispute between Cremona and
　　　　　　　　　Lodi over control
Consolidation:　　United with Osp Maggiore 29 December1499

Hospital:　　　　　Osp. S. Maria di Arlino
Location:　　　　　Located in Paullo
Founder:　　　　　It is mentioned in documents from 885 with a
　　　　　　　　　monastery by the same name
Administrators:　　Administered by *Humiliati*
Consolidation:　　United with Osp. Maggiore in 1471

Hospital:　　　　　Osp. S. Maria dei Tizzoni
Founder:　　　　　Named for ancient Lodi family Tizzoni
Administrators:　　Attached to a convent of *Humiliati* called *Dei
　　　　　　　　　Danari*. It was administered by *frati* with the
　　　　　　　　　supervision of the family Tizzoni who had
　　　　　　　　　the right to elect the *rettore*
Consolidation:　　27 March 1459 consolidated with Osp. Maggiore

Hospital:　　　　　Osp. Santa Maria di Virolo (S. Mariae)
Founders:　　　　　Wealthy family Virolo
Founded:　　　　　1224
Administration:　　Romano Paccaroli was the last minister
Consolidation:　　19 February 1459 with Osp. Maggiore

Hospital:　　　　　Osp. SS. Marthae et Gualterii
Founded:　　　　　1388
Consolidation:　　Absorbed with Osp S. Croce in 1396

Hospital:　　　　　Osp. S. Michaelis Atastaverne
Location:　　　　　On the ancient Roman road to Piacenza,
　　　　　　　　　probably more of an inn, but late
　　　　　　　　　documentation suggests the presence of an
　　　　　　　　　earlier hospital there probably connected to
　　　　　　　　　monastery di Brembio

Founders:	Rector sells land to two people – explicitly called patrons and founders of the hospital
Founded:	1261 or 1265

Hospital:	Osp. San Michele di Brembio (possibly the same as S. Michaelis Atastaverne)
Location:	Near the ancient Roman station on the Roman road
Founder:	Founded by noble family Alboni
Founded:	The oldest mention is 1265 but by that time it was in decline so probably much older
Consolidation:	Consolidated with Osp. S Maggiore 1471 and 1472, but not completed until 1473

Hospital:	Osp. S. Nazarii (later called Leonardi)
Founder:	Ruggero de Cerro, son of Alberto. Erected after his death by his *vassals*. Affiliated with the canons of S. Nazario di Milano. The hospital was to exist under the authority of the Milanese episcopate. De Cerro's bequest was to be split. One half of which was to go to the cannons themselves, and one half to the hospital workers. After he died in March 1132 his widow enjoyed the *usfrect* from the rents on hospital property
Founded:	10 October 1127

Hospital:	Osp. di San Pietro di Senna (Osp. di Senna)
Location:	Large old hospital in area of Senna. Outside the walls and along the Roman Road to Piacenza. It was named for its location along this major road
Founders:	A few families whose names are not recorded
Founded:	Was in existence from at least 1152
Administrators:	On 13 July 1152, it was placed under leadership of twelve *frati* who were independent of bishop. The *frati* promised to obey jurisdiction of the Bishop of Lodi as long as he didn't interfere or charge them or subject them to a different jurisdiction. It was

Lodi continued

connected to a monastery. In fifteenth century it was placed under the order of S. Jerome. It was under the protection of the dukes of Milan and became very prosperous. Also under the protection of Bianca Maria, Dowager of Francesco Sforza

Consolidation: It was not suppressed until 1801

Hospital: Osp. de Quado di Tavazzano (later called Giovanni)
Founders: A man of some notoriety – Ordrado Mondalino – who placed it under the jurisdiction of the Bishop of Lodi with an obligation to pay an annual income from the Bishop to the brothers
Founded: 1170

Hospital: Osp. di San Salvatore di Grafignana
Location: On the road to Grafignana near the township of San Colombano. On the road to Milan, Pavia, and Lodi possibly the Via Emilia headed to Piacenza
Founded: 1186 is the earliest reference
Consolidation: 25 May1472 incorporated into Osp. Maggiore

Hospital: Osp. SS. Sepolcro and Croce
Founder: Founded by a crusader Giselberto Cainardo
Founded: 1096
Administrators: Entrusted to the canons of the nearby church S. Lorenzo, but also a suggestion of their association with Cluniacs

Hospital: Osp. di Santi Simone e Giuda
Founder: Seems to have been founded by the Vistarini family who, in 1449, exercised patronage. Near *Porta Pavese*
Founded: 1355
Administrators: Independent *frati*
Consolidation: Duke of Milan, 7 August 1489, ratified union with Osp. Maggiore

Hospital:	Osp. S. Spiritus de la Caritate
Founder:	Once it was called Domus Fratris Facii. Probably a *Humiliati* house. Earliest reference 1242. 1302 transformed into hospital
Administration:	Once it became the Osp. S Spiritus it was administered by brothers under Rule of Santo Spiritus and with protection and favour by the Bishop of Lodi and the Visconti family

Hospital:	Osp. della SS. Trinita
Founder:	Probably the confraternity of the same name
Administration:	Administered by confraternity. Had been called S. Sepolcre

Hospital:	Osp. Sancto Vito (S. Giovanni)
Administration:	Affiliated with Benedictine of the monastery of SS. Vito e Modesto

List of additional hospitals with little information after 1261
  S. Petri a Pirolo
  De Remitta
  S. Bassiano, a Lodi Vecchio (1308)
  S. Maria d' Aurona a Pauilo (1334)
  S. Bassiano a Boffalora d' Adda (1365)
  S. Antonio a Tevenzano

Milan

Hospital:	Osp. S. Ambrogio
Founded:	Tradition says it was founded during Carolingian reign, but only evidence is from 1153

Hospital:	Osp. S. Barnaba
Founded:	Probably founded in 1140 at time of building the church of S. Barnaba
Administrators:	Consortium led by *decani* represented by a minister of the *converse*
Other notable families:	Cattaneo de Casate, da Marliano, Albeertus de Raude

Milan continued

Hospital: Osp. SS Benedetto e Bernardo (later called Sette
                     Conventi)
Founded: Founded 14 April 1346
Founders: Founded by archbishop, given to the tertiaries
                     of seven *convenia of Humiliati*
Administration: *Humiliati*

Hospital: Osp. Brolo
Location: Near the river Muzza
Founded: Evidence of two hospitals founded at Brolo in
                     1145 by Goffredo da Bussero
Administration: 1161 Oberto took charge and merged two
                     hospitals. Administered by *conversae* and
                     decani of the *corstia*. Became very large and
                     prosperous. Benefitted from the protection of
                     wealthy, powerful Milanese families including
                     the Visconti
Consolidation: Was not consolidated and survived into the
                     sixteenth century

Hospital: Osp. Colombetta
Founders: Credit is given to it being founded by the
                     Augustinian brothers *della Misericordia*.
                     However, evidence suggested it existed earlier
                     and benefitted from donations from wealthy
                     individuals
Founded: It appears from other sources it existed prior to
                     1279
Administration: Lay brothers of the confraternity *Misericordia*.
                     Lay men and women worked in the hospital.
                     Evidence for married couples working in the
                     hospital as converse. Given privileges in 1337
                     for visiting prisoners and other 'shameful
                     poor'

Hospital: Osp. San Dionigi
Founders: Probably founded by Bishop Ariberto or at least
                     associated with the monastery of the same
                     name

Consolidation:	Rettore of the hospital was included on the commission to unify hospitals in 1445

Hospital:	Osp. Saint' Eustorgio

Hospital:	Osp. San Gerardo di Monza
Founded:	1175
Founders:	Gerardo Tintore a layman
Administration:	The institution's *converse* were subsequently governed by statutes enacted in 1319 by capitulary officials, but these women elected their own minister and were protected by an advocate selected by the commune and invested by the archbishop

Hospital:	Osp. San Giacomo di Pellagrini
Location:	Porta Vercellina in the parish of Santa Maria alla Porta. At the crossroads of Magerla and via San Giovanni sul Muro
Founded:	1332. Founded specifically for pilgrims

Hospital:	Osp. San Simpliciano
Founded:	1091, near the church S. Michele
Founders:	Founded by a testament bequest from Lanfranco and Frasia della Pila
Administration:	They requested that hospital be administered by 'boni hominess' of the neighbourhood of Porta Comasina and for them to choose a minister for the hospital

Monza

Hospital:	Osp. di San Gerardo
Founded:	19 February 1174
Founder:	Gerando Tintore, a layman known for his charitable works
Administration:	Affiliated with a *Humiliati* house in the fourteenth century

Hospital:	Osp. San Bernardo in Monza (*Humiliati* third order)

Padua

Hospital:	Osp. S. Giacomo di Monselice
Founded:	1162
Administration:	Lay brothers and sisters

Hospital: ca di Dio

Parma

Hospital:	Osp. di frate Alberto
Founded:	1279
Founders:	In honour of Alberti di villa d'Ogna, a wine merchant from Bergamo

Hospital:	Osp. S. Bovo
Founded:	1312
Administration:	In 1347 placed under the protection of the town and the people of Parma

Hospital: Osp. S. Giovanni Gerosolimitano

Hospital:	Osp. S. Giacomo
Founded:	Late twelfth century

Hospital:	Osp. S. Ilario
Founded:	1266
Founders:	The *Societa della Croce* who came to power in the city in the year of the defeat of the ghibellines

Hospital:	Osp. dei Quattro Mestieri
Founded:	1322
Founder:	By Judge Ugolino da Neviano and contracted out to guilds of furriers, shoemakers, blacksmiths, butchers, which represented the major guilds of Parma

Hospital:	Osp. Rodolfo Tanzi
Location:	South of the city on *via Emilia* in *Capodiponte* – suburbs beyond river area

	incorporated in the thirteenth century within new city walls
Founded:	1201 and 1202. In December of 1201 Rodolfo Tanzi rented lands and buildings in Borgo Taschieri, in the district of *Capodiponte*. In April 1202 Bishop of Parma Obizzo Fieschi gave approval to Rodolfo Tanzi to build a new church to serve the needs of the community hospital
Founder:	Rodolfo Tanzi
Administrator:	Tanzi acted as rector of the hospital
Consolidation:	Activity diminishes after a flood in 1415

Hospital:	Osp. S. Sepulchre
Founded:	1140
Location:	Probably attached to monasteries of S. Alessandro and S. Ulderico
Founders:	Gonduino Calzolarius and his wife became converts to O. S. Sepulcre in 1140, and are credited with founding but possibly dates back to crusader foundation 1100–01

Other hospitals in Parma
  S. Giovanni Evangelista (1226)
  di dominus Isacchus (1230)
  di S. Paolo (1245)
  di. S. Francesco (1251)
  di. S. Edigo in Burgo (1255)
  della Misericordia (1255)
  di. S. Giorgio de Partis (1255)
  di. S. Ulderico (1255)
  di. S. Bartolomeo (alla strada rotta) (1266)
  di. S. Damiano or della disciplina vecchio (1289)
  del Consorio dello Spirita Santo (1300)
  di. S. Angelo (1331)
  di. S. Ambrogio della disciplina nuova (1341)
  di. S. Antonio (1347)
  dei. SS. Cosma e Damiano (1347)
  di. S. Michele de arcu (1347)
  di. Milites (1347)

Parma continued

S. Ilario
di Fizte Alberto
S. Bovo
dei Quatitro V. Nestiev

Pavia

Hospital: Osp. Santa Caterina
Location: By the Porta Ticinies
Founded: 31 March 1335
Founders: Moderno Caccialepre

Other hospitals in Pavia
  Osp. G. Giustina
  Osp. San Matteo

Piacenza

Hospital: Osp. S. Pietro della Cadè
Location: Outside the city on the *via Emilia* between
                    Piacenza and Fiorenzuola
Founded: 1100 by individuals

Hospital: Osp. S. Raimondo
Founded: 1170
Founder: Founded by local man Raimondo who was
                    a pilgrim to holy land. Later made a saint

Hospital: Osp. S. Spiritio and S. Misericordia
Location: In the eastern suburbs
Founded: 1090
Administration: Regular canons

Other hospitals in Piacenza
  S. Antonio (1172)
  S. Matteo (1106)
  S. Maria di Betlemme (S. Anna) (1172)
  S. Marco (1093)
  S. Vittoria (1110)

Treviso

Hospital:	Osp. Ognissanti di Treviso
Location:	Outside city walls by gate of S. Teonisto on the southwest road to Pavia
Founded:	11 December 1204
Administration:	Administered by a mixed group of brothers and sisters, some who lived within the community and others who were *extrinseci* owning property and living with their families in the city

Bibliography

Manuscript collections

Bergamo
Archivio di Stato (ASBg)
    Notarile F. Zenaglia
    Notarile G. Fanconi
    Notarile G. Soyarius
Biblioteca Civico Bergamo (BCBg)
    Misericordia Maggiore (MIA)
    Notarile G. Parvis
    Notarile V. da Poma

Como
Archivio di Stato di Como (ASCO)
    Archivio Ospedale di S. Anna (ASCO s.a.)
    Lettere Ducali

Cremona
Archivio di Stato di Cremona (ASCr)
    Ospedale S. Maria della Pietà (ASCr, OSM)
Codice diplomatico Cremonese (CDC)

Lodi
Codice diplomatico Laudense (CDL)
Fondi Minori Lodigiani

Milan
Archivio di Stato (ASMi)
    ASMi, Antiche diplomatica
    ASMi, Arch. Ospedale. Maggiore Milano (AOM)
    ASMi, AOM, Aggregazione Colombetta
    ASMi, AOM, Origine e dotazione, S. Simpliciano

ASMi, AOM, Origine e dotazione dei SS. Benedetto e Bernardo
ASMi, AOM, Consiglio degli orfanotrofie
ASMi, Carte Miniate
ASMi, Consiglio degli Orfanotrofi e del pio Albergo Trivulzio, Orfanotrofio Maschile (OM)
ASMi, Consiglio degli, Ospedale S. Giacomo dei Pellegrini

Monza
Archivio di Stato di Monza (ASM)
   Biblioteca del capitolare del Duomo di Monza (BCM)

Parma
Archivio Capitaolare
Archivio di Stato di Parma (ASPr)
   Antiche Ospizi Civili, Rodolfo Tanzi (RT)
   Diplomatico

Pavia
Archivio Comunale Pavia (ASPv)
   Archivio Ospedale San Matteo (OSM)

Treviso
Archivio di Stato di Treviso (AST)

Rome
Archivio Segreto Vaticano (ASVat)
   Registro Vaticano
Archivio di Stato Roma (ASR)

Other
Archivio di Stato Firenze (ASF)

Printed sources

This list includes secondary texts that contain printed editions of documents or translations of original documents.

Albertanus of Brescia, 'A Sermon to a Confraternity (1250)', introduced by J. Powell and translated from Latin by G. Ahlquist, in K. Jansen, J. Drell and F. Andrews, *Medieval Italy: Texts in Translation* (Philadelphia, PA, 2009), 393–9.
Astegiano, L. *Codice dipomatico Cremonese*, 2 vols. (Torino, 1895–98).
Augustine, *On Christian Doctrine*, D. W. Robertson (trans.) (New York, 1958).

Banzola, M. *L'Ospedale Vecchio di Parma: Notizie Storiche e Vicende Costruttive Precedute da una Sintesi della Formazione Urbana di Parma, Cenni sulle Origini e sulla Storia degli Ospedali nell'Occidente, Elementi di Storia dell'ospitalità a Parma /Maria* (Parma, 1980).

Bescapé, G.C. (ed.) *Antichi diplomi degli arcivescovi di Milano e note di diplomatica episcopale* (Firenze, 1937).

Bonelli, G. *L'archivio dell'Ospedale di Brescia. Notizia e inventario* (Brescia, 1916).

Cava, A. F. *Liber regulae S. Spiritus. Regola dell'Ordine Ospitaliero di S. Spirito. Testo e commento a cura di A. Francesco La Cava* (Milan, 1947) (LR).

Codice diplomatico della Lombardia medievale secoli VIII–XII. http://cdlm.unipv.it/progetto/piano

Constiutiones dedicatorum familiarium servitilium et omnium in Hospitali Santi Spritus de la Cittàte Civitatis Laude Commoriantum. Archivio Storico Lodigiano.

de la Riva, B. *De Magnalibus Mediolani.* Ed. M. Cort. (Milan, 1974).

Dinelli, P. *Dei sinodi della diocesi di Lucca, Memorie e documenti per la storia di Lucca* (Lucca, 1834).

Drei, G. *Le carte degli archivi Parmense de secolo XII* (Parma, 1950).

Frati, L. *Statuti di Bologna dall'anno 1245 all'anno 1267* (Bologna, 1869).

Friedberg, E. *Corpus Iuris Canonici.* Editio Lipsiensis Secunda (Leipzig, 1879).

Gli archive storici degli ospedali Lombardi: censimento descrittivo. Regione Lombardia (Milan, 1982).

Grazlioli, L. *La cronacca di Goffredo da Bussero in Archivio Storico Lombardo.* s. 4a v (1906).

Grossi, A. *Fondi minori Lodigiani* (CDLM, 2006).

Luibheid, C. *Pseudo-Dionysius: The Complete Works* (New York, 1987).

Manaresi, C. *Gli atti del comune di Milano* (Milan, 1919).

Mansi, J. D. *Sacrorum concilorum nova et amplissima* (Venice, 1784).

Migne, P. *Patrologia Latina.* Final release (Alexandria, VA, 1996).

Papal Encyclicals Online. Third Lateran Council 1179. http://www.papalencyclicals.net (2002).

Roncalli, A. G. and Forno, P. *Gli atti della visita apostolica di San Carlo Borromeo a Bergamo, 1557*, 2 vols (Florence, 1936–57).

Rovelli, G. *Storia di Como, descritta dal Marchese Giuseppe Rovelli: Divisa in tre parti* (Milan, 1789).

St Augustine. *The Summa Theologica*, D. Sullivan (ed.) (Chicago, IL, 1955).

St Gregory the Great. *The Book of Pastoral Rule*, G. Demacopoulos (trans.) (Crestwood, NY, 2007).

Statuta jurisdictionem Mediolani. Collected and printed in *Historia Patriae Monumenta, Leges Municipales* (Torino, 1876).

Bibliography 195

Statuto del comune di Lucca dell'anno MCCCVIII, ora per la prima volta pubblicato (Lucca, 1867).
Vignati, C. *Codice diplomatico Laudense* (Milan, 1879). http://cdlm.unipv.it/edizioni/io/grossi

Secondary sources

Abulafia, D. *Frederick II, A Medieval Emperor* (London, 1988).
Agnelli, G. *Ospedale di Lodi: Monographia Storica* (Lodi, 1950).
Alberzoni, M. and Grassi, O. (eds), *La carità a Milano nei secoli XII–XV: Atti del convegno di studi Milano, 6–7, novembre 1987* (Milan, 1989).
Albini, G. *Carità e governo della povertà: secoli XII–XV* (Milan, 2002).
Albini, G. *Città e ospedali nella Lombardi a medieval* (Bologna, 2009).
Albini, G. 'Dallo sviluppo della comunità ospedaliera alla sua crisi (secoli XIV e XV),' in Roberto Creci, *L'ospedale Rodolfo Tanzi di Parma in età medievale* (Bologna, 2004) 29–78.
Albini, G. El rostro asistencial de las ciudades: la Italia septentrional entre los siglos XIII y XV', in T. Huguet-Termes (ed.), *Ciudad y hospital en el Occidente europeo (1300–1700)* (Lleida, SP, 2014), 115–35.
Albini, G. 'Fondazioni di ospedali in area Padana (secoli XI–XIII)', in *La conversione alla povertà nel Italia dei secoli XII–XV: Atti del XVII convegno storico internazionale Todi, 14–17 Ottobre, 1990* (Spoletto, 1990).
Albini, G. 'L'assistenza all'infanzia nelle Città del Italia Padana (secoli XII–XV)', in *Città e Servizi Sociali* (Pistoia, 1990) 115–40.
Albini, G. 'Ospedali e società urbana: Italia centro-settentrionale secoli XIII–XVI', in F. Datini and F. Ammannati (eds), *Assistenza e solidarietà in Europa, secc. XIII–XVIII: Atti della 'quarantaquattresima Settimana di Studi, 22–26 Aprile 2012* (Florence, 2013), 384–99.
Affo, I. *Storia della cita di Parma, Parma 1793* (Bologna, 1908).
Ambrosioni, A. 'Gli arcivescovi e la città nel secolo XII', in M. Alberzoni and O. Grassi (eds), *La carità a Milano nei secoli XII–XV: Atti del convegno di studi Milano, 6–7, novembre 1987* (Milan, 1989), 47–66.
Ammannati, F. *Assistenza e Solidarietà in Europa, Secc. XIII–XVIII = Social Assistance and Solidarity in Europe from the 13th to the 18th Centuries: Atti della 'quarantaquattresima Settimana di Studi,' 22–26 Aprile 2012* (Prato, 2013).
Andrews, F. *The Early Humiliati* (Cambridge, 1999).
Anversa, E. *L'ospedale Rodolfo Tanzi di Parma nei documenti membranacei di privilegi, indulgenze e concessioni (1214–1368)* (Bologna, 1985–86).
Ballarini, F. *Compendio delle croniche della città di Como* (Bologna, 1968).
Banker, J. *Death in the Community: Memorialization and Confraternities in an Italian Commune in the Late Middle Ages* (Athens, GA, 1988).
Bassi, A. *Storia di Lodi* (Lodi, 1977).

Bianchi, F. *La Ca' di Dio di Padova nel Quattrocento: Riforma e Governo di un Ospedale per L'infanzia Abbandonata* (Venice, 2005).

Bianchi, F. 'Italian Renaissance Hospitals: An Overview of the Recent Historiography', *Mitteilungen des Instituts für Österreichische Geschichtsforschung* 115 (2007), 394–403.

Bischof, F. *Helvetia sacra gli umiliati, le comunità degli ospizi della Svizzera Italiana. Di Antonietta Moretti* (Bern/Basel, 1972).

Bolton, B. *Innocent III: Studies on Papal Authority and Pastoral Care* (Aldershot, 1995).

Bolton, B. '*Qui fidelis est in minimo:* The Importance of Innocent III's Gift List', in J. Moore, *Pope Innocent III and His World* (Brookfield, VT, 1999), 128–30.

Bongars, J. 'Gesta dei per Francos', in O. J. Thatcher and E. Holmes McNeal (eds), *A Source Book for Medieval History* (New York, 1905), 513–17.

Borghino, A. 'L'esempio di un ospedale: La Colombetta', in M. Alberzoni and O. Grassi (eds), *La Città a Milano nei secoli XII–XV, atti del convegno di studi Milano, 6–7 novembre 1987* (Milan, 1989, 1987), 225–38.

Bornstein, D. and Rusconi, R. (eds) *Women in Religion in Medieval and Renaissance Italy* (Chicago, IL, 1996).

Borromeo, F. and Torno, A. *La peste di Milano del 1630: La cronaca e le testimonianze del tempo del Cardinale Federico Borromeo* (Milan, 1987).

Boswell, J. *The Kindness of Strangers: The Abandonment of Children in Western Europe from Late Antiquity to the Renaissance* (New York, 1988).

Bowers, B. *The Medieval Hospital and Medical Practice* (Aldershot, 2007).

Bratchel, M. *Medieval Lucca and the Evolution of the Renaissance State* (Oxford, 2008).

Brasher, S. *Women of the Humiliati: A Lay Religious Order in Medieval Civic Life* (New York, 2003).

Bressan, E. and Rumi, G. *L'ospitale e i poveri: La storiografia sull'assistenza: L'Italia e il 'caso Lombardo* (Milan, 1981).

Brezzi, P. 'Le relazioni tra i comuni italiani e l'impero', in *Questione di storia medioevali* (Milan, 1964).

Brodman, J. W. *Charity & Religion in Medieval Europe* (Washington, D.C., 2009).

Brodman, J. W. *Charity and Welfare: Hospitals and the Poor in Medieval Catalonia*. Middle Ages series (Philadelphia, PA, 1998).

Brown, P. *Through the Eye of a Needle: Wealth, the Fall of Rome, and the Making of Christianity in the West, 350–550 AD* (Princeton, NJ, 2012).

Capitani, M. 'Il volto urbano di Como in età medievale', in *Tracce della memoria: Una storia delle territorio Comasco* (Como, 1982).

Caretta, A. 'Gli ospedali altomedievali di Lodi', in *Archivio Storico Lodigiano Ser. II Anno XV* (Lodi, 1967).

Caretta, A. '*L'assisstenza Diocesi di Lodi*', in *Archivio Storico Lodigiano Ser. II Anno XV* (Lodi, 1967).

Cavalcabó, A. and Gualazzini, A. *Bollettino storico Cremonese: miscellanea di scritti roiginali* (Cremona, 1965).

Città e servizi sociali nell'Italia dei secoli XII–XV, Pistoia, 9–12 ottobre 1987: dodicesimo convegno di studi. Centro Italiano di studi di storia e d'arte (Pistoia, Italy). Dodicesimo Convegno di Studi (Pistoia, 1990).

Chiesi, G. 'Gli Umiliati, la proprietà fondiaria dell'ospizio di collegio e l'ospitalità nelle valli ambrosiane', in *Il Medioevo nelle carte: Documenti di storia Ticinese e Svizzera dalle origini al secolo XVI.2* (Ticino, 1993).

Cippo, R. 'Le piu antiche carte dell'ospedale di San Giacomo (secolo XIV.)', in M. Alberzoni and O. Grassi (eds), *La Città a Milano nei secoli XII–XV, atti del convegno di studi Milano, 6–7 novembre 1987* (Milan, 1989), 239–72.

Cipolla, C. *Public Health and the Medical Profession in the Renaissance* (Cambridge, 1976).

Cohn, S. *The Cult of Remembrance and the Black Death: Six Renaissance Cities in Central Italy* (Baltimore, MD, 1992).

Colm, I. *Pseudo-Dionysius: The Complete Works* (New York, 1987).

Conrad, L. *The Western Medical Tradition: 800 B.C.–1800 A.D.* (Cambridge, 1995).

Cosmacini, G. *L'Ospedale Sant'Anna di Como: Nella storia della città* (Como, 2005).

Cossar, R. 'The Confraternity of the Misericordia Maggiore in Bergamo: Three Texts, 1282–1362', Roisin Cossar (trans.), in K. L. Jansen et al. (eds), *Medieval Italy: Texts in Translation* (Philadelphia, 2009) 400–04.

Cossar, R. *Transformation of the Laity in Bergamo, 1260–c.1400* (Leiden, 2008).

Cracco, G. 'Dalla misericordia della Chiesa alla misericordia del principe', in M. Alberzoni and O. Grassi (eds), *La Carità a Milano nei secoli XII–XV, atti del convegno di studi Milano, 6–7 novembre 1987* (Milan, 1989), 31–47.

Crane, T. *The Exempla or Illustrative Stories from the Sermones Vulgares of Jacques De Vitry* (London, 1890).

Cunningham, A. and Grell, O. *The Four Horsemen of the Apocalypse: Religion, War, Famine, and Death in Reformation Europe* (Cambridge, 2000).

Cunningham, L. *Brother Francis: An Anthology of Writings by and about St. Francis of Assisi* (New York, 1972).

D'Alessandro, V. *Le pergamene degli Umiliati di Cremona* (Palermo, 1964).

D'Andrea, D. M. *Civic Christianity in Renaissance Italy: The Hospital of Treviso, 1400–1530* (Rochester, 2007).

De Vitry, J. and Crane, T. *The Exempla or Illustrative Stories from the Sermones Vulgares of Jacques De Vitry* (London, 1890).

Epstein, S. *Genoa & the Genoese, 958–1528* (Chapel Hill, NC, 1996).

Epstein, S. *Wage Labor & Guilds in Medieval Europe* (Chapel Hill, NC, 1991).

Faladori. *L'ospedale Milanese di S. Simpliciano dalla fondazione all'inizio dal trecento: Aspetti economica, religiosa* (Tesse di Laurea, 1990–91).

Farmer, S. *Surviving Poverty in Medieval Paris: Gender Ideology and the Daily Lives of the Poor* (Ithaca, NY, 2002).

Farmer, S. and Rosenwein, B. *Monks and Nuns, Saints and Outcasts: Religion in Medieval Society, Essays in Honor of Lester K. Little* (Ithaca, NY, 2000).

Ferrari, Giovanni. *L'Ospedale Sant'Anna di Como nella storia della città* (Como, 2005).

Frederick, J. and Hinnebusch, J. *The Historia Occidentalis of Jacques de Vitry: A Critical Edition* (Freiburg, 1972), 146–51.

Galli, S. *Gli archive storica degli ospedali Lombardi* (Como, 1982).

Gazzini, M. *L'ospedale a Parma nei secoli XII–XIII* (Parma, 2002).

Gazzini, M. *Reti medievali Rivista*, 13:1 (2012): http://rm.univr.it/repertorio/rm_gazzini_ospedali_medioevo.html.

Gazzini, M. 'Rodolfo Tanzi, l'ospedale e le società Cittadina nei secoli XII e XIII', in R. Greci, *L'ospedale Rodolfo Tanzi di Parma in età Medievale* (Bologna, 2004), 3–28.

Gazzini, M. 'Una comunità di 'fratres' e 'sorores'', in R. Greci (ed.), *L'ospedale Rodolfo Tanzi di Parma in età Medievale* (Bologna, 2004), 259–307.

Geremek, B. *The Margins of Society in Late Medieval Paris* (Cambridge, 1987).

Glass, D. *Portals, Pilgrimage, and Crusade in Western Tuscany* (Princeton, NJ, 1997).

Goodson, C., Lester, A. and Symes, C. (eds) *Cities, Texts and Social Networks, 400–1500: Experiences and Perceptions of Medieval Urban Space* (Farnham, 2010).

Grant, E. *God and Reason in the Middle Ages* (Cambridge, 2001).

Grazlioli, L. 'La cronaca di Goffredo d Bussero', in *Archivio Storico Lombardo*, s. 4a v (1906), 211–40.

Greci, R. *L'Ospedale e la società cittadina nei secoli XII e XIII* (Bologna, 2004).

Greci, R. *L'Ospedale Rodolfo Tanzi di Parma in età Medievale* (Bologna, 2004).

Greenaway, G. *Arnold of Brescia* (Cambridge, 1931).

Grieco, A. and Sandri, L. *Ospedali e città: L'Italia de centro-nord, XII–XVI secolo* (Florence, 1997).

Grundmann, H. *Religious Movements in the Middle Ages: The Historical Links between Heresy, the Mendicant Orders, and the Women's*

Religious Movement in the Twelfth and Thirteenth Century, with the Historical Foundations of German Mysticism (Notre Dame, IN, 1995).

Guenza, M. 'La formazione della propreita fondiaria dell'ospedale Rodolfo Tanzi', in R. Greci (ed.), *L'ospedale Rodolfo Tanzi di Parma in età Medievale* (Bologna, 2004), 137–78.

Henderson, J. *Piety and Charity in Late Medieval Florence* (Oxford, 1994).

Henderson, J. *The Renaissance Hospital: Healing the Body and Healing the Soul* (New Haven, CT, 2006).

Herlihy, D. and Cohn, S. K. *The Black Death and the Transformation of the West* (Cambridge, MA, 1997).

Hinnebusch, J. *The Historia Occidentalis of Jacques de Vitry: A Critical Edition* (Fribourg, 1972).

Holman, S. *The Hungry Are Dying: Beggars and Bishops in Roman Cappadocia* (Oxford, 2001).

Horden, P. *Hospitals and Healing from Antiquity to the Later Middle Ages* (Aldershot, 2008).

Horden, P. 'The Earliest Hospitals in Byzantium, Western Europe, and Islam', *Journal of Interdisciplinary History* 35 (2005), 361–89.

Howe, E. *The Hospital of Santo Spirito and Pope Sixtus IV* (New York, 1978).

Huguet-Termes, T. *Ciudad y hospital en el occidente Europeo, 1300–1700* (Lleida, 2014).

Hyde, J. K. *Society and Politics in Medieval Italy; the Evolution of the Civil Life, 1000–1350* (New York, 1973).

Jansen, K., Drell, J. and Andrews, F. (eds) *Medieval Italy: Texts in Translation* (Philadelphia, PA, 2009).

Johnson, P. *Equal in Monastic Profession Religious Women in Medieval France* (Chicago, IL, 1993).

Larius, *la città ed il ago di Como delle descrizione e nelle immagini dall'antichità classica all'età romantica* (Anthology directed by Gianfranco Miglio) (Milan, 1959).

Little, L. *Religious Poverty and the Profit Economy in Medieval Europe* (Ithaca, NY, 1978).

Little, L. and Buzzetti, S. *Liberty, Charity, Fraternity: Lay Religious Confraternities at Bergamo in the Age of the Commune* (Bergamo, 1988).

Londero, A. *Per l'amor di Deu: pietà e profitto in un ospedale friulano del quattrocento (San Michele di Gemona)* (Udine, 1994).

Lynch, K. *Individuals, Families, and Communities in Europe, 1200–1800: The Urban Foundations of Western Society* (Cambridge, 2003).

Mambretti, R. *Le Carte dell'ospedale di San Biagio in Monza: (secoli XII–XIII)* (Milan, 1999).

Mambretti, R. 'L'ospedale di San Gerardo nei secoli XIII e XIV', in M. Alberzoni and O. Grassi (eds), *La carità a Milano nei secoli XII–XV, atti del Convegno di Studi Milano, 6–7 novembre 1987* (Milan, 1989), 187–223.

Marshall, R. *The Local Merchants of Prato* (Baltimore, MD, 1999).

Martines, L. *Violence and Civil Disorder in Italian Cities, 1200–1500* (Berkeley, CA, 1972).

McCormick, M. *Origins of the European Economy: Communications and Commerce, A.D. 300–900* (Cambridge, 2001).

Meersseman, G. *Ordo Fraternitatis: Confraternite e Pietà dei Laici nel Medioevo*, Vol. 3 (Rome, 1977).

Merlo, G. *Esperienze religiose e opera assistenziali nei secoli XII e XIII* (Torino, 1987).

Merlo, G. 'Religiosità e cultura, religiosa de laici nel secolo XII', in *l'Europa de secoli XI e XII* (Milan, 1989), 200–20.

Meroni, U. *'Cremona Fedelissima': Studi di Storia Economica e Amministrativa di Cremona Durante la Dominazione Spagnola* (Cremona, 1951).

Miglio, G. *Larius: La Città ed il Lago di Como nelle Descrizioni e nelle Immagini dall'antichità Classica all'età Romantica* (Milan, 1959).

Miskimin, H. *The Medieval City* (New Haven, CT, 1977).

Mollat, M. *Etudes sur l'histoire de la pauvrete: moyen age-XVIe siècle*, 2 vols (Paris, 1974).

Mollat, M. *The Poor in the Middle Ages: An Essay in Social History* (New Haven, 1986).

Moore, J. *Pope Innocent III and His World* (Brookfield, VT, 1999).

Morris, C. *The Papal Monarchy, the Western Church from 1050–1250* (Oxford, 1989).

Nicholas, D. *Urban Europe, 1100–1700* (Basingstoke, 2003).

Noto, A. 'Per la tutela dei legati elemosinieri Milanesi nel secolo XV', in *Studi in onore di Armando Sapori* (1957).

Numbers, R. and Amundsen, D. *Caring and Curing: Health and Medicine in the Western Religious Traditions* (New York, 1986).

Nutton, V. 'Medicine in Medieval Europe, 100–1500', in L. Conrad (ed.), *The Western Medical Tradition: 800 B.C.–1800 A.D.* (Cambridge, 1995), 139–207.

Orme, N. and Webster, N. *The English Hospital 1070–1570* (New Haven, CT, 1995).

Osheim, D. 'Conversion, *Conversi*, and the Christian life in medieval Tuscany', *Speculum*, 58:2 (1983), 368–90.

Owen Hughes, D. 'Kinsmen and Neighbors in Medieval Genoa', in H. A. Miskimin (ed.), *The Medieval City* (New Haven, CT, 1977), 121–45.

Paxton, F. *Anchoress and Abbess in Ninth-century Saxony the Lives of Liutbirga of Wendhausen and Hathumoda of Gandersheim* (Washington, DC, 2009).

Pecchiai, P. *L'ospedale Maggiore di Milano nella storia e nell'arte. Con notizie documentate su le origini e su lo sviluppo della organizzazione spedalieri Milanese, etc. [With Illustrations.]* (Milan, 1927).

Pellicelli, P. *Storia dell'Ospedale Maggiore di Parma, fondata del Rodolfo Tanzi nel 1201* (Parma, 1935).

Pennington, K. *Pope and Bishops; the Papal Monarchy in the Twelfth and Thirteenth Centuries* (Philadelphia, PA, 1984).

Pullan, B. *Rich and Poor in Renaissance Venice; the Social Institutions of a Catholic State, to 1620* (Cambridge, MA, 1971).

Racine, P. 'Il Sistema Ospedaliero Lombardo (secoli XII–XV)', in *Città e servizi sociali nell'Italia dei secoli XII–XV. Dodicesimo Convegno di Studi: Pistoia, 9–12 Ottobre 1987* (Pistoia, 1987), 355–80.

Rando, D. 'Laicus Religiosus' tra strutture civili ed ecclesiastiche: L'ospedale di Ognissanti in Treviso (sec. XIII)', in G. Merlo (ed.), *Esperienze religiose religiose e opera assistenziali nei secoli XII e XIII* (Torino, 1987), 43–83.

Rawcliffe, C. *The Hospitals of Medieval Norwich* (Norwich, 1995).

Rawcliffe, C. *Leprosy in Medieval England* (Woodbridge, 2006).

Rawcliffe, C. *Medicine for the Soul: The Life, Death, and Resurrection of an English Medieval Hospital: St Giles's, Norwich, C. 1249–1550* (Stroud, 1999).

Rawcliffe, C. *Sources for the History of Medicine in Late Medieval England* (Kalamazoo, MI, 1995).

Reynolds, R. L., Herlihy, D., Lopez, R. and Slessarev, V. *Economy, Society, and Government in Medieval Italy: Essays in Memory of Robert L. Reynolds* (Kent, OH, 1969).

Ricci, A. 'Nuovi contributi sulle fasi costruitile dell'ospedale di Santa Maria del Pietà nel Quattrocento', in A. Cavalcabo and U. Gualazzini (eds), *Bollettino storico Cremonese: miscellanea di scritti originali* (Cremona, 1965).

Ricci, A. 'La realizzazione della riforma e la sorte degli ospedali minori', in R. Greci (ed.), *L'ospedale Rodolfo Tanzi di Parma in età medieval* (Bologna, 2004), 79–136.

Ricci, G. 'Naissance du pauvre honteux: Entre l'histoire des idées et l'histoire sociale', in *Annales. Histoire, Sciences Sociales Ahess*: 158–77.

Ricci, G. 'Povertà, Vergogna e Povertà Vergognosa', in *Società e Storia*, Vol. 2 (1979), 305–37.

Rocca, E. *Ospedali e canoniche regolari* (Milan, 1959).

Rocca, E. 'Ospedali e canoniche regolari', *La Vita Comune del Clero nei Secoli XI e XII* (Milan, 1962).

Rothrauff, E. 'Charity in a Medieval Community: Politics, Piety and Poor-relief in Pisa, 1257–1312', PhD thesis (Berkeley, CA, 1994).

Rubin, M. *Charity and Community in Medieval Cambridge* (Cambridge, 1987).

Ruelle, P. *Le Besant de Dieu* (Bruxelles, 1973).

Scott, A. *Experiences of Charity, 1250–1650* (Farnham, 2015).

Simons, W. *Cities of Ladies Beguine Communities in the Medieval Low Countries, 1200–1565* (Philadelphia, PA, 2001).

Siraisi, N. *Medieval & Early Renaissance Medicine: An Introduction to Knowledge and Practice* (Chicago, IL, 1990).

Swanson, R. N. *Religion and Devotion in Europe, c.1215–c.1515* (Cambridge, 1995).

Sweetinburgh, S. *The Role of the Hospital in Medieval England: Gift Giving and the Spiritual Economy* (Dublin, 2004).

Sweetinburgh, S. 'The Role of the Hospital in Medieval Kent, c.1080–c.1560', dissertation (1998).

Thompson, A. *Cities of God: The Religion of the Italian Communes, 1125–1325* (University Park, PA, 2005).

Tierney, B. *Medieval Poor Law. A Sketch of Canonical Theory and Its Appreciation in England* (Berkeley, CA, 1959).

Trexler, R. 'Charity and the Defense of Urban Elites in Italian Communes', in F. C. Jaher (ed.), *The Rich: The Well Born, and the Powerful: Elites and Upper Classes in History* (Urbana, IL, 1973).

Trexler, R. *Power and Dependence in Renaissance Florence* (Binghamton, NY, 1993).

Varanini, G. 'Gli Ospedali dei 'malsani' nella società veneta del XII–XIII secolo', in *Città e Servizi Sociali nell'Italia dei Secoli XII–XV*. Centro Italiano di studi di storia e d'arte (Pistoia, Italy). Dodicesimo Convegno di Studi (Pistoia, 1990), 141–65.

Vauchez, A. and Bornstein, D. *The Laity in the Middle Ages: Religious Beliefs and Devotional Practices* (Notre Dame, IN, 1993).

Vio, G. *Le scuole piccolo nella Venezia dei Dogi* (Venice, 2004).

Wallis, F. *Medieval Medicine: A Reader* (Toronto, 2010).

Watson, S. 'City as Charter: Charity and the Lordship of English Towns', in C. Goodson, A. Lester and C. Symes (eds), *Cities, Texts and Social Networks, 400–1500: Experiences and Perceptions of Medieval Urban Space* (Farnham, 2010)

Waley, D. P. *The Papal State in the 13th Century* (London, 1961).

Waley, D. P. and Dean, T. *The Italian City Republics*, 4th edition (Harlow, 2009).

Welch, E. *Art and Authority in Renaissance Milan* (New Haven, CT, 1995).

Wickham, C. *Early Medieval Italy: Central Power and Local Society, 400–1000* (Princeton, NJ, 1981).

Wickham, C. *Sleepwalking into a New World: The Emergence of Italian City Communes in the Twelfth Century*. The Lawrence Stone Lectures (Princeton, NJ, 2015).

Zanoni, L. *Gli Umiliati neilLoro Rapporti con l'eresia, l'industria della Lana ed i Comuni nei Secoli XII e XIII Sulla Scorta di Documenti Inediti* (Roma, 1970).

Index